OPIUM
FIEND

VILLARD Ⓥ NEW YORK

OPIUM FIEND

A 21ST CENTURY
SLAVE TO A
19TH CENTURY
ADDICTION

A MEMOIR

STEVEN MARTIN

Published in the United States by Villard Books, an imprint of The Random House Publishing Group, a division of Random House, Inc., New York.

VILLARD BOOKS and VILLARD & "V" CIRCLED Design are registered trademarks of Random House, Inc.

Grateful acknowledgment is made to Richard Curtis Associates for permission to reprint excerpts from "The Big Smoke" by Emily Hahn (*The New Yorker,* February 15, 1969), copyright © 1969. Reprinted by permission of Richard Curtis Associates.

Library of Congress Cataloging-in-Publication Data
Martin, Steven.
    Opium fiend: a 21st century slave to a 19th century addiction / Steven Martin.
        p. cm.
    Includes bibliographical references.
    ISBN 978-0-345-51783-8
    eBook ISBN 978-0-345-51785-2
1. Martin, Steven.   2. Drug paraphernalia—Collectors and collecting—United States—Biography.   3. Antiques—United States—Biography.   I. Title.
    NK4897.M36   2012
    362.29'3092—dc23   2012006896
    [B]

Printed in the United States of America on acid-free paper

www.villard.com

9 8 7 6 5 4 3 2 1

First Edition

Book design by Liz Cosgrove

Dedicated to the memory of my sister,
Lynn Lee Martin (1967–2010)

A Note from the Author

This memoir chronicles my experiences as a collector of antique opium-smoking paraphernalia. I do not advocate the use of opium. I do not wish to convey that anyone who smokes opium will have the same experiences that I had. I am not suggesting that anyone do or not do any of the things that I have done. My aim is simply to share what has happened to me. Most of the names in this memoir have been changed, the notable exceptions being Roxanna Brown, Karl Taro Greenfeld, and my own. Some locations and biographical details have also been altered to preserve the anonymity of the persons discussed. All research conducted for this book was my own, and any errors contained within it are also my own.

Map of Mainland Southeast Asia★

★Traditional English-language place names reflect those used in the text.

OPIUM
FIEND

Once upon a midnight dreary, while I pondered weak and weary,
Over many a quaint and curious volume of forgotten lore . . .

—Edgar Allan Poe, "The Raven" (1845)

Halloween, that day of symbolic horrors, seemed an appropriate time to stop. I had already stocked the refrigerator of my apartment in Bangkok's Chinatown with nutritious, easy-to-digest food such as goat's milk and yogurt, even though I knew it would be days before I could eat again. The flush lever on my toilet had long before rusted tight, and I'd become accustomed to lifting the lid of the water tank and pulling up on the little chain. Within a day or so that porcelain lid would be too heavy for me to lift, so I took it off and put it behind the toilet where I wouldn't trip over it.

The door to my ninth-floor flat was situated down a dark corridor and next to a little-used stairwell that was marked as a fire escape. Like most doors in Chinatown, mine was barred against intruders with a wrought iron outer door. From inside the apartment it was possible to reach out through the bars of the outer door and fasten a large padlock on its latch, giving the impression that nobody was home. My bedroom window looked out on the corridor, and it, too, was barred. In addition to the bars, this window had layers of opacity to ensure privacy: on the inside heavy drapes, and on the outside a tinted windowpane completely obscured by a screen covered with dust so thick it might have been mistaken for a curtain of ash-colored velvet. From outside my apartment it was all but impossible to tell that I was inside.

For months I had been a recluse to the extent that my face-to-face social obligations were almost nil. But this situation was masked by the fact that I worked from home—people rarely saw me in person anyway. Communications didn't worry me. Everybody knew that email had become my preferred method of keeping in touch. What they didn't know was that I'd discovered email was perfect for preserving a façade of normalcy no matter how crazy things got. I could take as long as I needed to reply while fabricating plausible excuses as to why I couldn't leave my apartment. If I became too addled to talk coherently, I could dodge telephone calls by simply ignoring them. Roxanna was the one person whose calls would be difficult to ignore, but her invitations had fallen off as my downward spiral had become more and more apparent.

As I waited for the symptoms to start, I began to think of ways to occupy my mind. I was no stranger to this scenario: I had twice tried to put a halt to my daily smoking. My first attempt might have succeeded if only I'd been more disciplined. Backing off from the habit wasn't as difficult as I'd thought it would be, and this had made me confident that I was still my own master. But then I lost control. Two months of restrained dabbling on weekends had descended into a daily orgy of indulgence.

A second attempt at cutting back was harder, but I'd managed to abstain for a whole month before finding the perfect excuse for a relapse. And thus began my free fall. Subsequent attempts to quit were painful ordeals that lasted a single harrowing night and ended at dawn, when I would crawl back to the mat, light the lamp, and smoke with a voraciousness that shocked me. I watched as my own hands prepared pipe after pipe, both thrilled and terrified to know that a line I'd memorized from a Victorian-era book now applied to me: I had "succumbed to the fascinations of opium."

By Halloween 2007, I had been smoking opium continuously for months—as much as thirty pipes a day. I decided to try to quit again. This time, I told myself, I would not fail. I knew I would be in for a rougher ride; I had let my habit get so out of hand that the withdrawal would be many times worse than my previous ordeals. I recalled those days of soul-piercing pain, the nights of sweat-soaked insomnia, and I tried to imagine how anything might be worse.

To steel myself for the storm, I pretended that I was going to suffer a bout of malaria in the days before quinine. The idea appealed to my sense of the romantic—here was another age-old affliction that had to be weathered stoically. But I knew very well that malarial fevers were never as ugly as what I would soon experience. Among my small library of century-old books with gilt leather bindings I had discovered a paragraph or two that described in clinical prose what I was about to endure.

I had read about the all-encompassing pain that drove opium addicts to beg for the relief that could be had only via a few draws on the pipe. I had read of people tightly trussed to their beds and locked in rooms by loved ones who then stopped their ears with raw cotton to block out the tortured screams. There were tales of prayers shrieked through the night; pleas for a hasty death that were sometimes answered by a body too shocked to function beyond a few days without opium. The morning after would be no scene of poignant demise; no *Death of Chatterton* angelically sprawled across his bed high above London. It would

more resemble the aftermath of a cholera victim's death throes—
a room defiled by the performance of a macabre, bone-twisting
Watusi to the rhythms of explosive farts and geysers of liquid
shit.

And if I survived the physical pain, once it began to diminish,
the mental anguish would take over: a dense boom of depression
lowered onto a brain already exhausted by long nights of sleep-
lessness. This desperate funk manifests itself in many ways and is
seemingly tailor-made to suit the fears and phobias of each and
every addict. Just as your body turns against you during the days
of physical withdrawal, so, too, your mind will conspire with
opium to unleash mental torment at its most intolerable. Whatever is most likely to unhinge you, that is what you will experience. Imagine the sound of a thousand babies crying inconsolably
for hours and hours on end. If I survived the physical pain, for
how much longer would my opium-deprived brain persecute
me? A month? A year?

The very thought of this had in the past been enough to
make me give in before even starting. But this time I was determined. Savor what Halloween was meant to be, I told myself.
Savor your nightmare. When it is all over you will be free of
opium . . . forever.

My provisions were stocked, and the most important preparation was in place: my opium-smoking layout. Should I need it,
the hardwood tray with all the necessary accoutrements meticulously arranged upon it was waiting under my coffee table in the
living room, together with a bottle of the finest liquid opium.
Some might think it self-defeating to have a quick fix at hand,
but I was unsure of whether the accounts in those old books
were exaggerated. If they weren't, and if death was as real a possibility as the books suggested, I needed to have the antidote at
the ready.

It was late evening, nearly twenty-four hours since my last pipe, when the "opium cold" began, an array of flu-like symptoms—sneezing, watery eyes, and runny nose—that announces the body's first signs of falling to pieces. This is a common event for opium addicts, something I had many times experienced whenever I got too busy to recline and prepare some pipes—a simple reminder that opium was needed to tighten things back up. This time, the arrival of these symptoms caused me to retreat to my bedroom with its single blacked-out window. I wanted no part of the outside world. The bustling sounds of nighttime in Chinatown floated up to my flat on waves of heat emanating from the sunbaked concrete, but I had no desire to stand at a window and look at the city below. I had long before become too detached to enjoy something as worldly as a room with a view, and had hung blankets over the windows to promote the illusion of perpetual twilight.

In order to keep my mind off the steadily intensifying symptoms, I got online—YouTube—and did some searches. I looked up an old cartoon that I'd stumbled across days before while looking for Halloween fare, a Fleischer Studios gem from 1930 called *Swing You Sinners!* I watched the clip over and over that night until the manic jazz and snatches of menacing dialogue became imbedded deep in a part of my brain that specializes in turning catchy songs into maddening little ditties.

Spook #1: "Where you want your body sent?"

Spook #2: "Body? Ha! There ain't gonna *be* no body!"

Oh, yes there would. I began to dwell on morbid visions of my corpse being discovered, the centerpiece of a room that looked as though it had been ransacked by a madman. Whoever found me would also find my collection of antique opium-smoking paraphernalia—those pieces that had survived my thrashing about like a headless chicken. There was a time when

I would have died before putting my collection in peril—no exaggeration—but of late it had become just another source of convenient income: a way to pay for more opium.

At some point I lay down on my bed and fell into a fitful sleep. I woke up just before dawn on November 1—All Saints Day—with a loud buzzing in my ears and a dull headache. My immediate thoughts were recollections of nightmares: vague scenes based on long-buried memories of celebrating Todos Los Santos as a young man in Manila; images of crowds among concrete crypts in candlelit cemeteries. Those real-life events had been joyous occasions, but my dreamed version was suffused with loss and a bitter longing.

That first night without the pipe was a taste of what I was to lose: Never again would sleep be so delicious; never again would dreams be so real. The scene in the cemetery felt as though the dreams themselves were aware of their imminent demise, that without opium my dreamed events would never again enjoy as much importance as my predictable waking life. That overlap— the blurring of lines between sleep and wakefulness that I experienced with daily opium use—would soon cease to exist. I couldn't help but feel I was giving up half my life.

Those first waking thoughts set the tone for the morning of that second day. Feelings of impending loss kept resurfacing, and all thoughts led to opium. I tried to watch movies on my laptop, but they served only to anger me. Who were these people and what did they know about life? My principal feeling toward nonsmokers was scorn. Opium arrogance kept me engaged, but just barely. I stared at the performances meant to evoke emotions such as love and loneliness but I could not relate. Watching people interact was like being forced to watch a mime—I felt as though I lacked the patience to understand the message. I had lost interest in the activities of everyone but a couple of opium-smoking friends. The rest of humanity I could ignore in the same way that one tunes out the speakers of a foreign language.

When I could no longer look at the images on my computer screen I tried to read, but this was equally difficult for my opium-starved brain. I found uniquely silly the articles in the many back issues of *The New Yorker* that littered my apartment. Focusing on unread pieces was impossible, and when I tried to reread articles that I'd enjoyed in the past, they now seemed insultingly dull. I could read no more than a paragraph or two before launching the magazine at the wall like a fluttering missile. If only *The New Yorker* were heavier, I thought to myself, I could break its spine.

As the day wore on these feelings of anger and alienation were usurped by a riotous fever. Around me the tropical city sweltered while I wrapped myself in blankets and shivered with exaggerated spasms that might have looked comical had anyone been there to witness them. Time seemed suspended, and I had unplugged the clock so I wouldn't be tempted to look and gauge time's progress. I do not know how long I shuddered with cold before a rising heat replaced it, drenching me with sweat and compelling me to throw the blankets to the floor. After some time had passed I frantically gathered them up again to shield myself against a bracing cold that was all in my mind. My skin was studded with pebbly goose bumps—the inspiration behind the term "cold turkey." Despite the chill, blankets felt loathsome against my body, and when I was broiling with fever even the breeze from the electric fan made my skin crawl. I seemed to have lost the ability to enjoy even the slightest bit of comfort.

Several times that night I was visited by these brutal seasons, and then sometime before dawn I actually prayed—doubled up like some slave waiting to be fetched a cruel kick. I had never before in my life felt desperate enough to pray, but that night I did so with a fluency and sincerity that surprised me.

It must have worked. When I awoke a few hours later my pillow and bedclothes were sticky with opium-laced sweat, but the fever had mostly subsided. Feelings of celebratory relief were premature, however. What had woken me up were cramps in my stomach—gut-wrenching pains that brought me to my feet almost involuntarily and propelled me toward the bathroom. Depth bombs of shit began exploding out of me, punctuated by gas bursting into the toilet bowl. The force and noise were such that it seemed as though my bowels were bellowing angry obscenities, and I found myself answering each anal exclamation with an oral one of protest and awe: "Whoa! What the fuck?!"

So frequent were these violent purges that my strength was quickly drained, flowing down the toilet with torrents so copious that I thought my insides had liquefied. I would have sat there and waited out the waves of diarrhea had my legs and arms not become racked with cramps that demanded movement. Here it comes, I thought to myself, the beginnings of the uncontrollable thrashing that was described in old accounts—this was what might kill me. From the bathroom into the bedroom and back. How many trips had there been? Enough so that raw skin could no longer be wiped with toilet paper. I used a hand-held showerhead to rinse myself clean, but the taxing cycle of constantly disrobing, washing, drying off, and getting dressed soon became too much, and so I paced my bedroom wet and naked, waiting for the return of stomach pains that again and again sent me running back to the toilet.

Then all hell broke loose. My arms and legs felt as though they were being pulled from their sockets. My guts bloated inside me, forcing up vomit followed by gobs of greenish bile. Even my testicles ached with nauseating pain. Mentally I was reduced to directing the most basic actions, trying to steer clear of walls and furniture while flailing my arms and legs about as if I were on fire.

However, there was one task at which my brain functioned as usual—that frantic tune from the old cartoon on YouTube played in my head in an endless loop. Naked, I jumped around the room to the private strains of a Harlem jazz band. Like a human pogo stick I bounced. Completely exhausted, I aimed for the bed and tried to rest and catch my breath, but I could not stay still. The opium was working its way out of my system, squeezing through the walls of every one of my cells, causing me to howl in agony and leap to my feet after lying motionless for mere seconds.

I don't know how long I was in this state, but at some point I decided that I could go no further—and by my simply having made up my mind to give in, some of the pain instantly began to subside. But I did not renege on my decision. I heard Jean Cocteau's advice from 1930 above the ringing in my ears: "Do not persist. Your courage is to no purpose. If you delay too long, you will no longer be able to take your equipment and roll your pipe. Smoke. Your body is waiting only for a sign."

Hobbling to the living room on legs bruised from countless barks against furniture, I dropped to my knees and crawled toward the woven-cane mat. With hands that seemed to belong to someone else, I jerked the layout tray from under the coffee table. I scratched through several wooden matches before one lit, burning myself in the process, and needed both hands to steady the flame in order to light the opium lamp. Once that was done, I gathered all my remaining concentration to prepare a pipe.

My brain and body were on my side at this point. I felt strength return and a sharpening of mind at the mere thought of getting some opium vapors into my lungs. While preparing that first pipe I overcooked the pill—a botched job that normally I would never have carried through with, but on that day I sucked greedily at the thick white smoke and held it in my lungs while shakily beginning the preparations for my second pipe. This next one was better—the opium vaporized as it was supposed to, and the sweet vapors swirled about me as I exhaled gratefully. I rolled the third pipe with much less urgency. I even remembered to exhale through my nose to let the vapors pass along moist membranes, absorbing just a trace more opium. Every little bit counted.

"Yah dee," I whispered to myself in Lao, repeating the words that Madame Tui used to pronounce over my supine body after her pipes had done their work. "Good medicine."

Indeed. Closing my eyes for a moment I savored a miracle: the total banishment of pain. The vacuum was instantly replaced by a deliciously tingling wave that crept up the base of my neck and caressed my head with something akin to a divine massage. Whereas moments before my muscles had felt like they were being pinched by countless angry crabs, there now was a soothing sensation of calm and well-being. I prepared one more pipe—this time with almost no shakiness—and held the vapors deep in my lungs before exhaling slowly through my nose.

With the torment quickly fading from memory, I noticed my naked and disheveled state. I rose from the mat with restored agility and calmly went into the bathroom to take a leisurely, hot shower, washing away the oily sweat and traces of vomit, mucus, and feces that covered my skin and clotted my hair. Refreshed, I dried and dressed for comfort in a clean cotton sarong and a linen guayabera before returning to the mat and reclining once more.

I took a moment to admire my opium-smoking layout, a collection of rare and elegant paraphernalia that took years to gather and was worth thousands of dollars. Equal parts Asian artistry and steampunk science, like props from a scene concocted by a Chinese Jules Verne, the heavy nickel accoutrements waited on the wooden tray before me. There were picks and awls of obscure provenance, reminiscent of antiquated dentists' tools; odd brass receptacles resembling miniature spittoons; pewter containers lidded with delicate brass openwork; tiny scissors with gracefully looping handles; dainty tweezers adorned with ancient symbolism denoting luck and wealth and longevity; strange implements with handles of ivory and blades of iron resting on a small brass tray etched with a detailed depiction of a young scribe offering tea to a robed mandarin. There was a tiny nickel-handled horsehair brush and a matching pan for sweeping up bits of ash. Enveloping everything was the warm glow of the opium lamp, the shining centerpiece of the layout tray. Second only to the pipe in importance, my oil lamp had a bubble-flecked glass chimney shaped like a fluted dome.

The crowning glory of my entire layout was perched lightly upon the chimney of the lamp: a hammered silver lamp shade in the form of a cicada. Slivers of lamplight shone through filigree work in the insect's abdomen and—most magically—illuminated its red ruby eyes.

Lying on my back with my head propped upon a porcelain pillow, I hefted the opium pipe in my left hand like a gun, my index finger curled around its silver fittings as though on a trigger. The Chinese word for opium pipe translates to "smoking-gun," and this one had just killed all my pain. With my right hand I lifted a tiny copper wok by its ivory handle and placed it upon the opium lamp. I measured five drops of opium into it. Within seconds the small pool of liquor began to boil and its heady sizzling was all I could hear.

Once again I was the alchemist, the one who had rediscov-

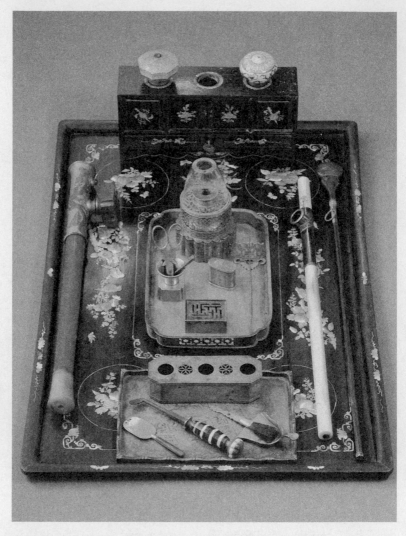

Complete layout of paraphernalia for opium smoking from the author's collection. The components date to the late nineteenth and early twentieth centuries and were crafted in China. (Photograph by Paul Lakatos)

ered how to work these long-forgotten implements. I was one of just a handful alive who could manipulate the elixir in the old Chinese manner and create bliss-inducing vapors. I was a high priest, one of the last still vested with the powers to perform these mysterious rites. After years of patience and persistence I had relearned the ancient craft and brought these hallowed rituals back from near extinction. This exclusivity of knowledge—watching my own deft hands use esoteric accoutrements to work a rare vintage of opium—gave me as much joy as the narcotic itself.

As I began cooking and rolling another pill for the pipe, I smiled to myself as though amused by the foolish antics of a young child. "Why on earth did you put yourself through all that?" I said aloud.

It had been barely thirty-six hours since I had begun my last attempt to quit on my own. Of course opium had won. Opium always won.

Though I had always wanted to be an opium addict, I can't claim that as the reason I went to China.

   —Emily Hahn, "The Big Smoke," *The New Yorker,* February 15, 1969

Tench was a forgettable character with an ugly, monosyllabic name—a booze-sotted British dentist trapped in a Mexican backwater partway through a novel. The only reason I mention Tench is because of an idea put forth by his creator, Graham Greene—an idea that he uses the wretched dentist to illustrate. According to this premise, the course of the character's life is set when, as a small boy, he finds a dentist's plaster cast of a set of teeth in a wastebasket. The discovery led to Tench's growing up to become a dentist—and then down a slow, steady path toward his eventual self-exile and ruin far from home.

   Is it possible that a person's childhood fascination with some object could subtly influence every other decision made during his or her life, a snowballing of interests, propelled by obsession and compulsion, that rolls on long after the initial discovery is forgotten?

   And if this were possible, would it then happen only to the most obsessive and compulsive of us? I bring up the idea because I believe I remember the source of my own Tenchian fixation— the beginnings of an early fascination with things Asian. A fascination that, many years later, would inspire me first to travel in Asia and then to live there. A fascination that would eventually drive me to accumulate so much knowledge that I became the world's foremost authority on a shadowy Asian ritual. A fascination that over time was to become so nuanced and narrow, it would lead me to become a slave to that most Asian of vices.

But that's all a long way down the road. Let me first explain how I believe I was instilled with a curious proclivity that affects a very small percentage of Westerners. Let me tell you how I was "bitten by the Asia bug."

When I was a small child my paternal grandparents had a glass display cabinet that contained, among other things, one of those colorful silk shoes that Chinese women with bound feet used to wear. There was only a single shoe in the cabinet and I remember during each visit, as I pressed in for a closer look, my grandmother would tell me that a whole race of women once wore tiny shoes just like this one. She never explained the part about the women being full sized, and I just assumed that their stature was in proportion to that silk shoe—a population of miniature women, perhaps related to the people who once inhabited the porcelain pagodas at the bottom of the adjacent fish tank.

Now, lest anyone get the idea that my childhood was something that Bruce Chatwin might have invented, I must admit here that I had no spinster aunts who chatted about Samarkand over tea. I do not have an exotic family history; at least it's hard for me to imagine anyone finding anything exotic about my past. I was born and raised in San Diego. My family on both sides had lived there a generation or two before I was born, but all had originally come from somewhere else.

The San Diego of my youth—roughly the 1960s and '70s—was a very livable place. I gather that most people have a favorable view of my hometown, and I think it's deserved if weather and location are what makes a city pleasant. Like nearby Los Angeles, San Diego is blessed with a climate that can pass for subtropical much of the year. In truth, most of Southern California is a desert and rain is almost unheard of, but by diverting water from faraway rivers, city planners have allowed anyone who can afford the water bills to turn their properties into faux-tropical jungles that are the envy of much of the rest of the country.

As I remember it, even the city's poorer residential areas were picturesque and interesting. There was street after palm-lined street of crumbling stucco bungalows, the foliage in their yards often a clue to whether the residents were locals or some recently arrived immigrants. Mexicans were partial to lemon trees; Filipinos planted clumps of banana trees; and, after 1975, Vietnamese immigrants arrived and began nurturing stalks of sugarcane. These were things I noticed because as a kid I was interested in tropical foliage. I knew the species of the palm trees that grew in my neighborhood, and during rides around the city I kept my eyes open for types of palms that I'd never seen before. Once home, I'd thumb through the *Sunset Western Garden Book* in order to identify them. Anything new that I had spotted went on a list, and if anyone asked me, I would have rattled off the varieties of palms that could be found growing around San Diego County.

Palm spotting was not my only pastime. I also entertained myself by making exhaustive lists of anything that caught my fancy—an embryonic form of collecting that was my first childhood hobby. While poring through the family set of encyclopedias, I drew up lists of World War I biplanes; lists of breeds of toy dogs; lists of Old West outlaws. I spent hours gazing at the illustrations in my many children's handbooks authored by Herbert S.

Zim, books that inspired lists of Native American tribes and species of insect pests. I made a list of what kinds of sharks you were
likely to come across if you swam off the California coast, and I
lamented over my list of birds that had become extinct in North
America.

My parents must have wondered what to make of it. In one
of those "school days" memory books that people used to keep,
my mother wrote that in the third grade I wanted to be a "statistician." She got it wrong. I wasn't looking for patterns. It was
nothing more than an impulsive gathering of information. Once
I was old enough to do minor chores and wheedle an allowance
out of my parents, I stopped making lists and began to collect
objects.

Despite my early fascination with the silk shoe, my first boyhood collections had nothing to do with Asia and were rather
unoriginal. I look back now and realize that these initial attempts at collecting were simply an exercise in gathering and
categorizing that is common among young boys: a cardboard
box filled with seashells and colorful stones, followed by an
album of foreign postage stamps and, later still, a bureau drawer
full of the persistent offerings of the Littleton Coin Company.

My first coin collection was a lesson in how the urge to acquire can cloud one's judgment. I came across an advertisement
for the Littleton Coin Company in the back of a comic book. I
signed up and soon had a handful of tiny manila envelopes, each
with a coin from some struggling or recently extinct country,
such as the Republic of Biafra. "Pay for the coins you wish to
keep," said the accompanying letters from Littleton, New Hampshire. "Send back the coins you don't want."

I wanted them all—despite having no way of paying. A new
coin showed up in the mailbox every few days. I examined each
one carefully before hiding it in a bureau drawer. Before long

the coins began arriving with letters written in tones of polite urgency, which over time became curt and vaguely threatening. I simply stopped reading them. Finally there was a phone call. My father stuffed all the little manila envelopes into one large manila envelope, and my whole coin collection was mailed back to New Hampshire.

I did better with fossils, which I dug out of the ocher-colored dirt in the backyard of my grandparents' house. In the distant past the area must have been the bed of a shallow sea, because the fossils were recognizable as seashells—mostly bits and pieces but now and then a whole clam or snail shell looking as though it had been made from the same sandy earth, pressed in a mold and baked solid. The sheer excitement of finding a well-formed fossil was enough to keep me in the backyard for hours, troweling away in the shade of a huge rubber tree. I wrapped each fossil in a length of toilet paper and kept them all in a box, and as soon as I got home it was time to consult Herbert S. Zim. After a time I no longer needed the book because I'd committed to memory all the text and illustrations that applied to my finds.

At this young age I was like a hyperdedicated sports fan who hungrily memorizes the professional statistics of a favorite athlete. As soon as I found something that caught my interest, I would read about it until I had exhausted all my resources: the family encyclopedias and books around the house, and later books at the school and public libraries. When I felt I'd learned all that I could, my obsession would start to cool and eventually burn out, but while blazing it was about the only thing on my mind.

In my early teens I began to collect foreign banknotes, and with these I rediscovered my attraction to Asian imagery and iconography. This collection, gathered while I was in junior high school, contained samples of the worthless paper currency of the recently defunct South Vietnam, and of Cambodia and Laos, as well as earlier banknotes from when the three countries were part of colonial French Indochina. These mid-century bills, with their colorful and idealized images of native peoples, elephants, and pagodas, were miniature works of art.

Travel was also a big part of my childhood. In 1972, when I was ten, my parents decided to buy a Volkswagen bus and hit the road. National parks were the primary destinations of the trip, and we—my parents, myself, and two younger siblings—visited the major parks in the western United States as well as lesser-known national monuments. We made subsequent road trips in the '70s, each with a different theme. One trip took in the ghost towns of California and Nevada. During another, we made stops to explore ancient ruins left by Native Americans—sites in the Southwest with names like Casa Grande and Tuzigoot and Montezuma Castle. I remember enjoying the natural beauty of the national parks and monuments, but for me it was the historical human settlements that inspired. There was something about the mystery of these places that gave me a fascination for dwellings that had once sheltered past lives.

This fascination also included antiques. As a boy I was convinced that certain inanimate objects had feelings. Okay, admittedly I was a weird kid, but I could not accompany my mother into a thrift store or junk shop without feeling sorry for some of the items that had been banished from the lives of their previous owners. At times these discarded things seemed to call out to me, and their pleas for a new owner were especially heart wrenching if the objects were damaged. My mother was patient but firm. "No, you can't have that," she would say. "It's broken!"

In an episode of the early 1970s television show *Nanny and the Professor,* the children found an enchanted antique radio that could somehow pick up music and events that had aired many

decades previous. After watching the program I became convinced that the idea was plausible. I wanted a radio like the one
on the TV show, one of those wooden cathedral-shaped models
from the 1920s with a dial that glowed like a peephole into the
past. I gabbed about it until my parents inquired at a couple of
antiques stores, but by this time such radios were already collectibles, and if they still worked they did not run cheap.

To console me my mother bought some record albums that
were recordings of radio programs from the 1930s and '40s—
The Shadow, The Great Gildersleeve, and *Fibber McGee and Molly.*
She then made some drawings, and my father took these into
the garage and, using a piece of plywood and a jigsaw, made a
convincing copy of the face of an old cathedral radio. After
staining and lacquering it, he stapled a scrap of grille cloth to the
back of the plywood to simulate a speaker, and then glued Ba-
kelite knobs onto the front. There was even a dial that lit up via
a tiny bulb connected to an AA cell battery. When finished, we
propped the replica radio façade up on the hi-fi cabinet and
spent evenings listening to the recorded radio shows. The effect
was perfect. Unlike the radio in the television show, however, I
didn't imagine that mine was miraculously picking up broadcasts
from the past. Instead, I used the scene to pretend that I was *in*
the past. From what I remember, that imaginary radio was the
first instance of my trying to feel nostalgia for a past that I had
not known.

I was also a Disney geek. Being only an hour and a half away
from Disneyland was, in my mind, one of the best things San
Diego had going for it. From about age five until adolescence
convinced me that it was no longer cool to do so, I went with
my family on annual day trips to the vast amusement park. Of
the themed sections that the park was divided into, Adventureland was an early favorite. Like the thousands of "tiki bars" that

were all the rage in post–World War II America, Adventureland was not an attempt at replicating any cultural accuracy or geographic coherence. Instead it seemed to be based on the tales of sailors returning from voyages in the South Seas, or the stories of great-uncles who had passed through European colonial outposts in tropical Africa and Asia. This was not something that I realized at the time, of course. To me Adventureland was simply the most exotic place I had ever been—like being able to jump into a Saturday morning episode of *Danger Island*.

The landscapers at Disneyland took full advantage of the Southern California climate, creating riotous jungles where before there had been groves of orange trees in orderly rows. The centerpiece of Adventureland is the Jungle Cruise, a ride on a cleaned-up and canopied version of Bogart's *African Queen* steamboat. A cleverly designed maze of artificial waterways and islands, the ride quite convincingly made me feel as though I were chugging first through the rivers of tropical Asia and then Africa.

The usual animatronics that Disney has long been famous for—depicting both animals and people—are the highlights of the ride, but I remember being most intrigued by some of the simpler visual effects, specifically the ruins of an ancient Khmer temple and a shrine to the Hindu deity Ganesha. The latter consisted of a concrete statue of the elephant-headed god—suitably detailed to appear carved from sandstone and clad in the patina of age—that the boat's steersman pointed out and explained was the guardian of the "sacred elephant bathing pool" that lay just beyond the next bend in the river. The passengers of the steamboat got a fleeting glimpse of the shrine, a smiling Ganesha atop a plinth and surrounded by emerald stalks of giant bamboo, before the boat rounded the bend and the vision was gone.

It was one of my favorite sights in all of Disneyland—that

benevolent Asian deity upon his throne on the bank of a tropical river, shaded by jungle canopy and covered with moss. I don't know if anyone else my age was affected by this image, but it must have made an impression on me: Some thirty years later I had made several journeys up and down both the Mekong and Irrawaddy rivers, and had published details of my travels in guidebooks and magazines; I had visited all the major Khmer ruins in Cambodia, Thailand, and Laos—remnants of stone temples that radiated out like milestones from Cambodia's Angkor region to the far corners of Indochina, and I had gathered a substantial collection of images of the Hindu deity Ganesha from all over Southeast Asia. It has become fashionable to belittle Disney's theme parks for being sterile and artificial, but my childhood experiences at Disneyland sparked some of my adult life's most exotic adventures and eclectic pursuits.

Adolescence changed my interests somewhat. Is there something about the hormonal assault that goes on within the bodies of adolescent boys that gives so many of them a fascination with things military? I began spending less time reading about fossils and seashells and more time studying the details of World War II fighter planes and Nazi uniforms. There was no hope of trying to gather a collection of either. By the mid-1970s, even such offbeat collectibles as Nazi daggers were being reproduced and sold via ads in the backs of magazines, but I had little interest in collecting reproductions of any sort. Luckily for my parents, my interests were largely thwarted. If the old radio shows had seemed a tad odd, how would they have viewed a sudden urge to acquire Nazi weapons? The one thing I could afford were American military medals. The Vietnam War had only recently ended and, as long as I limited myself to collecting medals from that conflict, there were plenty on offer, and they were cheap. Perhaps because of the war's outcome there seemed to be no shortage of veterans who were willing to sell their military-issued decorations for a pittance.

The imagery on one of these awards seemed as though it had been designed especially to fire my imagination. The Vietnam Service Medal had a green, yellow, and red ribbon—the latter two colors symbolizing the flag of South Vietnam—and was embossed with a dragon half hidden in a thicket of bamboo. How could I say no when such baubles were selling for little more than a buck apiece? There were other things to acquire: hat devices and shoulder devices and once a cigarette lighter engraved with a map of Vietnam. The war may have been unpopular with much of America, but in it I saw adventure.

Had I been born a decade earlier I might have signed up for a tour. Instead, I watched movies. In 1980, the year I graduated from high school, I saw Francis Ford Coppola's *Apocalypse Now* for the first time. Whatever the director was trying to say about the waste and futility of the Vietnam War—or war in general—was pretty much lost on me. Instead I was enthralled by the beauty and grandeur of the settings. Jungle scenes in which the protagonists were dwarfed by giant banyan trees left me in awe. Once the story moved upriver and came upon Colonel Kurtz's headquarters in the ruins of a Khmer temple, I was completely captivated. Where was this land of misty jungles and hydrogen-bomb sunsets? When the movie was over I didn't get up to leave. Instead, I sat there awestruck by the experience and watched as the credits rolled up the screen. Then I saw where *Apocalypse Now* had been filmed. Not in Vietnam, of course, but in the Philippines.

I was familiar with the Philippines because I had Filipino friends in school. San Diego is a navy town with a number of naval bases, and because the Philippines was once an American colony, its citizens were allowed to serve in the U.S. Navy even after independence was granted the archipelago in 1946. For that reason San Diego had, and still has, large numbers of Filipinos in residence. The ones in school were pretty much the only Asians I knew—although I don't remember when I realized they were Asian. Their last names were usually Spanish; they shared many of the same surnames that were common among the large number of Mexican kids in school.

During the summer between my junior and senior years in high school, an American-born Filipino friend accompanied his immigrant parents on a trip to their homeland. The following school year he told me stories about his experiences in the islands. Crazy stories. This was a country whose rich were so wealthy they seemed like comic book parodies of billionaires, and whose poor partied as though each day was their last; a land of epic natural disasters, but whose heartbreaking tragedy was always suffused with an element of buffoonery. Still, my ideas about the place were vague. After watching *Apocalypse Now* I was suddenly able to superimpose visual images onto the crazy stories I'd heard about the Philippines—images that to me were tantalizingly exotic. I made up my mind that I had to see the place.

Upon my graduation from high school, my parents gave me a gift of a thousand dollars. What would I do with it? I was undecided on a major and so college seemed to be something I should postpone. I wanted to be an archaeologist, but guidance counselors told me to forget the idea. Take lots of math, they advised. In the future everything will be run by computers, and you'll need lots of math to get a good job. Of course they were right, but I hated math.

After barely a semester at a community college, I dropped out and began to travel—and the Philippines became my stepping-stone from California to mainland Southeast Asia. By the time I was twenty-one I had visited twice.

Back then the Philippines got even fewer Western tourists than it does now. Most "tourists" going to the Philippines are really emigrant Filipinos returning home to visit relatives. The tourists who aren't Filipinos are usually middle-aged Western men looking for a cheap place to drink and carouse with prostitutes. The country is not on the backpacker circuit because its beaches and culture cannot compete with Southeast Asian destinations such as Thailand and Bali. To most Westerners, the Philippines suffers from a lack of exoticism. Simply put, Philippine culture is just too accessible. To a young Western backpacker, sharing a bus ride with a saffron-robed Buddhist monk reading the sacred Pali texts is exotic. Sitting next to a Catholic nun reading the Bible is a lot less so. When the Buddhist monk takes out his prayer beads, closes his eyes, and chants under his breath, the Westerner swoons. When the Catholic nun pulls out her rosary and says her Hail Marys, the backpacker squirms.

However, I wasn't put off by the accessibility of Philippine culture—to me its mix of the familiar and the exotic was a draw. I brought the address of some relatives of a high school friend and was supposed to contact them as soon as I arrived. They lived a few hours south of Manila, but I chose instead to check into a hotel in Manila's tourist district and do some exploring on my own. Having grown up so close to the Mexican border and Tijuana, I was no stranger to poverty or the trickery it often spawns when a seemingly rich outsider appears on the scene. I was on my guard, but the rush of being alone in unfamiliar surroundings was more invigorating than frightening. Certainly my familiarity with Filipinos in California allowed me to feel more at ease than I would have had I just touched down anywhere else in Asia.

The road trips with my parents were based on destinations, and their approach to travel had rubbed off on me. On my first visit to the Philippines I made it a point to see the sights, including a flight up to the former American colonial hill station at Baguio and then a drive down to La Union where there were beaches lapped by the warm waters of the South China Sea. I also made a pilgrimage to a location where *Apocalypse Now* was filmed, taking a canoe up the river where the Khmer temple scenes were shot.

After returning to San Diego I kept in contact with friends I had made in Manila, and during my second trip to the Philippines, nearly two years after the first, they insisted that I stay with them. This didn't surprise me. What was surprising was the depth of their hospitality: They insisted that I stay with them the entire time I was there. I was able to save so much on accommodations that my trip lasted six months. Besides saving money, this arrangement fit in with my travel priorities for the second trip, which were different from my first. I was less interested in destinations and more keen on understanding the people.

So instead of seeing the sights, I parked myself in front of the little mom-and-pop shop that my Filipino "family" tended and learned their language and culture by watching the transactions. The narrow lane out front was a constant parade of pedestrians and gliding pedicabs, and people invariably greeted me as they passed—the women and girls with shy smiles and the men with casual, upward nods of their heads. I was the only Westerner in the neighborhood, and everyone knew my name. I sat in front of that little store every day for months and never tired of the view.

It was a thoroughly enjoyable way to spend the twenty-first year of one's existence.

Collecting experiences was easy in Manila, but collecting objects was more of a challenge. The Filipinos whom I knew and lived among were relatively poor, and there were very few objects lying about that struck me as collectible. Things got used until they were useless and then they were tossed into a heap in a vacant lot that served as the neighborhood dump. There discarded items sat until the scavengers with wooden pushcarts made their rounds, picking through the piles. Anything recyclable—bottles, wire, any kind of scrap—was carted away to a vast and stinking shantytown in another part of the city where there resided what seemed to be a caste of trash pickers who made a living from recycling Manila's refuse.

In Ermita, Manila's tourist district, there were a handful of antiques shops that gave an idea of what Filipinos thought about antiques. The old furnishings and knickknacks—many of them made in the United States or Europe—were no different from what one could find at flea markets in Baltimore or Seattle—except that they were ten times the price.

One thing Filipinos collected that I found interesting were old Catholic icons: carved wooden santos ranging in size from small figurines of saints, friars, and nuns to larger-than-life images of Christ dying in agony on the cross. Some of the shops in Ermita specialized in Catholic antiques, their shelves crowded with dusty santos. The more primitive images—probably taken from rural churches—had an appealing folk-art look to them.

I was especially impressed by the fine old icons with smooth ivory faces whose features mirrored those of the Chinese artisans who had carved them: Marys and Christs with mournful expressions that were amplified by high cheekbones and slanted eyes. The images were fascinating to look at, but if the asking prices of the Western bric-a-brac seemed unreasonably high, the Catholic icons were astronomically so. Clearly these were already well-established collectibles among the Filipinos themselves. Instead of santos I settled for *anting-anting,* small brass amulets with Catholic imagery said to possess magical powers that protected the wearer from danger. There were stalls near Quiapo Church where old ladies with skin like Brazil nuts sold these talismanic charms for a few pesos each.

In August 1983, Benigno "Ninoy" Aquino returned to the Philippines from exile in America to challenge the rule of President Ferdinand Marcos. Before he could even set foot on the tarmac at Manila International Airport, Aquino was assassinated. I heard the news while attending a birthday party in my neighborhood on Manila's outskirts. During the tumultuous months that followed I accompanied friends to political rallies in Manila's version of Central Park, where tens of thousands of people wearing yellow T-shirts chanted for the resignation of Ferdinand Marcos.

However, by the time the downfall finally happened in 1986, I was in Hawaii. On television the humiliated dictator and his family were shown arriving at the Honolulu airport. The haste of their departure could be seen in their luggage—their worldly possessions packed into scores of cardboard boxes that had once contained Pampers disposable diapers. I watched the events unfold and wished I were in Manila to witness the citywide celebrations that were taking place.

After my money had run out in 1984, I left the Philippines and returned home to San Diego. Nearly four years had passed since I'd graduated from high school. My parents wanted to know what I was planning to do with my life. One day I walked into a naval recruiter's office and got into a conversation with the man behind the desk, who claimed that I could get stationed in the Philippines if I enlisted for a minimum of four years. He also told me that submariners made an extra hundred dollars per month and suggested that I volunteer for submarine duty. Both propositions sounded reasonable to me.

People who grow up in navy towns don't usually have high opinions of sailors. The ones I saw as a kid in San Diego seemed horribly unhip. In the age of long hair their heads were shaved so close you could see the pimples on their scalps. They traveled in loudmouthed bands at Sea World and Old Town, but no amount of attitude could make up for those clownish uniforms. My father, who like me was born and raised in San Diego, was not at all impressed by my idea of joining the fleet. "Do you want to be bossed around by those pinheads?" he asked. But it was too late. I'd already signed the contract.

As it turned out, the recruiter was wrong about there being submarines based in the Philippines. I ended up at Pearl Harbor, but I didn't complain much. At least I would be closer to the Philippines than if I had been stationed on the mainland, and I could fly there while on leave.

The navy was a four-year holding pattern for me. I did no collecting while I was in. I barely had time to sleep, so hobbies were out of the question. There was some travel but mostly it was work and more work. My primary duty was navigating the submarine. I have always loved maps, but the navy used charts— which are essentially maps of bodies of water. Maps have land, settlements, people, and history, but charts—unless they overlap some coastline—consist mostly of soundings: thousands of tiny numbers indicating the depth of the water. For me there was nothing more boring than a deepwater chart. I worked and squirreled away my money, telling everyone that I was going to get out after my four-year enlistment and retire in the Philippines at the age of twenty-six. I doubt many took me seriously. After I was discharged in 1988, I did go back to Manila, but I didn't stay there long.

The gloriously corrupt Ferdinand Marcos was long gone, and President Corazon Aquino, who had stepped into her martyred husband's shoes and led the drive to oust the dictator from the Philippines, was making an effort to rid the country of the jobbery and petty corruption that many Filipinos believed was Marcos's dirty legacy. I was staying in the Philippines on a tourist visa, which after an initial twenty-one days could be extended to give me a total of sixty days in the country. Then I would have to leave. Of course, flying out of the Philippines every two months would have been a real expense—except that I had found a way around it.

A friend of a friend who worked at the Bureau of Immigration and Deportation indicated to me that she could extend my visa under the table if I would have a new polyester bowling suit tailor-made for her. She sent me her measurements, and when the suit was finished, I gave it to her. That done, all I had to do was show up every couple of months at the immigration office with a carton of "blue seal" made-in-the-USA Marlboros, and my passport was quickly and efficiently stamped with another two-month extension. It was one of those arrangements that made me smile anytime I heard somebody cursing corruption in the Philippines. This worked fine for a few months. Then one day I showed up for my usual visa extension but my friend the Marlboro-smoking bowling enthusiast was nowhere to be found. I made a discreet inquiry, "Is Estrellita sick today?"

"No," came the reply. "Fired for corruption."

An immigration officer asked to see my passport and began thumbing through it. He was joined by another officer, and then another and another. Finally they all moved out of earshot and examined my passport in a huddle. I braced myself for a hefty fine, but when the passport was returned I was told, "You have five days to leave the Philippines."

When I got back to my apartment I looked at a map of Southeast Asia. In 1989, Vietnam, Cambodia, and Laos were closed to the casual tourist. Burma allowed tourists a mere seven days of visa time, and on arrival there was a mandatory currency exchange of two hundred U.S. dollars for worthless Burmese kyat. The remaining Southeast Asian capitals were Bangkok, Singapore, and Jakarta. Hong Kong wasn't too far from Manila, but it was expensive and I had little interest in going there. Singapore, too, was known as a costly place to visit. Thailand and Indonesia would be the most economical destinations, and so I chose Thailand. While in the navy I'd heard plenty of stories about ports of call in the Pacific, and Thailand, because of its wild nightlife and pristine beaches, was always high on the sailors' rave-about list.

I spent two weeks in Thailand: a few days at the beaches in the south, a few days in the mountainous north, and the remainder in the sprawling capital waiting for my fresh Philippine visa. The climate was similar to the Philippines', and the Thais physically looked very much like Filipinos, but the similarities ended there. The Thai language was totally incomprehensible and, unlike Filipinos, very few Thais seemed able to speak English. I wasn't ready to learn a new language. A nice place to visit, I thought as I was boarding the flight back to Manila.

Two months later I was back in Bangkok. President Aquino's anticorruption crusade was still in full swing, and I had again been told to leave the Philippines to obtain a fresh visa. Then something happened. In Bangkok I found work as an extra in a movie being shot by the Hong Kong director John Woo, just as

Manila was experiencing a particularly violent coup attempt. I decided it was a good idea to park myself in Thailand and wait out the political flare-up. Chiang Mai, a city in northern Thailand, was experiencing a boom in tourism, and after the film shoot was finished I went to check it out. While there, I was offered a job teaching Thai tour guides to speak Spanish—a language I'd learned while growing up in San Diego. It was a decision that would have lasting consequences. The rent in Thailand was cheap, visas were easy to obtain, and the months segued into years.

After a few years in Chiang Mai, I relocated to Bangkok. My teaching jobs gave way to writing gigs—first for a local magazine, then for the in-flight magazine of Thai Airways. This led to freelance journalism for the wire services Agence France-Presse and the Associated Press. Later, along with features for the wires, I began penning travel pieces for the Asian edition of *Time* magazine. Then came the guidebooks: For nearly a decade, I paid the rent by doing updates for Lonely Planet and Rough Guides, contributing to biennial editions of guidebooks about Thailand, Burma, Cambodia, Malaysia, Singapore, Brunei, and the Philippines.

Not long after arriving in Thailand I began collecting again. The writing jobs meshed perfectly with my old hobby: Suddenly I was getting paid to travel all over the region and had ample opportunities to scour its antiques shops. Based in Bangkok, I lived frugally in a small apartment in the city's Chinatown, spending less than five dollars a day on food and channeling the rest into whatever I was collecting at the moment. I owned no television and, except to browse Bangkok's Saturday night thieves market, rarely went out at night. After some initial exploration, I found the allure of the city's famed nightlife easy to

resist. Some people collect hangovers and sex partners. My fol-
lies were less fleeting.

Thailand and the surrounding countries offered seemingly
endless collecting possibilities. It wasn't just that the cultures of
mainland Southeast Asia had been producing collectible artifacts
for thousands of years. Even if you took away the antiques shops
and discounted old things altogether, the simple fact that Thailand, Laos, Burma, and Cambodia used non-Roman scripts to
write their respective languages made their modern products
exotic—and hence collectible—in my eyes. In the Philippines, a
Coke bottle looked just like a Coke bottle did in the States. In
Thailand, the Coca-Cola logo had been rendered into the Indic-
based Thai script—voilà! Instant collectible.

After a couple years in Thailand I began collecting something that was inarguably an art form: textiles. One would have
to be blind to spend any time in Southeast Asia and not notice
them. Many of the different ethnicities in the region have long-
held weaving traditions and have been producing works of art in
silk and cotton for centuries. What I found most interesting was
that historic events, such as forced migrations in the aftermath of
war, could be traced by reading what experts referred to as the
"grammar" of the region's textiles.

Prices could go as high as tens of thousands of dollars for
museum-quality pieces, but I found that during my travels I
often passed through villages in rural Laos, Cambodia, and
Burma whose inhabitants would part with interesting textiles—
usually sarongs—for just a few dollars each. In southern Laos, in
the bamboo jungles along what was once the Ho Chi Minh
trail, I visited a village whose weavers had produced cotton blankets with motifs that could not be misidentified: American
fighter planes and "Huey" helicopters. It was as though I had

found the exact opposite of a World War II cargo cult. This iso-lated culture living along the former Ho Chi Minh trail—one of the most heavily bombed pieces of real estate in history—had produced talismanic blankets in the hope that those wrapped in them would be protected from the terrible rain of bombs and bullets.

After a few years I had built up a respectable collection of textiles, but then my interest started to wane. One thing that turned me off was my fellow collectors. From afar they looked harmless enough. Some were matronly Thai women with big hair, titled according to the kingdom's system of ever-diminishing nobility. The Thai men were either moss-backed academic sorts or flamboyantly gay. They were an elite crowd and often spoke excellent English, and you wouldn't earn any points for speaking Thai to them unless it was flawless. There were also Westerners who collected the region's textiles, a bohemian-looking lot who had lived in the region for decades. Yet this was no polite circle of tea-sipping friends. According to stories I heard, the eccentric façades masked a cutthroat competitiveness. Okay, most serious collectors of just about anything will be able to tell you eye-popping stories of greed and deceit, and with the sums of money involved it came as no surprise that the Southeast Asian textile crowd had some real scoundrels among them.

Take, for example, the Thai university professor who ap-proached a woman from Chiang Mai—a friend of mine—who was selling off a collection she had inherited. The collection it-self contained some rare pieces, particularly from northern Thai-land, an area that had been officially a part of the kingdom for less than a century and whose textiles reflected cultural influ-ences from neighboring Laos and Burma. As established collect-ibles, such textiles had a high market value and could sell for thousands of dollars. The professor explained that he was writing a book, and he requested a selection of relevant pieces from the woman's collection that could be professionally photographed to illustrate it. My friend agreed but immediately there was a glitch: The photo shoot would take much longer than expected. When the textiles were finally returned to her months later, many of the best pieces were nowhere to be seen. Instead, similar but inferior textiles had been substituted. The professor was an acclaimed expert on northern Thai textiles, and my friend with the inherited collection was a nobody. Guess who never saw her textiles again?

Such tales were disturbingly common. Southeast Asian textiles were beautiful, but I had little affinity for the people who collected them. Perhaps I was afraid that if I kept at it, I would become just like them. Or perhaps I was simply bored with textiles. After some years of collecting, I abruptly stopped. I wanted to collect something new; something romantic without being common or clichéd; something whose collectors were not snobby or grasping but open to sharing knowledge and enjoyable to be around. I also felt I should be helping to preserve the old ways of Asia—ways that were fast disappearing. I didn't set out to actively look for my next collectible. It wasn't necessary. These things just have a way of finding me.

*The most direct road and speediest conveyance to Paradise . . . is by
means of that subtle drug, opium.*

—Mordecai Cubitt Cooke, *The Seven Sisters of Sleep* (1860)

No matter when you visit the capital of Laos it always seems half
a century behind the times. Vientiane has changed little since
John le Carré used it as a backdrop for his spy thriller *The Honor-
able Schoolboy.* All the monuments that commemorate Laos's role
as a Cold War pawn are still standing. There's the tawdry copy of
the Arc de Triomphe, built with concrete donated by the United
States for the construction of an airport runway. There's the
huge bronze statue of a Lao king presented by the Soviet Union
in 1972. Perhaps the statue possessed some Trojan horse
quality—a few years after receiving it, the Lao monarchy was
dead and the Kingdom of Laos was a Communist state.

Not that you'll get much revolutionary fervor out of the Lao.
The residents of Vientiane are an easygoing, unpretentious lot,
living in the shadow of pompous monuments about which they
know little. Their capital is a dust-blown, low-rise city that clings
to such French colonial traditions as shoulder-shrugging bu-
reaucracy and the after-lunch *sieste.* The Lao temperament kept
the Communist revolution from sliding into the draconian. The
royal family's demise notwithstanding, it was nothing like the

toxic Maoist experiment in neighboring Cambodia. Instead of fanaticism, the new leaders of Laos continued the Lao tradition of asking for and living off foreign aid.

By 1991 restrictions on visiting Laos had begun to ease up, and in April of that year I went to Vientiane for the first time to obtain a fresh Thai tourist visa. I was excited to see that heavy reliance on Soviet charity had clapped a bell jar over the country and preserved traditional aspects of life that had all but vanished in Thailand. While strolling about Vientiane taking photos one cool morning, I stumbled across a procession led by a white elephant. Where else could one see such a sight? No hype, no tourists, nothing for sale—just this near-mythical beast of the old Orient, draped in silks and being lured at a stately pace by handlers clutching bananas. The encounter was both unexpected and typical. It was later that day that somebody pointed out to me one of Vientiane's opium dens.

Laos was well known in the 1990s as the only place in Southeast Asia where opium could still be experienced in the Chinese manner. Sure, there were (and still are) plenty of opium-smoking tribal peoples, such as the Hmong, who inhabited villages on Southeast Asia's mountain slopes, grew their own poppies, and smoked their own harvest. But to find a genuine, urban, Chinese-style opium den that was open to the public—one of those storied haunts of yore—you had to go to Laos. In fact, Vientiane is the only Southeast Asian capital where Chinese-style opium dens survived into the twenty-first century—all the way until 2002, when an antidrug crusade funded by the French government shut down the last one for good. These establishments were very basic and run by ethnic Chinese and Vietnamese, most of whom had fled North Vietnam for Laos in the 1950s when the French quit their former colony.

The two dens that I occasionally visited during visa runs in the early to mid-1990s were rooms set aside in private residences. One was run by Madame Tui, who with her husband had come from Hanoi in the late 1950s. Madame Tui looked like an Asian version of Grandmama Addams from the 1960s television sitcom *The Addams Family.* She always dressed in black and had that signature shock of ghostly gray hair parted down the middle. Her husband was once the principal opium pipe maker in Vientiane but had retired by the time I met him. Although he had been living more than forty years in Laos, he never learned to speak Lao, and so I never had the opportunity to converse with him. Not that my spoken Lao was anything near fluent, but the Lao and Thai languages are, with some good-humored patience, mutually intelligible. I have always had a knack for picking up languages, and after a few years in Thailand I was getting adept at Thai. I also found that whenever I stayed in Laos more than a few days, my ears would begin to recognize the patterns of substituted consonants and tonal shifts that largely differentiate Lao and Thai. The Lao unfailingly take delight in hearing Westerners try to speak their language, so it was always worth the effort.

Unlike her husband, Madame Tui spoke flawless Lao and could always be found reclining beside her lamp in the upstairs room of her shophouse opposite the newly opened Tai-Pan Hotel. The shophouse door was always open, and the number of flip-flops at the threshold gave an idea of how many smokers Madame Tui was entertaining. I used to walk in and softly announce my arrival saying, *"Mae thao yu baw?"* ("Is grandmother home?") to nobody in particular while heading through the room on the ground floor to reach the stairway. Muffled sounds coming from the ceiling—the bump and scratch of bodies shifting on the floorboards in the room above—confirmed that Madame Tui was awake and tending her pipe.

The upstairs room was always dark, the windows tightly shuttered even on sunny days. I don't remember seeing any furniture—at least none as far as the circle of lamplight extended. The rectangle of floor set aside for guest smokers was covered with a thin, musty mattress that was off-putting at first, but which became more and more accommodating with each pipe smoked.

At the time, my interest in smoking opium was nothing more than enjoying an exotic thrill every couple of years, a bit of Tintin-esque adventure whenever I was in Vientiane. Opium takes some getting used to, and those initial attempts to smoke always made me dizzy and nauseous, but I was doing it for the experience, not the intoxication. While doing research for *The Rough Guide to Laos* in the late 1990s, I was in Vientiane more frequently and made it a point to spend an hour or two at Madame Tui's every time I passed through the capital on my way to and from Bangkok. By then I had learned to avoid the nausea by not smoking to excess, and I began to enjoy opium's subtle effects. I always tried to time my visits so that I arrived just around dusk. It seemed like the right time to be visiting an opium den.

Since there was only Madame Tui preparing pipes, the den could not practically accommodate too many smokers—unless they were content to wait their turn. A pipe of opium took about five minutes to prepare and smoke. That meant if there were five smokers including Madame Tui, there was approximately a twenty-minute wait between pipes. This was not usually the case when I first began visiting her, but as Laos caught on in popularity with backpackers in the late 1990s, word about Madame Tui's soon got around. And since she was the one opium den proprietor in town who allowed entry to foreign tourists, it soon got so crowded that instead of a pair or two of rubber flip-flops neatly parked at the front door, I would arrive to find a mass of dusty, oversized Tevas piled atop the locals' smaller, tidily arranged footwear. Madame Tui charged foreign visitors the equivalent of one dollar per pipe, and she was making too much money to turn the backpackers away. However, more than once she complained to me that the novice smokers vomited in her den, and she asked me to translate her pleas that they stop being so greedy. On the one occasion I did this nobody listened.

About that time I began avoiding the scene at Madame Tui's and instead visited the den of Mister Kay, whose freestanding wooden house on stilts was closed to the backpacking hordes but allowed expatriate Westerners, most of whom were French. The smoking at Mister Kay's den took place in a large room facing the street, and the pungent smell of opium was noticeable long before one arrived at the front door.

The room was devoid of decoration or furniture with the exception of woven reed mats on the creaking wooden floorboards. Mister Kay's paraphernalia was rustic, and in many cases crudely repaired with such incongruous materials as cellophane packing tape. During a typical visit I would recline and smoke a few pipes prepared for me by one of the elderly Chinese smokers who were fixtures in the place. The cost was fifty cents per pipe if I paid the smoker directly, less if I bought a pellet of opium from Mister Kay's wife, a bawdy old Lao woman who kept the pellets in a pocket in her brassiere and dispensed them to patrons with a merry cackle.

About a two-hour drive north of Vientiane is the town of VangVieng—a popular stop for backpackers traveling through Laos. There, too, opium could be found, but unlike the long-established dens in the capital, the opium dens of Vang Vieng were only a couple years old and little more than shacks. Cobbled together from wood scraps and roofed with corrugated tin, most were bare rooms about ten feet square. When not in use as a venue for opium smoking, the typical Vang Vieng opium den served as a living space for the den proprietor and his family. All of the dens had some sort of business operation out front— which was nothing more than a front. These tiny shops were manned by the woman of the house so she could keep a lookout while her man made pipes for the tourists inside. Surely every Lao in town—including every cop—knew which of these shanties were serving up crudely rolled pills of opium to be inhaled by wide-eyed backpackers, but to the uninitiated the dens were not so obvious.

A couple of the more brazen local addicts—and all the den keepers of Vang Vieng were addicted to their offerings— employed touts to bring in customers. The touts, usually teenage boys, could sometimes be seen loitering around Vang Vieng's restaurants and guesthouses, and were most active at night when crowds of backpackers settled in at the open-air eateries to watch the latest Hollywood fare on pirated DVDs. If a tout was around when you got up to wander outside to stretch your legs or have a cigarette, he would try to strike up a conversation—which might lead you to an opium den.

But for the most part you had to look for opium in Vang Vieng—it didn't look for you. Those who wanted to experiment could quite easily find it, of course, but for every tourist who did seek out opium, there were perhaps ten who were oblivious to the scene—and were just as happy to be sipping margaritas from plastic cups as they floated on inner tubes down the lazy tropical river along which the town of Vang Vieng gently sprawled.

In March 2001, I was in Vang Vieng with Karl Taro Greenfeld, who at the time was based in Hong Kong as second in command at the Asian edition of *Time* magazine. Karl was researching a story about the resurgence of opium smoking in Laos due to its popularity among backpacking tourists. Although he hired me to be something of a fixer, Karl had been kicking around Asia almost as long as I had, and he didn't really need my help getting most things done—except to translate now and then. There was, however, one thing that needed doing that Karl himself could not do: He needed me to smoke opium. Karl had at one time been hooked on heroin while living in New York City, and although he had been clean for years, he still harbored a strong fascination for drugs—opiates in particular. This seemed a little odd to me at the time, but I didn't waste much thought on it. I was getting paid two hundred dollars a day plus expenses. My mission was to get myself and Karl into a working opium den, and then for me to smoke some opium so Karl could observe and later work the details into his story. It was the sort of assignment that one prayed for.

I had worked for Karl on a handful of occasions and always enjoyed myself as much for the opportunity to hang out with him as for the unusual subject matter of the articles he researched. Karl had one foot planted in Asia and the other in America. His ethnic background—Japanese mother, Jewish American father—and the years he had spent living and working in Asia meant that our conversations weren't limited to the predictable questions about the continent that newcomers always needed answered. Indeed, Karl knew much more about some parts of Asia than I did.

Karl's article for *Time* magazine was going to be about Vang Vieng, a small town whose stunning scenery—it was surrounded by those impossibly vertical limestone mountains that one associates with Chinese scroll paintings—and easy accessibility to cheap liquor, marijuana, and opium had made it a must-stop destination on the Laos backpacker circuit. It was an economical place to party and relax amid gorgeous vistas, where rooms could be had for a couple dollars a night, and the amiable locals would smile tolerantly if you spent your entire vacation stoned and swaying gently in a hammock beneath the mango trees.

In 1996, a mere five years before Karl and I were there for his story, I had overnighted in Vang Vieng and found little more than bowls of *pho* (Vietnamese noodles) available for a transient to satisfy his hunger. The town was poor and lacked electricity and refrigeration. There were no restaurants other than the handful of noodle joints that ringed a flyblown market where every morning at dawn the locals came to buy the ingredients necessary to prepare that day's meals.

A few years of tourism had changed all that—the accommodations and food had improved hugely. As often happens in Southeast Asian tourist boomtowns, a number of the foreign visitors had decided to stay and try their hands at entrepreneurship. Usually an Italian would start up a restaurant, a Brit would open a bar, and if there was an ocean nearby and the possibility of diving, Scandinavians would quickly corner that market. Vang Vieng was different, however, in that the predominant foreign nationality, both as visitors and expats, were Canadians.

The most popular nightspot in town—Hope's Oasis—was run by a Canadian named Alfie, a strapping and permanently ballcapped guy in his late twenties, who seemed to be genuinely enjoying himself. He had a good rapport with the Lao staff, and had one or two Canadian girls working for him for free— hipsters with nose rings and obvious crushes on the young proprietor—who were content to make salads for a week or two before the dwindling days remaining on their visas forced them to move on. The menu, music, and décor of Hope's were sophisticated, and the place was packed nightly with young backpackers.

It would have been impossible for me to imagine a place like Hope's Oasis when I first passed through Vang Vieng less than a decade before, but parts of Southeast Asia were like that. The years between 1990 and 2000 saw great change in what was formerly known as French Indochina, a region that had been embroiled in decades of civil war, stunted by fifteen years of Communism, and then suddenly forced to embrace tourism after the collapse of the Soviet Union in 1991.

Karl and I found accommodations in the form of a small collection of bungalows on the riverbank, and then walked around the town. Vang Vieng was small and it didn't take us long to notice Hope's Oasis. Within an hour of arriving, we were sipping Cokes at Hope's, where the after-dusk scene was reminiscent of a popular restaurant and bar near a typical North American university. Alcohol was by far the intoxicant of choice with a discreetly passed bong making an appearance now and then. The opium dens we had come to report on seemed as far removed from Hope's as they would have from a Señor Frog's in Waikiki.

Later that evening, Karl and I took a stroll to see if we could locate one of the dens. Once we were off Vang Vieng's main tourist street the town resembled a typical lowland Lao settlement in which the inhabitants are in bed and asleep by nine. Nothing I saw looked like a place where opium was being smoked, and I couldn't detect the smell of it in the cool night air. After walking around for half an hour, we decided to call it a night and head back to our bungalows. On the way, we passed a small cinder block building that stood out because lights were still burning inside. It was the telephone exchange office. Karl mentioned that he wanted to go inside and ask about long-distance calls.

Waiting outside, I was approached by a young Lao man with larcenous eyes. "What you want I help you find," he said with a cadence so flat that I knew the sentence was simply a series of sounds he'd memorized. I answered him in Lao. "I'm looking for the police station."

He laughed and replied in Lao, "Asleep already!" He held a small plastic bag up to his face and breathed in and out of it, causing the bag to rapidly collapse and inflate with a brittle crackling noise. I saw then that his eyes were not those of a petty thief as I had initially thought, but the restless eyes of a glue sniffer.

"Where's an opium den?" I asked in Lao.

"Closed already," he replied. "They're asleep."

"I'll come back tomorrow then. Which way is it?"

The young man rubbed his stomach through a rag of a shirt. "Brother, please help. I haven't eaten yet."

I pulled a wad of kip from my pants pocket and gave him a five hundred note. I'm so bad at calculating exchange rates in my head that I wasn't sure if the amount was a prize or an insult. The young man pocketed the bill and pointed toward the river. "Ton's place is at the fork in the road. He won't cheat you. He's Lao. All the others are Vietnamese."

When Karl came out of the building, the glue sniffer was still hanging around, perhaps hoping for another handout. "What's up?" Karl asked.

"Our friend here just pointed out a den to me."

"Excellent. Should we go have a look?"

"He says it's closed, but at least I know where to look tomorrow."

The Lao language has two ways to say goodbye, one of which implies that the person being spoken to is staying behind. I used this on the glue sniffer lest he follow us all the way to the bungalows.

The next day Karl and I set out after lunch to find an opium den. Ton's place was a cabin-like structure of rough planks fronted by a mechanical press for making sugarcane juice. I poked my head into the doorway and asked for Ton, but an old woman told me he was out and wouldn't be back until evening. Feeling confident now that I had identified at least one place where I could come back and smoke opium, I suggested to Karl that we look around for another den. It didn't take long to find one.

A few yards up the road was a hut-like shanty that served as a tiny shop, its display of snacks in brightly colored foil packaging and cans of warm soft drinks lined up with their brand names visible. The cans of soda struck me as odd, and I remarked as much to Karl. "Who's going to buy a warm Coke?" I asked.

"Unless this stand is just a front for an opium den," Karl said with a sly smile.

Karl was right. No sooner had we approached the display of snacks than the shopkeeper—a wan-faced Vietnamese woman— leaned toward the bamboo wall behind her and spoke a few short words through it. Her husband—or a man I assumed was her husband—came from around back and hissed at us. Karl laughed. "Did you hear that? If that hiss wasn't an Asian cliché, I don't know what is."

The Vietnamese proprietor looked about forty and was half naked, wearing nothing but a pair of ragged shorts. He spoke no English but by using sign language—a mimed hit on the pipe—told us what Karl had already surmised. The man seemed very impatient to get us into the hut, and perhaps due to his pushiness, I felt we should first agree on a price. He spoke almost no Lao, so again he used sign language to indicate that he wanted one dollar per pipe. I thought the price was exorbitant and tried to talk him down, but Karl was eager to get started. "Just make him happy. At most you'll smoke, what, five pipes? I've got a five-dollar bill right here."

A door made of woven bamboo led into the boxlike room behind the snack stand. Once we were inside, the proprietor locked the door by twisting a length of wire around the door's frame and fastening it to the bamboo wall. As my eyes adjusted to the gloom, I took in the tiny room, barely twelve feet square. There were no windows. A handful of meager household items had been pushed into a corner, clearing the dirt floor so that a straw mat could be spread out upon it. The den keeper produced a blob of opium sandwiched within a piece of wax paper. The sticky mass looked something like tar.

He motioned for us to sit down on the mat as he began arranging a crude brass lamp whose glass chimney had been replaced by a perforated Pepsi can. The opium pipe was a simple bamboo stem, one end of which was stuck into what looked like a small porcelain vase. The vase had a tiny hole in its side, and this is where the opium would vaporize. I watched as the den keeper pulled the vase from the bamboo stem and used a wire to scrape out the opium ash that coated the vase's inner surfaces. Known in English as "dross," this black residue is a by-product of the vaporization process and, depending on the humidity of the surrounding atmosphere, can be sand-like and dry or moist and sticky. While the den keeper was cleaning and preparing the pipe, we could hear a conversation through the thin bamboo walls. Two Australian women—youngish from the sound of their voices—were trying to buy something from the Vietnamese woman manning the "snack shop" in front:

"How much for the Pringles, darl?"

There was what seemed like a long silence before the same voice spoke up again.

"I want to buy some crisps. How much?"

Another long pause followed, and then the same voice was heard again, this time raised and with some exasperation.

"Look. We give you kip. You give us Pringles."

Yet more silence ensued. Then a second Australian voice piped up.

"Bloody stupid, isn't she? How's she expect to make any money?"

Karl and I struggled to keep from laughing out loud. After the frustrated Australians left, I found that Karl was thinking the same thing I was. "Those cans of Pringles are probably empty. What do you want to bet they were picked out of the trash behind Hope's Oasis?" he said.

My eyes had adjusted to the darkness inside the den. Karl eschewed the mat and was instead sitting in a corner as far away from the smoking as possible. He had his arms around his legs and his chin resting on his knees, and he was watching me and the den keeper with a famished look. "I'm jealous," he said.

Karl loved to tempt the devil. His morbid fascination with narcotics reminded me of those combat veterans who spend their lives trying to relive the rush of past battles.

"Don't even think about it," I said. "You've got a wife and a kid, remember? That's why you're paying me to do this."

After I had smoked a few pipes, we departed the Vietnamese-run den to go back and see if Ton had returned. Karl needed to get some quotes from a den keeper but we were unable to communicate with the Vietnamese beyond hand signals. When we arrived at Ton's den he was there and hosting three college-age Italian men. The inside of Ton's was larger than the Vietnamese den and the floor was made up of wooden planks instead of dirt. The Lao, like the Thai, will not tolerate a dirt floor, and they traditionally construct their homes raised up off the ground. The plank floor had been covered with wide plastic sheets printed with a tile-like pattern, and a thin mattress covered with a cloth was laid out for guest smokers. Ton's was a class act, and his fee per pipe was half what the Vietnamese had charged.

After the Italians had left, I introduced myself and Karl to Ton and we got the interview that Karl needed. Ton told us that he came to Vang Vieng specifically to sell opium to tourists, and that his Vietnamese competitors were also recent arrivals to the town. He said that the police did a sweep every few months and locked up all the den proprietors in the town's tiny jail, a shack made of corrugated steel. Ton went on to explain that the police always let them go after a couple of days, when opium withdrawal caused the prisoners to have diarrhea in unison, horribly fouling the one-room cell.

Back at Hope's Oasis later that evening, Karl did a few more interviews. After several hours talking to backpackers, he said he almost had enough for his article. "If we could just talk to some authority figure like a cop or something. I need to know what the official take on this situation is."

"How about the village headman?" I suggested. "I think we'd be better off avoiding the police. They're likely to throw us in that little jail before deporting us."

"You think?"

"Yeah, we'd better not. Give me another day to find the headman and I'll also look into hiring a car to take us back to Vientiane," I said.

The village headman was accommodating, and the interview went well. A shirtless old man with talismanic tattoos across his back, he had nothing but good to say about Vang Vieng's tourist invasion. As for opium, however, it didn't even exist. "There's no opium here," the old headman corrected me when I asked how many dens were in operation.

Karl and I had to spend the night in Vientiane in order to catch
the early flight to Bangkok the following morning. This left us
with half a day to kill. I suggested that we go to Mister Kay's den
to see if I could get both of us in, but Karl said he'd seen enough
opium smoking. "I hope you never have to find out what being
hooked on opiates is like," he said without further explanation.

Instead, I took Karl to a no-name antiques shop, just opposite
the old Hotel Constellation on Samsenthai Road. A couple
years earlier I had spent half an hour in this very shop looking
over old medals that once adorned the uniforms of the military
and police of pre-Communist Laos. I found the Hindu iconography appealing—especially the three-headed elephant that was
once the official symbol of Laos. The Hindu symbolism was a
reminder that, culturally, Laos was on the farthest eastern reaches
of Greater India. I also remembered there being some opium
pipes in a display case, and this was the reason I thought Karl
might find the shop interesting.

"What a great idea for a souvenir," Karl said as the old Vietnamese couple tending shop opened a glass case and began lay-
ing opium pipes on the countertop. "Do you think I can get one
of these through U.S. customs?"

"That's a good question," I said. "I mean, they're antiques,
right? I guess if you tried to bring in ten of them you might have
some questions to answer, but not just one."

Karl's enthusiasm for the dusty relics prompted me to give
them a closer look. The pipes were more elaborate than the
simple bamboo-and-vase rigs used in Vang Vieng. These were the
classic Chinese design of opium pipe that I had smoked from in
Vientiane. Perhaps they once belonged to some of the old smokers who frequented Mister Kay's. I asked if the pipes were genu-

ine antiques, knowing full well what the answer would be whether they were or not. The shopkeepers did not disappoint me. "Old," said the man in Lao. "Very old," said the woman for emphasis.

Karl chose a pipe with jade end pieces and I offered to haggle a good price for him. I reminded the woman that I'd bought some medals from her a couple years before, but she didn't seem to remember me. No matter. When I asked the price, I was surprised by how reasonable it was—and I decided to buy a souvenir pipe for myself as well. The pipe I chose was a simple bamboo stem with end pieces carved from water buffalo horn. The pipe bowl was shaped like a discus, about three inches in diameter, and made from a terra-cotta colored clay. Tiny Chinese characters had been pressed into the clay when it was still wet, and these I surmised were the chop marks of the artisan who had crafted the bowl a century or so earlier.

The shopkeepers wrapped our pipes in newsprint as Karl and I counted out dollars onto the glass countertop. Back at the hotel and exhausted, we turned in early to our respective rooms after making plans to meet for breakfast the next morning. Before going to bed, I opened my travel bag and began rearranging my clothes so that I could fit the two-foot-long opium pipe inside. The pipe was still wrapped in newspaper with small red rubber bands around the stem at two-inch intervals. At first I had no intention of unwrapping the pipe until I got back to Bangkok, but I became curious to see it under the warm incandescent light of the hotel room.

The rubber bands were so thin that most broke and dropped to the floor as I tried to remove them. I almost changed my mind about unwrapping it, seeing that I'd need to come up with more rubber bands or perhaps some tape. But then I thought, what the hell, the smudged newsprint wrapper was already halfway open. I pulled off the remaining paper and then held the pipe in both hands at arm's length. Its smooth, unadorned stem gave it a streamlined look, and the discus-shaped bowl added to this effect. It looked nothing like a pipe for smoking tobacco. Without any obvious decoration to identify it as Chinese, this opium pipe could have been mistaken for a highly evolved war club or even some species of musical instrument. Yet it was neither. This was an opium pipe, a potential instrument of self-destruction that was technically illegal in most countries. To me, it was also a symbol of the old Orient—as archaic as rickshaws, Chinese junks, and man-eating tigers.

I put off rewrapping the pipe until morning and instead put it on display atop a chest of drawers next to the television set. I was smitten with my new souvenir. While reading myself to sleep, I many times looked up to admire the pipe's crisp lines. The following morning I was delighted when my new opium pipe was the first thing I saw upon waking. Then and there I had a collector's epiphany: Why had I never thought to collect opium pipes? The pull on my interest was so strong that I wondered how I could not have noticed their collectibility until that very moment. An opium pipe was a rare thing—it evoked all the mystery of the old Orient. There was an aspect of outlaw chic about it. It was a decidedly cool thing to collect, too, perhaps the coolest thing I had ever considered collecting. And in that instant I knew I had to have more of them.

As vague and incorrect ideas of the immediate and remote effects produced by opium-smoking are held by the people generally as there are regarding the kind of pipe used and the manner of smoking.

—H. H. Kane, *Opium-Smoking in America and China* (1882)

Usually when collectors first take notice of something, when some object catches their fancy and they want to see, learn, and acquire more, there is a book on the subject—all the collector has to do is read up on it. For collectors of Asian antiques in particular there is no shortage of books, no matter how arcane the subject matter: Chinese snuff bottles, Indian betel nut cutters, even Japanese *tsuba*—the intricately crafted hand-guard fittings found on samurai swords. For potential collectors of these and sundry other artifacts there are illustrated guides ready to educate and advise. But my efforts to find anything published about opium pipes turned up next to nothing.

A Hong Kong–based magazine called *Arts of Asia* ran three short illustrated articles pertaining to opium-smoking paraphernalia during the 1990s. I obtained back issues of two of these, one with an article about opium pipes and another about opium lamps. The latter article was quite good. I was impressed by the author's having taken the time to scout out some intriguing tidbits—such as discovering a Chinese general store in Manhattan's Chinatown that sold opium lamps all the way into the late 1970s. According to the article, the Chinese merchant pretended to have no idea what this unlabeled inventory was used for. The opium lamps illustrated in the piece belonged to the author, and it was obvious that he had spent much time trying to ascertain the function of each and every component of his complex little lamps.

Arts of Asia seems to rely heavily on self-made experts to supply the magazine's articles, and, as in the case of the piece about opium lamps, this can be a boon when collectors who might otherwise have difficulty getting published are able to share their knowledge. On the other hand, the *Arts of Asia* piece about opium pipes was an example of what happens when an author who knows very little about a subject has his words published. It would take me years to separate the facts from the misinformation conveyed in this article. The piece did have one exceptional saving grace, though: It was liberally illustrated with photographs of opium pipes and paraphernalia from the collection of one Trevor Barton.

I would later learn that, like the author of the article, Barton was primarily a collector of tobacco pipes—an established collectible with thousands of devotees in Europe and North America. As you might guess, the vast majority of tobacco pipe collectors are older men, and many of them have been at their hobby for decades. Trevor Barton was typical. Over time I was also able to learn that he had been gathering tobacco pipes from all over the world since the 1940s. An Englishman, he earned his living as a manager for a firm that sold natural gas equipment, a job that kept him traveling and gave him access to antiques shops and flea markets on four continents. Most serious collectors of tobacco pipes have at least one example of an opium pipe among their hoard; an outlaw curiosity amid the law-abiding calabashes and meerschaums; something sure to resurrect the conversation after sips of single malts and puffs on favorite briars have made old men quiet and contemplative. Trevor Barton, however, was different from the usual tobacco pipe collector in that he was not content to garnish his collection with a single opium pipe. He had many examples, and their photographs in the *Arts of Asia* article were a revelation to me.

I had already found and read shrill Victorian-era essays against smoking opium, written at a time when the habit was common yet believed to be the wickedest vice known to man. Almost none of these old tracts were illustrated with opium paraphernalia. It was as though the implements of opium smoking were unworthy of mention—deadly tools that were better left unseen. But there was nothing ominous looking about the pipes in Trevor Barton's collection. Their carnival-like adornment in polychrome porcelain, multicolored enamel, and bejeweled silver seemed meant to garner attention with a promise of hedonistic celebration. I was fascinated by these most colorful and ornate examples of opium paraphernalia and needed to learn more.

A few months after reading this pair of articles, a trip to the bathroom led me to an unlikely source of information—an article in *Vanity Fair.* For years in Thailand I had been living on tourist visas, exiting the country every three months to visit a Thai embassy abroad and obtain a fresh visa. The trips were something of a hassle, but having to leave Thailand regularly kept me from getting too lazy, and it was a great way to see firsthand how things were changing in the region. Often I took notes and turned them into articles that I could sell to magazines or the wire services, and in doing so I could recoup the cost of the journeys. Any neighboring country would do, but Cambodia in the late 1990s and early 2000s was my visa-run destination of choice because a good friend had taken a job running the Phnom Penh bureau of Agence France-Presse.

Dan had a spacious flat in a French colonial-era building overlooking the confluence of the Mekong and Tonle Sap rivers. His verandah alone was half the size of my Bangkok apartment, and the famed Foreign Correspondents Club of Cambodia—at the time my favorite restaurant in all of Southeast Asia—was just around the corner. At "The F," as the restaurant was known to expats, I typically had an unhurried breakfast before excusing myself to the privacy of Dan's nearby bathroom for a mid-morning respite. It wasn't that the restaurant's restrooms were unclean. In some ways the men's room was as atmospheric as the rest of the establishment (felt-tip pen graffiti: WHO THE HELL IS AL ROCKOFF?), but it was also as busy as the rest of the establishment. Going back to Dan's was a way to break up the morning, and I knew that when I returned to my table at the restaurant everything would be just as I had left it—the waiters knew my routine.

As it happened, the aforementioned issue of *Vanity Fair* was doing duty as potty fodder in Dan's bathroom. Leafing through the table of contents of the magazine, my eyes rested on a piece titled "Confessions of an Opium-Seeker" by author Nick Tosches. I scanned the article for illustrations and then took the magazine back to the restaurant and began reading it there, parking myself in an oversized planter's chair beneath the caressing breezes of an ancient ceiling fan. When the Sunday brunch crowd became too boisterous, I paid the check in dollars, received my change in riel, and then spent the rest of the morning reading on Dan's verandah.

When an outsider covers territory with which I'm on intimate terms, it's often a recipe for disappointment. I know what's real and what's just colorful prose, so when authors overly embellish surroundings that I know well, I feel as though some dilettante stranger has buttonholed me at a party and made extravagant and doubtful claims about a close friend. Parts of "Confessions of an Opium-Seeker" made me feel this way once the author's narrative took him to Southeast Asia and he began describing settings I knew well. On the other hand, I could easily relate to the hunger to experience the old Orient that seemed to have driven the journey.

Tosches searched the capitals of Southeast Asia looking not just for opium but for an *opium den*. He claimed diabetes had driven him to seek out opium, but he also insisted on having his medicine administered in exotic surroundings. His search led him through places that he felt were likely to still have opium dens: Hong Kong, Bangkok, Phnom Penh. Of course, the drug was available in the region's boondocks. In northern Thailand and Laos, backpacking tourists went on organized "treks" to mountain villages inhabited by ethnicities such as the Hmong, and a pipe or two of opium was almost invariably a part of the package.

Tosches, however, wanted the experience of an urban opium den—an establishment specifically for opium smoking, not the rural hut of some tribal highlander who happened to be an opium smoker. He wanted a place of sophistication where any member of the public might enter and recline and be served opium by an attendant who could masterfully prepare the narcotic before his eyes and wield the pipe with a flourish. He yearned for the charm and decadence of the old Orient, but no such place seemed to exist—all had been closed long ago. All but one apparently, and once the author found it, this opium den that ended his quest was lovingly described but vaguely located. I read this and felt that Tosches must have made a promise not to reveal the den's location. A year or so later, his expanded *Vanity*

Fair article was published as a seventy-two-page book called *The Last Opium Den.*

I knew where the opium den was. At the time the article was written there was only one city in Southeast Asia where such an establishment still existed. I might have finished the article and then forgotten about it, but upon doing some online research about Tosches I read that his *Vanity Fair* piece had supposedly received more positive feedback than any previous article in the magazine's history. Apparently I wasn't the only one interested in opium. I gave the story a second read.

One thing that caught my attention was the prominent mention of a book about opium smoking by a writer called Peter Lee. I made a note of it and began looking for a copy. Finding it took some time. Coincidentally, the book had been published in Thailand, but I could find almost no information about the publisher or the book on the Internet. Thinking that the author might be living in Thailand, I put my full attention toward obtaining a copy, and when I finally found one, *The Big Smoke* turned out to be one of the strangest self-published books I had ever read. The book's title was lifted from an article written for *The New Yorker* in 1969 by the American author and adventuress Emily Hahn. In it she told about her experiences with opium in 1930s Shanghai. Peter Lee's *The Big Smoke* did not describe the author's long-past experiences with opium as had Emily Hahn's excellent *New Yorker* piece. Instead, it was a modern how-to book for would-be opium smokers.

Peter Lee's *The Big Smoke* boasted detailed descriptions of opium smoking and even photos of some of the steps necessary to prepare the pipe. Opium was, according to the author, a miracle cure-all for modern society's woes. Paradoxically, he then went on to describe opium addiction in tones so sober that I felt he must have experienced withdrawal firsthand. He also offered a list of remedies for addiction. Some of them, including the "Clear Light, or universal free energy" method, sounded questionable to me. This cure could be performed only by a certain San Francisco spiritualist who would put the opium addict into a trance and then order the narcotic to "return to the cosmos for recycling." Withdrawal via this method was said to be fast and painless, but there was no name or contact information for the one person the author claimed could perform it.

The author's bio said he was a Chinese educated in America, but after reading the book I felt that something was off. There were quotes from famous opium smokers such as Emily Hahn and the French writer Jean Cocteau, but when I found and read these quotes in their original publications, it seemed that their highly selective use in Peter Lee's book was an attempt on the author's part to show opium smoking only in the most favorable light. Who was this guy?

The book's New-Agey tone sounded very American to me, as did the author when he sometimes dropped the spirit-healer persona for that of the outraged conspiracy theorist. There were rants about the U.S. federal government's antidrug policies as well as diatribes against pharmaceutical conglomerates whose greed and failure to somehow eliminate opium's addictive properties kept it from being a natural alternative to synthetic drugs. When I contacted the author with questions regarding some photographs of opium paraphernalia illustrated in his book, he admitted that he did not collect antique paraphernalia beyond what he needed to smoke opium at home, and that his own layout did not contain any antique pieces other than his pipe and lamp. But in the back of the book he did include a selection of color photos of genuinely old paraphernalia belonging to a German collector. Peter Lee told me that this collector was not easy to contact. Credits on the photo captions did not disclose his full name—here I shall call him "Helmut P."—and gave no other information about him.

Over a few weeks Peter Lee and I exchanged a handful of emails. The man was an odd mix of characteristics. He was a booster for opium smoking and proud of his knowledge (he sometimes followed bits of information with "Remember where you heard that"), but he also seemed to understand that promoting the use of a drug that was illegal in just about every country on earth might get him into serious trouble. I got the feeling that whoever this guy was, he was of two minds: hiding behind a pen name and fictitious biography and yet wanting to be the Timothy Leary of opium.

I decided to cut things off. I had gotten little information about opium paraphernalia that I hadn't already figured out myself, and Peter Lee kept pressing me to look for and sell functional pipes and lamps to him—something I didn't care to do. Instead, I made a gift of a small brass opium lamp that I had bought at an antiques shop in Bangkok and mailed it to the author at his home in a country outside continental Asia. My aim was to break things off in a polite way but also to be remembered if in the future I needed to get in touch again. Peter Lee was pleased with my offering and rewarded me with the name and phone number of somebody living in Southeast Asia who he claimed could teach me more about antique paraphernalia.

I was put off by my brief dealings with Peter Lee, however, and something told me to steer clear of him. I had come to the conclusion that his book was an attempt to garner widespread interest in opium smoking, the wished-for result being increased supply to meet increased demand. To go to such lengths in hopes of seeing opium become as cheap and ubiquitous as it had been in the nineteenth century struck me as reckless. My own experimentation with opium had, up until that point, been largely agreeable. I wasn't convinced that all the historical warnings against the narcotic were accurate—indeed, I thought that much of the early writings about opium's dangers were exaggerated. Yet I still had a healthy respect for the drug's alleged risks, and if I were suddenly to find that for some reason I could never again smoke opium, I would not have shed any tears.

After breaking off my correspondence with Peter Lee, I cast aside and almost lost the contact information for that supposedly knowledgeable source that he had given me. When, months later, I remembered the contact and finally made the effort to seek out and meet the man, he not only turned out to be a very important source of information about the effects of high-quality opium, but he also became a very good friend.

❧

I spent hours looking at the photographs in the opium-related articles from *Arts of Asia* magazine. I did the same with the how-to book, memorizing the details in the photos of Helmut P.'s collection. I heard about a museum catalog from an exhibition that was held at the Stanford University Museum in 1979. The exhibition was mostly put together from the collection of a professor named Ralph Spiegl. During a visit to San Francisco, I persuaded a friend to drive me to the museum where I was able to get a copy of the catalog as well as see a handful of opium pipes that were in the permanent collection. The catalog's illustrations were small and the descriptions of the pipes on display were brief, but at least I was able to glean some information by comparing the dimensions of each pipe. It seemed the average opium pipe was an astonishing twenty-two inches long.

Emily Hahn's story in *The New Yorker* was charming, but there were no illustrations and little description of the paraphernalia she and her friends used. Jean Cocteau's *Opium: Journal d'une désintoxication (Opium: Diary of a Cure)* from 1930 was illustrated with Cocteau's own line drawings—edgy self-portraits of the author suffering through detox—but again, there was almost no description of opium paraphernalia.

In 1882, a New York doctor published a book called *Opium-Smoking in America and China.* Claiming to have spent years in the opium dens of Manhattan, Dr. H. H. Kane wanted to cure opium addiction, and his book was a warning to American readers about how quickly the vice of opium smoking was spreading. Kane described the smoking process in detail, and his book featured a single engraving of a typical opium pipe, opium lamp, and other requisite opium-smoking accoutrements.

Besides these publications and a handful of magazine articles, there was nothing—at least not in English. It seemed that almost nobody had written in detail about opium paraphernalia—even during the heyday of opium smoking. Much, of course, had been written about the scourge of opium addiction, but nobody had bothered to describe the instruments or the rituals of that addiction. At the time I couldn't figure out why, but after I began learning about opium's more recent history, the reason for the dearth of reliable information became rather obvious.

Before explaining why the culture of opium has been so thoroughly forgotten, I should dispel a commonly held modern misconception: Opium was not introduced to China by the British. Fans of simplified versions of history with clear-cut heroes and villains (as well as modern Chinese propagandists) may be distressed by this politically charged truth, but for the rest of us this is good news—the real history of opium in China is much more complex and, as a result, infinitely more interesting.

Opium arrived in China around the seventh century via Arab traders, whose opium-laden camels traveled east over the fabled Silk Road. The Arabic connection is most evident in the

Chinese word for opium, *yapian,* which is probably a corruption of the Arabic word for opium, *afiyun.* The Arabic word was, in turn, based on Afyon, the name of a province in what is now modern-day Turkey, where the Arabs believed opium originated. Following the narcotic's arrival in China from the west, hundreds of years passed and opium assumed a place among thousands of drugs—some indigenous, some imported—that made up the prodigious Chinese pharmacopoeia. Li Shizhen, the father of Chinese herbal medicine, described opium in the sixteenth century, noting the narcotic's ability to cure diarrhea and trumpeting its benefits as an aphrodisiac. This reputed attribute would greatly enhance opium's desirability in China and other parts of Asia but paradoxically would also stigmatize the drug once it arrived in America.

As an assumed aphrodisiac, opium gained popularity in Chinese society and by the mid-Ming dynasty (approximately 1450 to 1550) opium was worth its weight in gold. China began to demand that semi-vassal states such as Siam provide opium as a tribute item along with luxury goods such as elephant ivory and rhinoceros horn. Yet the magical substance was not without its drawbacks. Addiction was a known risk, but most users managed to avoid it due to the simple fact that opium was very rare and costly.

As in other regions of the world where opium was known, the Chinese method of ingestion was eating. If eaten frequently, raw opium wreaks havoc on the gastrointestinal system, causing severe constipation. The same side effect that made opium an effective treatment for diarrhea kept it from being enjoyed too often as an aphrodisiac. Then, sometime in the early seventeenth century—exact dates are impossible to know at this point—the Chinese began smoking opium recreationally.

Early attempts at smoking opium should not be confused

with the classic opium-smoking experience that evolved from it. Because raw opium is a sticky goo difficult to ignite and burn, the narcotic had to be mixed with tobacco in order to be smoked. While consuming opium in this way was somewhat easier on the digestive system, it was still problematic. Burning opium produced an acrid gray smoke that caused the smoker to choke and coated his or her teeth with an oily black residue.

There were other unpleasant side effects as well. Because it was difficult to gauge one's optimum dosage, all but the most regular smokers of the opium and tobacco mixture would have become nauseous every time they tried it. Smoke too much and toxic shock caused the body to involuntarily vomit, the smoker retching for hours even though there was no opium in the stomach to expel. Burning opium also changed its chemical makeup, destroying certain alkaloids that made opium intoxication pleasurable. So neither of these early methods of ingesting opium, eating nor burning, was suitable if opium was to be used recreationally as a thrill to the senses.

The innovations that would give opium users a sophisticated and pleasurable high wouldn't happen until the eighteenth century, when some nameless Chinese craftsman, whose creativity seems to have been surpassed only by his anonymity, came up with a design for a true opium pipe—an instrument whose purpose was not to burn opium but to *vaporize* it. In the West, this was known as "opium smoking," but the term is actually a misnomer since vapor, not smoke, is produced. Opium vaporizes at a relatively low temperature, which allows heat-sensitive alkaloids to survive and that, in turn, makes for a superior high. This is why confirmed opium smokers would never consider "smoking" the drug in any apparatus other than a true opium pipe.

The new and improved opium pipe's vaporization process took place in its unique "pipe bowl." Nothing about its shape

This diagram of an opium smoker illustrates how the opium pipe's unusual design facilitated the vaporization process. Based on a drawing from *Opium des fumeurs,* published by the Archives de Médecine Navale et Coloniale, Paris, 1890.

suggested a traditional bowl in which tobacco is deposited before being burned and inhaled. The typical opium pipe bowl looked more like a doorknob, with one tiny hole on its topside and a much larger hole on its bottom. This bottom hole had a metal fitting around it (the "collar") that attached to a second metal fitting (the "saddle"), which was permanently fixed to the pipe stem. This design allowed for the pipe bowl to be affixed to the pipe stem in an airtight manner, and it was easily detachable so the interior of the bowl could be periodically cleaned. If the opium pipe was not completely airtight, vaporization could not happen. The pipe stem was about two feet long, because a flame (the opium lamp) was needed to heat the opium for vaporization, and a long pipe stem allowed the smoker to stay a comfortable distance from the lamp.

The opium lamp was a simple oil-fueled burner upon whose squat, ventilated base sat a glass chimney designed to funnel heat upward. Vegetable oil was used instead of kerosene or alcohol because it produced a low-temperature flame that did not destroy those all-important alkaloids. In China, camellia oil was said to be the best for opium lamps. In Southeast Asia, coconut oil was the obvious choice, and after opium smoking was introduced to America, peanut oil became the preferred fuel for opium lamps there.

Once a dose of opium was prepared—the drug having been cooked, rolled into shape, and attached to the pipe bowl—the smoker then held the primed bowl just above the lamp while in a reclining position. This is the reason opium smokers are always seen lying down in old photographs. Their position had less to do with opium making them drowsy—although after many pipes it definitely did—and more to the fact that reclining was the best position for the smoker to comfortably hold the pipe steady over the lamp while monitoring the opium as it vaporized. The smoking process was delicate and took some concentration, and was all but impossible to do for long periods unless lying on a horizontal surface. That surface was often just a floor covered by a mat or carpet, but sometimes it was a wooden "bed" built specifically for the purpose of opium smoking.

I know nothing about physics, but the thing that impresses me most about the opium pipe and lamp is that they are a simple solution to a complex problem—how to efficiently get heat-sensitive opium alkaloids into human lungs where they can pass into the bloodstream and create almost instantaneous pleasure. Somebody in China was taking opium intoxication very seriously during the eighteenth century when this type of pipe was invented.

Some historians believe that these novel developments were a result of a tobacco ban enacted by Chinese officials. Having been recently introduced to China from the New World, tobacco was seen as a greater evil than opium. Whatever its inspiration, this new pipe design opened the door for opium to become a national sensation among China's artistic and elite classes. As the drug's popularity increased, the smoking experience improved. The Chinese learned to refine opium especially for the newly invented pipes by boiling it, filtering it, and allowing it to age. The result was *chandu,* a potent form of opium made specifically for vaporizing.

During the early nineteenth century, the vanguard of Chinese society—artists, poets, and even the attendant eunuchs of the imperial palace—were inspired enough by their fondness for opium smoking to fashion a new lifestyle around it. Later, respected scions of the elite such as nobles, scholars, and mandarins lent their sense of taste and sophistication to create rites and procedures for this novel pastime.

Despite opium having been known to some of the most inventive and trendsetting cultures of the ancient world—Egypt, Greece, Persia, and India immediately come to mind—it was in China and later Vietnam that the paraphernalia of opium smoking saw dizzying innovation in both design and artistry. Pipes, lamps, and other tools made specifically for vaporizing opium were crafted from the finest materials—ivory, jade, porcelain, rare hardwoods coated with lustrous lacquers, and precious metals encrusted with valuable stones. In some circles, the ritual of opium smoking became as elaborate as that of tea drinking—not the stylized and formal pantomime of a Japanese tea ceremony, but the spontaneous and convivial version that is uniquely Chinese.

A casual opium smoker might become a committed addict after using the drug over a period of several months or years. Not all who smoked became addicts, but heightened availability made opium's pleasures difficult to resist. Among upper-class Chinese smokers, young men who were not yet financially stable were discouraged from taking up the pipe. It was, however, socially acceptable for older men and women of sufficient wealth to indulge on a frequent and regular basis—and these were the smokers most likely to spend lavish amounts on their paraphernalia in order to please themselves and impress their smoking friends. A retired merchant might have an opulently appointed private smoking room in a quiet part of his house. The truly wealthy might have two different smoking rooms, one for the summer months and another for the winter, in order to take advantage of the seasonal changes in sunlight and temperature that could subtly affect the opium-smoking experience. The smoking room might be outfitted with lavish trappings, including an opium bed of intricately carved hardwood, enclosed on three sides to create a cozy atmosphere.

In his book *Travels in China* (1855), the French missionary Abbé Huc described what he saw firsthand:

> At mansions of the rich there is usually found fitted up for accommodation of friends, a private boudoir, richly ceiled, and garnished with superb adornments, such as art only can achieve and wealth procure; and here rich paintings, with choice scraps from Confucius, adorn the walls, and carvings in ivory with other articles of vitù, grace the tables. Here also provided in chief the gilded opium-pipe with all its appurtenances; and here host and guests, unrestrained by curious eyes, deliver themselves up without concern to the inebriating chandoo and its beatific transports.

After the Chinese invented the vaporization process, a simplified version of the Chinese opium pipe went west along some of the same trade routes that had originally brought opium to

China with the Arabs. In other words, the Arabs brought opium to China, but the Chinese taught the Arabs how best to enjoy it. This probably happened during the nineteenth century, and to this day a localized version of the Chinese opium pipe is clandestinely used to vaporize and inhale opium in some countries of the Middle East. Instead of using an oil lamp as a heating source, Middle Eastern smokers used a glowing piece of charcoal held with a pair of metal tongs, a method that to me seems wasteful, but perhaps in regions where there was an abundance of raw opium this was not an issue. Because they did not use an opium lamp, Middle Eastern smokers were able to indulge sitting upright—there was no need to recline in order to monitor the pipe's distance from the flame.

Understanding opium's effects on its users is key to understanding its popularity in China and other parts of Asia. High-quality opium ingested in small quantities was conducive to both mental and physical work. Candidates for official positions smoked opium before they sat for the imperial exams. Merchants conducted business while smoking opium, agreements being sealed with some leisurely draws on the pipe. Opium thus served much the same function in social situations as did alcohol, but with an important difference. The symptoms of moderate opium intoxication were difficult to detect. Unlike drinkers of alcohol, experienced smokers could easily hide any evidence of their indulgence. There was no reckless casting off of social inhibitions that could sometimes lead to embarrassment. Opium also lacked any kind of hangover.

Chinese and other Asian cultures value self-control, order, and decorum. For many of China's elite, opium was the perfect drug. By the early nineteenth century, opium smoking was already an integral part of Qing dynasty high culture—a rare treat for those whose could afford it.

Then along came the British. Tea is what they were after, and China had plenty of it, but the Chinese would take only silver in trade. Such was the insatiable British thirst for the caffeinated joys of tea that London's silver reserves were rapidly depleted. The British scrambled to find some item that the Chinese lacked, but it seemed there was little demand in China for any of Britain's manufactured goods. To Chinese eyes, Britain's exports were crude and shoddy—British woolens looked barbaric when compared to Chinese silks. Some European-made goods such as timepieces became status symbols in China, but few could afford such luxuries. Britain combed her colonies in search of something that might suitably excite Chinese cravings equal to the British demand for tea. In time, opium was hit upon.

From her Indian colony, Britain oversaw the cultivation of the opium poppy and the harvest of its medicinal sap with an efficiency that ensured raw opium from Bengal and Bihar was consistently of the finest quality and purity. Patna, especially, was considered to produce the Château d'Yquem of opium. Balls of the raw narcotic were packed in mango wood crates and shipped to ports along the south China coast. Chinese brokers and merchants then processed the raw opium into *chandu* and repackaged and sold it under such brands as Fook Lung (Abundant Luck) and Lai Yuen (Source of Beauty).

British India's opium was well received in China and proved to be so popular that the British could demand payment in silver—thus turning the tables on the Chinese tea monopoly. American traders tried to get in on the act by importing opium to China from Turkey—and some New England families prospered as a result—but Turkish opium was considered inferior to that of British India by China's discriminating smokers.

When Chinese officials became aware that the flow of silver had reversed, they attempted to stop the opium trade by force,

Postcard made from a portrait depicting "opium smoking" posed in a studio in China circa 1910. Although not depicting actual smoking, images like this are historically important for the paraphernalia on display. (From the author's collection)

not once but twice. Both Opium Wars—the first of which ended in 1842 and the second in 1860—were disastrous for China. Not only was China outgunned by the British, but many port cities such as Canton, complicit in the lucrative opium trade, were invested in seeing China defeated so that the flow of opium would continue unrestricted.

What Britain gained, besides the right to openly trade opium with Chinese wholesalers, was a rocky, barely inhabited island near the mouth of the Pearl River, 110 miles southeast of Canton. This island became the British colony of Hong Kong. Over time, this shimmering jewel in Queen Victoria's crown prospered while China grew ever more addicted, corrupt, and ungovernable.

To this day, China and many Chinese around the world view opium as a dastardly British trick that kept their country poor and backward long after the British opium trade had ceased. This lingering taste in Chinese mouths—as bitter as a lump of opium melting on the tongue—seems to have kept them from saving any record of opium's cultural importance for posterity. Apart from endless retellings of historic episodes that show China as a victim heroically struggling to throw off the foreign narcotic plague, there is no hint in the official version of Chinese history of opium's important place in the social life of the imperial past; no mention of the hundreds of tons of opium that were being cultivated in the Szechwan and Yunnan provinces by the mid-nineteenth century. In fact, some historians surmise that by the 1880s, China was growing two times more opium than it imported.

If ever there was any great Chinese language tome on the art of opium smoking, it no longer exists—at least I have been unable to uncover any evidence of one. Surely this was the main reason I was having such difficulty finding reliable information about antique opium pipes. Any such work written in China during the height of the drug's popularity would have been banned and then destroyed by the end of the Cultural Revolution.

With all this official Chinese historical revisionism in mind, I can't help but wonder, What if? Had the Chinese not perfected the art of opium vaporization and thus vastly improved the quality of opium intoxication (which, in turn, increased demand for the drug), would the historic British opium trade ever have happened?

Of course there's no way to know the answer to this question, but one fact is certain: Whereas before the Opium Wars the narcotic sap of *Papaver somniferum* was a rare cerebral delicacy whose devotees ranked among China's wealthy and privileged, the British victory suddenly made opium available to nearly everyone. Even the lowliest rickshaw puller could now afford a cheap, adulterated form of the drug. This caused an epidemic of addiction that, in China with its teeming millions, was obvious even to visiting foreign observers.

Christian missionaries targeting China for conversion found in opium a ruthless demon as shocking as foot binding and female infanticide. By writing books and articles and giving public talks aimed at Westerners, particularly North Americans and Britons, the missionaries helped generate the public outrage that eventually gave rise to a global, American-led movement to halt the opium trade and prohibit opium smoking in nearly every country worldwide.

But the commercially shrewd British and their lopsided Opium War victories also inspired another movement—a short-lived one that has been all but completely forgotten, and this was the rise of skilled Chinese craftsmen who began producing tools for a diverse and fast-growing market. It was during this time, roughly from 1850 to 1910, that Chinese artisans created opium-smoking paraphernalia of previously unseen artistry.

Because of opium's relatively new and semi-outlaw status, the adornment of opium paraphernalia did not have to conform to the strict and proper parameters that were based on ancient Chinese art forms. Much latitude was given to the craftsman, and, just as important, to the patron for whom a piece was being made. Adornment on an opium pipe could be custom-made to the whims of an individual smoker.

Traditional Chinese art is often stylized and repetitive. Apprentices copied their masters so closely from generation to generation that, to the layman's eye, the decorative motifs seem barely to differ from one dynasty to the next. The adornment of opium paraphernalia, on the other hand, was like visual jazz: It didn't conform to rigid convention and so comes across as spontaneous, festive, and fresh. In fact, artisans so broke from tradition when making opium paraphernalia that contemporary experts of Chinese art often mistake their works for provincial art created in Southeast Asia by ethnic Chinese who had no formal training in the arts of the mother country.

In my opinion, the crafting of opium-smoking accoutrements reached its apex in what is now Vietnam. There the craftsmen—many of them ethnic Chinese—were exposed to European decorative motifs brought over with the French who began colonizing Indochina in the 1860s. The artisans of Vietnam preferred silver over the hard, nickel-like alloy called *paktong* that was the Chinese material of choice for metal parts and fittings on opium pipes and lamps. The Chinese liked *paktong* for its durability, and the alloy was also used to make scholarly objects such as containers for calligraphic ink.

Silver is softer than *paktong,* and its malleability enabled Vietnamese artisans to use both repoussé and chased work techniques, hammering out ornamentation in the minutest detail. Their designs sometimes dispensed with Chinese convention altogether, replacing it with realistic Art Nouveau depictions of flora and fauna. But more popular was a harmonious combination of Chinese and European art. An example of this cross-culturalization is an obscure mammal whose image was probably imported from France and first applied to Vietnamese opium paraphernalia. The dormouse is a nocturnal rodent similar to the squirrel, fond of eating grapes by night and sleeping the day away in the shade of grapevines. The French phrase *"Dormir comme un loir"* ("Sleeping like a dormouse") implies a delicious, unhurried slumber. Thus, the dormouse on a cluster of grapes became a common European motif on opium pipes that were otherwise Chinese in adornment—a tiny image of the rodent curled up under the pipe bowl in celestial slumber, behooving the owner of the pipe to do the very same.

But Vietnam's most remarkable contribution to opium smoking was a unique style of lamp, and those who are able to view a lighted one are in for a visual treat. The Vietnamese love for dragons as a decorative motif is often evident, as these auspicious beasts writhe up the sides of the lamp's base and oil reservoir. Muscles bulge beneath scaly hides, wickedly hooked claws shred clouds, and gaping maws expose needle-sharp teeth and serpentine tongues. The dragon's legs sometimes form the base of the lamp, supporting a crystal chimney etched with bamboo stalks and leaves—giving the effect that the dragon is poised to burst forth from a glowing jungle lair.

Now imagine yourself in a room in old Indochina, reclining alone next to a layout tray upon which rests such a lamp. Your full attention is absorbed by this sculpture in silver and crystal, the centerpiece of a room becoming somber in the waning light of a tropical dusk. Soon the room is completely dark, and all you can see is the warm glow of the opium lamp's flame upon this meticulously detailed silver dragon. Slowly and meditatively begins the first act of a hedonistic ritual that will last until dawn. Is it any wonder that French citizens in their thousands fell under the trance of *la fée brune*, "the brown faerie," as opium came to be called among them?

Thanks in large part to the British, opium smoking was already common in Indochina when the French began to colonize it. The habit was introduced to Southeast Asia from China, both via Chinese immigrants who settled in ports along the coast of Vietnam, and by tribal peoples such as the Hmong who migrated south into the region's northern highlands. To ensure that profits from opium smoked in its colonies didn't go straight

into British pockets, France in 1881 established the Opium
Regie, a government-controlled monopoly that promoted local
poppy farming, imported the raw narcotic from India and China,
and oversaw refining and the licensing of opium dens. By 1914,
official records show that 37 percent of Indochina's revenues
were coming from the sale of opium. The drug made vast fortunes for the French, but it also tempted the very same coloniz-
ers with addiction. Smuggling opium from the colonies back to
France was a crime, but smoking the drug was not, and anywhere there was a demand for it, opium was soon to follow. By
the turn of the twentieth century, opium-smoking establishments had spread to France, mostly in coastal cities such as Toulon and Marseille and Hyères.

The French colonials' love for opium and attachment to their
opium accoutrements can be corroborated by the hundreds of
pieces of paraphernalia that made it back to the mother country intact—antique opium pipes and lamps that still occasionally turn up at auctions in cities outside of Paris. Some of these
pieces were quite obviously crafted by Vietnamese artisans specifically for French smokers. French naval officers are said to have
commissioned opium lamps attached to gimbals so that even
during the roughest transoceanic crossings, the all-important
flame was kept steady and upright, ready to gingerly toast each
pill of opium to perfection.

In fact, French naval officers came to like their opium a little
too much. In the late nineteenth century French officers caught
smoking it would find their dossiers marked with the initials
"F.O." (fumeur d'opium), scarlet letters that would severely curtail
their advancement up the ranks. In 1907, one French officer
charged with spying for the Germans blamed his transgressions
on his opium addiction. "L'affaire Ullmo," as it was called, re-

sulted in the accused being found guilty and exiled to Devil's Island, and the scandal led to official inquiries that concluded that the ranks of the French navy were filled with opium addicts. In a *New York Times* article from April 1913 titled "Opium Degrading the French Navy," a French admiral decried the fact that even the cadets on French training ships frequented the opium dens of Toulon. Besides her sailors, many of France's opium smokers were colonists returning from Indochina. Popular memory has it that most of these were the wives of French functionaries and businessmen, driven to smoke by *le cafard*— depression brought about by the tropical heat and monotony of life far from France. Perhaps because opium was introduced to France not by foreigners, but by the French themselves, it took some time before the authorities felt they had a problem on their hands.

By the time the famous Hungarian photojournalist Brassaï was capturing his seedy portraits of 1930s Parisian nightlife, the French love affair with the decadent stuff was officially over. In fact, Brassaï's handful of photographs of opium smoking do not show an opium den, but a session at a private home. By then, opium smoking, like the drinking of absinthe, had been banned in France—but not before the drug had left its mark on French culture.

Beginning in the late nineteenth century, a love for the exotic and a fascination with the Orient made opium smoking a favorite subject of certain French literary figures. Their writings—breathless passages that when translated into English sound alternately profound and ridiculous—are similar to French illustrations of the period in that they unabashedly attempt to exoticize and eroticize opium. Predictably, books with opium themes commonly featured drawings or photos depicting opium pipes posed with Buddha figurines, or opium lamps throwing dramatic shadows upon walls while gently illuminating Asian nudes.

Charles Baudelaire is the best known of the French writers who experimented with opium in hopes of enhancing their skills, but those who know opium say Baudelaire was a mere dabbler. A handful of French writers and poets *were* regular opium smokers, and thanks to these few, the French contribution to opium literature is easily the richest. There is the aforementioned Jean Cocteau, of course, and Claude Farrère's 1904 collection of short stories *Fumée d'opium* (translated into English under the title *Black Opium*). Better is the lesser known Louis Laloy, whose 1913 book *Le livre de la fumée* describes opium smoking in minute detail. Also of note is Georges-Albert Puyou de Pouvourville, who wrote under the Vietnamese nom de plume Nguyen Te Duc. His book *Le livre de l'opium* has an Orientalist flavor that causes some modern readers to grimace, but nonetheless shows an intimate knowledge of opium's effects:

> Opium plays a siren's tune on the piano of his nerves, and as he listens, the smoker forgets about the passage of time, and he also forgets about hunger, thirst, fatigue and sleep.

However, the most skilled at describing opium's pleasures in writing was Max Olivier-Lacamp. When his book *Le kief* (bliss) was published in the 1970s, its opium-sexy imagery is said to have caused a number of elderly reformed smokers—some of whom had not touched a pipe in decades—to abruptly leave their comfortable lives in France and brave a trip back to Asia in search of their old flame.

For the past decade I have lived in an apartment in Bangkok's
Chinatown, halfway up a building that, in the early 1960s when
it was built, was one of the tallest in the city. Its eighteen floors
look out over Chinatown to the north and the Chao Phraya
River to the west. The location of my apartment, nine floors up,
is just about perfect. I'm too high for most mosquitoes yet low
enough to be able to make out the faces lining passenger boats
that shuttle commuters and tourists up and down the muddy
river. Visitors to my place may notice that I have no television. I
don't need one. In the same way that some people leave the TV
on for companionship, the sights and sounds of the Chao Phraya
River keep me company even when I am not actively taking
notice of them.

My building, said to be the height of comfort and modernity
in 1964, is now an eyesore on a stretch of the river whose banks
are crowded with international luxury hotels. There is black
mold growing on the walls and laundry hanging limply inside
cages that enclose balconies. Yet, if I lean out my kitchen window and look downriver, I can see the Royal Orchid Sheraton,
the Hilton Millennium, the Bangkok Peninsula, the Oriental
Hotel, and, just beyond that, the Shangri-La.

Western tourists pay hundreds of dollars, sometimes thousands, per night for a penthouse view of the sluggish Chao
Phraya River. For me it's $275 a month, electricity and water not
included. In the early evenings I gather my dry laundry from a
wire affixed outside my window and hear the booze cruise
barges starting their motors so as to be warmed up and out on
the river in time for the sunset. Once darkness falls I no longer
need to look at the clock—I can tell the time by which songs are

being performed on board the party barges as they float up and down the river. Every night some Ricky Martin impersonator with a Filipino accent does "Livin' la Vida Loca" while going upriver at half past seven and then repeats the song while coming back down around ten. The river's acoustics are so fine that I can hear cocktail shakers rattling rhythmically and, when a bend in the river causes a barge's open stern to point in my direction, I can hear the whoops and shouts of Lao-speaking dishwashers playing grab-ass in the scullery.

Bangkok's Chinatown is the noisiest section of what is surely one of the noisiest cities in the world. The district where I live has one of those impossibly long Thai names—Samphanthawong—and is the most densely populated district in all of Bangkok. I live on the northern edge of what a century ago was a riverside village inhabited by Vietnamese Catholics. A couple minutes from my apartment is a late-nineteenth-century cathedral whose Art Nouveau embellishments include crocodile-head gargoyles. Some of the descendants of the original Vietnamese settlers live along the lanes near this old cathedral, and when they leave their front doors open to the street I can see household crucifixes tacked high on interior walls. This is something the casual visitor might not notice. Instead, what catches the tourists' eye are the heaps of used motor vehicle parts piled up in front of one shophouse after another. My neighborhood makes its money recycling old automobile engines. Some are refurbished and some are broken up for scrap and sold to Pakistani buyers. Here there are transmissions stacked like dead beasts bleeding oil onto the street; over there, man-size piles of greasy cogs sorted by size. All around is the noise of these old engines being broken into small, manageable pieces. I can hear these sounds with startling clarity in my ninth-floor apartment.

There are other noises—the cries of food vendors. One of

my favorites is a vendor of grilled squid who uses a small outboard canoe as his conveyance. There are two boatmen actually, one controlling the boat and the other grilling squid on a small hibachi approximately the size and shape of a one-gallon paint can. They putter along the river's edge, calling attention to themselves with a horn attached to a bicycle tire pump. When one of them pushes down the pump's plunger, the horn wails like some forlorn species of goose. These guys are certainly some of the last of the old river-based vendors, of which Bangkok once had thousands.

Another type of vendor, much more common and no favorite of mine, are farmers who drive pickup trucks filled with a single type of produce, such as oranges or pineapples or rambutans. To let the whole neighborhood know he's arrived, the farmer parks his vehicle and then, in a voice raspy from use, gives a repetitive monologue about his produce over a loudspeaker. Having your ears blown out by tinny speakers amplifying froggy voices is a very Bangkok experience.

After dark, the mechanics and vendors have gone home, and the noise abates. By midnight even the party barges have moored, and their drunken revelers have been shuttled back to their hotels by Bangkok's ubiquitous taxis. This is the best time to take in the view from my apartment. I look out over the rooftops of Chinatown and imagine that out there packed away in some attic or crawlspace under a stairway is the opium pipe of my dreams. Its stem is a solid piece of ivory carved to look like bamboo. The saddle is silver, chased with fluttering bats symbolizing happiness. Its pipe bowl is a chocolate-colored Yixing clay from the kilns of the eponymous city near Shanghai. The entire pipe is covered with the rich patina of age, and all edges have been buffed to a mellow smoothness by the loving caresses of a long-dead owner. It's out there somewhere, I tell myself. All I have to do is find it.

Great collectors have great focus. They not only collect, they
learn. Many people are simply gatherers, obtaining an example
of this and an example of that, getting a euphoric buzz at the
moment of acquisition but then losing interest in the object
soon after it's in hand.

An American friend living in Thailand once told me that
every time he went back to the States for a visit, his brother insisted that he bring him an elephant figurine for his "collection."
It didn't matter to the brother what the figurine looked like, as
long as it was an elephant. As my friend told me about this, it
was clear that he was annoyed with the task of having to buy
elephants for his brother. He explained his irritation this way:
"It's weird. When he sees me, it's the first thing he asks about:
'Where's the elephant? Where's the elephant?'" My friend mimicked his grasping brother, eyes bulging as he waited to see what
was brought to him from Thailand. "But as soon as I give him
the thing, he looks at it for a few seconds and then puts it on the

shelf with all his other elephants and forgets about it. He never mentions it again."

This mindless acquiring is common; everybody knows someone who does it. Most of these gatherers are simply enjoying a momentary high by obtaining something new. Like compulsive shoppers, their "collecting" is a form of compulsive behavior; they scratch their itch and then they're satisfied until they get the itch again. Some of these people go on to build large collections— they may have an example of every Barbie doll ever manufactured, or cover the walls of their homes with antique enameled metal signs advertising every conceivable product—but they rarely do much research about their collectible. Maybe the research has already been done and the findings are already set down in books, so there's no need. They buy a book and gather and gather and then, once they lose interest or die, their collections are packed away into basements or broken up and sold at garage sales. Perhaps these collectors or their heirs make some money in the process of de-acquisitioning, but no real knowledge has been gained from the exercise.

Real collectors—as opposed to mere gatherers—become so obsessed with their collectible that they can think of nothing else. They not only need to acquire, they must also know everything about what they are acquiring: every little detail of age and provenance; the story behind every little gouge or crack on its surface. And just knowing about it is not enough. They feel a need to tell others—to educate, to make others appreciate and admire certain objects in the same way they do.

Explained in this way, my hobbies become a noble cause— there's no shame in my weird behavior. But deep inside I still wonder. Is what I do no different from the hyperconsumer who tries to keep up with the latest technology? Or perhaps my collecting is just another manifestation of the compulsion that drives some people to obsessively wash their hands? I really don't know.

What would have happened to my newest collecting obsession if all the answers were easily found in a large selection of well-researched, -written, and -illustrated books? Would I have become bored with opium-smoking paraphernalia as I had with Southeast Asian textiles? Yes, probably. As it turned out, it took years to educate myself and by the time I had developed an eye, I was thoroughly hooked.

Using photos from the *Arts of Asia* magazine articles, I began by scouring the antiques shops of Bangkok for opium pipes and lamps. Bangkok is notorious for being a city where anything can be bought for a price. That reputation may no longer be wholly accurate, but illicit antiquities do occasionally turn up in Bangkok's antiques shops—although they are unlikely to be openly displayed.

Bangkok's first antiques shops began life as pawnshops in a gated section of Chinatown known as Woeng Nakhon Kasem. By the 1980s, a high-end shopping mall specifically for the retailing of antiques had been constructed, and many of the former pawnshops relocated there. The result was River City, a multistory, air-conditioned building filled with shops offering relics from all over Asia, displayed with lighting and sophistication worthy of the Metropolitan Museum of Art. Not surprisingly—this was still Bangkok after all—the new shopping center was not without some intrigue: Now and again plainclothes police officers would raid shops looking for antiquities looted from ancient sites in Thailand and Cambodia.

When it came to opium antiques, the offerings in Bangkok were slim, but they whetted my appetite. I also searched neighboring countries for opium paraphernalia when I was working on guidebooks. Of course, I immediately went through the typical amateur collector's apprenticeship—that is, getting ripped off by the local antiques merchants. However, much of this wasn't intentional. The merchants seemed genuinely clueless about what I was looking for. I was shown old Chinese water pipes used for tobacco, and the merchants would swear up and down they were for smoking opium. Long, thin tobacco pipes—the type whose length required a servant to apply a flame to the bowl—and even Middle Eastern hookahs were also being passed off as opium pipes.

The few opium pipes and lamps I managed to find in Southeast Asia that matched the photographs I had were either modern reproductions or poorly repaired pastiches. It was as if some tinker had gathered the remaining parts of old pipes and lamps and then patched them together with only a vague idea of what they'd originally looked like. I even came to realize that the first opium pipe I bought in Vientiane—my epiphany pipe—was also a modern reproduction. What was going on? How was it that something as quintessentially Asian as an old opium pipe could not be found in Asia? The answer, of course, was simple and obvious: As drug paraphernalia, nearly all opium pipes and lamps in Asia had long ago been destroyed.

In his book *The Changing Chinese* (1911), within a chapter titled "The Grapple with the Opium Evil," author Edward Alsworth Ross told of official campaigns to incinerate opium-smoking accoutrements in the Chinese city of Foochow:

> Eleven burnings have taken place and the pipes, bowls, plates, lamps, and opium boxes sacrificed by fire are upwards of twenty-five thousand. Nothing is spared and no curio seeker need hope to rescue some rare and beautiful pipe by a tempting bid.

It was after about a year of serious collecting, in the early 2000s, that I discovered a certain website for online auctions was practically awash in antique opium-smoking paraphernalia. On a whim I had done a few searches on eBay to see what would turn up, but I didn't strike gold in plain sight. Doing a search for "opium" rarely delivered anything authentic.

Instead, I had to be creative with my searches, using words that would reveal auctions by sellers—primarily in America— who had come across genuine opium antiques among their heirlooms but were unaware of what they had found. With an astonishing frequency I found opium pipes online that were simply listed as "Oriental pipe" or "Asian pipe," or in some cases labeled "Native American peace pipe." Opium lamps came up even more frequently than pipes. I often found outstanding examples listed as "spirit lamp" or "alcohol lamp" or even "whale oil lamp." Just as I myself had found almost no visual resources to clarify what was and wasn't opium paraphernalia, sellers using online auctions were also hindered by the dearth of information —especially on the Internet where these auctioneers were most likely to do their research. The result was that I had the online auctions pretty much all to myself. For the better part of two years I bid on and won scores of century-old pieces of opium paraphernalia at a tiny fraction of what they would have fetched if the sellers had known what they were selling. That solid-ivory opium pipe that I dreamed of finding in Bangkok's Chinatown turned out to be nestled in a small town in the state of Tennessee. The seller thought it was a peace pipe made of bone and it cost me just over seventy dollars.

I also began to notice patterns. By noting the location that the online sellers were shipping from and by asking them questions about where items were found, I could discern where the best pieces were turning up. America was by far the richest source—not surprising if one was familiar with history. But first, time to debunk another myth: The Chinese did not bring opium to America. Decades before the arrival of tens of thousands of Chinese sojourners seeking wealth in the California goldfields, Americans were already getting hooked on opium. Laudanum, the opium and alcohol concoction that Thomas De Quincey quaffed in order to quell such nineteenth-century causes of stress as "the absolute tyranny of the violin," was well known in America. But, like tobacco, alcohol is a poor delivery system for the narcotic—the enervating effects of liquor dull the energizing qualities of opium. Instead, what the Chinese introduced to America was *chandu* and their own ingenious paraphernalia and technique for vaporizing it.

Judging by numbers alone, there's a good chance that opium smoking became firmly established in California in 1852, three years into the Gold Rush. That year some twenty thousand Chinese from the environs of Canton, where opium use was prevalent, arrived in San Francisco. Still, it took another twenty years for the habit to catch on with non-Chinese. The first Americans to try opium smoking were probably gamblers, prostitutes, and other underworld figures who frequented the Chinatowns of San Francisco and other settlements in the American West. H. H. Kane, the doctor whose 1882 book *Opium-Smoking in America and China* warned about the rapid spread of opium smoking among Americans, claimed that the first one to experiment with it was a gambler named Clendenyn who tried the drug in 1868.

Whatever the actual names and dates were, once opium smoking caught on with the general public, it spread like an epidemic, advancing east to St. Louis, Chicago, and New Orleans. Kane estimated that opium smoking arrived in New York

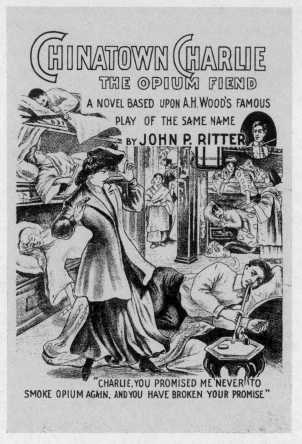

Dime novel with an opium-den theme. Beginning in the late nineteenth century, opium smoking found its way into Western literature, both highbrow and low. Published by J. S. Ogilvie, New York, 1906. (From the author's collection)

City in late 1876 or early 1877. He went on to write of the opium smokers that he interviewed in the dens of Manhattan:

> These people, whom I have questioned closely, tell me
> that there is hardly a town of any size in the East, and
> none in the West, where there is not a place to smoke and

Americans smoking. To be sure in many towns there is no regularly established opium-house, but there is always a Chinese laundry, the backroom of which serves the same purpose.

Jack Black, a former opium addict whose 1926 memoir *You Can't Win* gives a detailed account of his life of crime and vagrancy in the United States and Canada during the late nineteenth and early twentieth centuries, claimed that opium was "almost as cheap as tobacco" and that the drug was the medium of exchange at Folsom prison during his time incarcerated there.

In order for modern readers to understand how opium was received in America (and later in Canada), we must put ourselves into the rigidly competitive mindset of people of the day. The races did not mix, not only because it was thought to be degrading to intermingle with people whose culture was considered inferior to one's own, but because the "survival" of a race and its culture was of paramount importance. Because opium smoking arrived with an alien culture—and especially a non-European one—it was viewed as more of a threat than if it had come with Europeans. Americans, like the Chinese before them, reacted to the spreading vice by blaming the foreigners who had made the drug widely available.

Keep in mind that opium dens came about not because smokers necessarily craved one another's company (although that, too, would have been a draw), but because preparing an opium pipe was a skill that took much practice. Opium dens were usually run by Chinese, who always had attendants on hand that could be hired by American habitués to prepare pipes for them. China was also the principal source of the *chandu* and its peculiar paraphernalia. For all these reasons, the drug's association with Chinese people lingered long after opium became widely smoked among non-Chinese.

A search of the *New York Times* online archive turns up quite a few local news stories—columns so brief that it's obvious reports of another "opium joint" being raided in Manhattan's old Chinatown centered around Mott and Pell streets were not exactly headline news. Here is a typical article from May 1883, a mere paragraph in a "police blotter" column of crime stories from the previous day:

> Ah Chung, the Chinaman who kept an opium joint at No. 18 Mott-street, was committed for trial by Justice White in the Tombs Police Court yesterday, and Katie Crowley, the young girl who was found there, was held for further examination. Superintendent Jenkins, of the Society for the Prevention of Cruelty to Children, promised the Justice that he would look into the matter, but he expressed the opinion that there was "nothing new in it."

Cities such as San Francisco and New York tried to control the spread of opium smoking by passing ordinances to keep non-Chinese residents from frequenting opium dens in their respective Chinatowns with threats of jail time and fines for both smokers and den proprietors. The new laws were easy to enforce. Cops on the Chinatown beat cast a suspicious eye on any address that was suddenly very popular with non-Chinese visitors. But this diligent enforcement had an unforeseen result: Americans began to open opium dens specifically for American opium smokers beyond the borders of the cities' Chinatowns. Interestingly, the "Oriental" décor of these new establishments was sometimes described in news stories about the raids that shut them down. Apparently you could take the opium den out of Chinatown, but the American clientele still expected an evening of exotic escapism. Here are the headlines from an August 1899 article in *The New York Times* about the raiding of a particularly brazen establishment whose opulence warranted bold type and extra ink:

OPIUM SMOKERS ARRESTED

...

West Sixty-fourth Street Resort Raided by the Police.

...

A LUXURIOUS ESTABLISHMENT

...

Fitted Up in Oriental Style, with Many Attractions for Smokers, It Did a Thriving Business.

...

And excerpts from the story:

> Acting on a warrant . . . [police] yesterday morning raided an opium smokers' resort on the top floor of the flat house at 28 West Sixty-fourth Street. After breaking past the lookout they arrested John C. Ellis, the former proprietor of the "White Elephant," and thirty-one inmates, including four women. . . .
>
> The West Sixty-fourth Street place was known as one of the best-patronized and most luxuriously fitted-up establishments of its kind in the city. Ellis, who, when the raid was made, was found deeply under the influence of

the drug, and clad in Oriental costume, was not known to the patrons of the place as the proprietor. An undersized youth, answering to the name of "Joe" Cohen, figured as the manager. . . .

The place was opened only about two weeks ago, and no expense was spared to make it inviting to the smokers. The walls and ceilings were covered with red and gold cloth stamped with fleur-de-lis of gilt, and the corners of the rooms were hung with bright-colored flimsy silks . . . for the accommodation of smokers who cared to disrobe and wear the pajamas that were distributed. . . .

"Joe" Cohen was well known and popular among the opium smokers on the west side, and last week when a place on Broadway, between Sixty-sixth and Sixty-seventh Streets, run by a Chinaman called "Boston," was closed, the known smokers received cards of invitation to the Sixty-fourth Street establishment. The cards bore the name "Harry Hill," and their possession gave the entrée to the bearer whether he was known or not to Cohen. The place, which could accommodate about fifty smokers at one time, was crowded night and day, and the receipts averaged about $200 [about $5,000 today] every twenty-four hours.

If an inexperienced smoker came well recommended he was admitted, and after paying 50 cents for a card of opium, he received a "layout," and one of half a dozen "cooks" anxious to prepare the stuff in return for the privilege of smoking some of it would roll pill after pill for him. The layout consisted of a tin tray, a lamp, pipe, and a sponge to clean the bowl of the pipe, and a "yen-hok," or long piece of steel like a knitting needle, on which to cook the opium. The opium was carefully weighed out by the manager in an ante-room and then delivered on the back of a common playing card. One card sufficed for about twenty pills, and perhaps half a dozen cards would be used by a party of three during a smoking séance of about three hours, after which the smokers would retire and go to sleep. The place did also a good business in cigars, cigarettes, and liquors.

The patronage of the place had grown so large that the front flat on the same floor had been engaged, and the rooms there were being partitioned off for private smoking rooms, where select parties of smokers and sightseers could be accommodated. The addition was to have been ready this week, and every Chinatown guide had been apprised of the proposed opening.

As tame as this news story may seem to us today, opium was the methamphetamine of its day. The public was shocked by tales of just how far users would go to get a fix. If opium smoking had been contained to America's Chinatowns and underworld communities, it might not have caused much alarm. Instead, as the vice spread to the general public, husbands complained to police about wives who left their homes and children unattended to spend long hours reclining in smoky dens among strangers. When these places were raided, authorities were appalled to find women from "good families" in states of intoxication and partial undress, having discarded their hats, shoes, and corsets to be comfortable while smoking. That's when Victorian prudishness came into play. The Chinese belief that opium could prolong men's sexual staying power was perhaps misinterpreted. Americans whispered that the drug was an aphrodisiac that could turn a prim and proper lady into a scissor-legged slattern. H. H. Kane fretted that the scofflaw attitude of Americans in general drew them into the opium dens:

> The very fact that opium-smoking was a practice forbidden by law seemed to lead many who would not otherwise have indulged to seek out the low dens and patronize them, while the regular smokers found additional pleasure in continuing that about which there was a spice of danger. It seemed to add zest to their enjoyment. . . . Each new convert seemed to take a morbid delight in converting others, and thus the standing army was daily swelled by recruits.

Historical photographs confirm the popularity of opium with America's non-Chinese population. Photos of white smokers are relatively common, and social reformer Jacob Riis captured an image of an African American man smoking in a Manhattan den and included it in his groundbreaking series of photographs documenting New York City's poor. As authorities took to raiding opium dens across America, people of all races— Caucasians, African Americans, Latinos, and Native Americans, as well as Chinese—were caught in the act of smoking together. Knowing what we do about the bigotry of nineteenth-century Americans, is it any surprise that society was horrified by opium? Here was a drug that encouraged the mingling of different classes and races! In her book about drug use in Canada, *The Black Candle* (1922), Judge Emily F. Murphy remarked:

> A man or woman who becomes an [opium] addict seeks the company of those who use the drug, and avoids those of their own social status. This explains the amazing

phenomenon of an educated gentlewoman, reared in a refined atmosphere, consorting with the lowest classes of yellow and black men.

In San Francisco in the 1870s, an Irish immigrant named Denis Kearney led a disgruntled following of primarily Irish laborers who were competing with the Chinese for jobs in the building of railroads and other grand nineteenth-century projects. In time Kearney and his followers, known as the Workingmen's Party, were able to use anti-opium hysteria to whip up sentiments that led to the Chinese Exclusion Act of 1882—a series of laws that tightly curtailed Chinese immigration to the United States. These laws were left on the books until World War II, when America and China found a common enemy in Japan, and the anti-Chinese acts were revoked.

The irony of one foreign-born group telling another that it wasn't American enough to stay on American soil was not lost on some commentators of the day. A political cartoon titled "At Frisco" that appeared in *Harper's Weekly* in 1880 depicted Kearney as a thuggish leprechaun wielding a club and, in a thick Irish brogue, telling a rattled-looking Chinese that in "the words of George O'Washington and Dan'l O'Webster in regarrd to Furrin Inflooince, ye must go. D'ye understand? Ye must go!"

Right or wrong, the association of opium smoking with the Chinese stuck. Americans adopted Cantonese terms to describe opium smoking, opium paraphernalia, and states of opium intoxication and withdrawal. Got a "yen" for something? The term originally meant a craving for opium. Slang words and terms that associated opium with the Chinese found their way into everyday use via pulp literature and the lyrics of popular songs, first ragtime and then jazz and the blues. Opium smoking may have been on the decline in America by 1931 when Cab Cal-

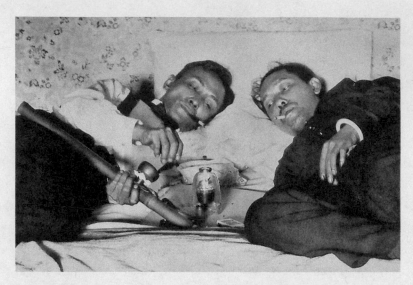

Opium smokers in a tenement in Manhattan circa 1910. In New York and other North American cities, the vice spread beyond the borders of China-town and caught on with locals and immigrants of all ethnicities. (From the author's collection)

loway sang about Smokey Joe going to Chinatown to look for his girl Minnie, who "gets her pleasure kicking the gong around," but listeners didn't have to be told that Minnie was an opium smoker. The slang term "kick the gong," meaning to smoke opium, had long been in use, and would be referred to again in songs by artists such as Slim & Slam and Hoagy Carmichael.

Even cartoons for American children produced all the way into the 1930s—the fare of Saturday matinees—featured the obligatory opium-smoking scene whenever a Chinatown theme was employed. Terrytoons Studios' cartoon short *Chop Suey* from 1930 is a typical example. Using San Francisco's China-town as a setting, it depicts two mice in Chinese attire and pig-tails whispering about their "yen" through a peephole in the door of a Chinese laundry and then being handed two opium pipes by the proprietor—a cat, also in Chinese attire. The mice take a couple pulls on their pipes (erroneously without the use of lamps) and then go floating away on the clouds.

An unfortunate result of these cultural remnants of opium smoking is that however forgotten (or misremembered) the vice may be in the minds of the modern-day general public, some Chinese Americans are likely to be irked by what they feel is a negative stereotype. On the other hand, many non-Chinese Americans seem to view historic opium smoking not in a negative light, but as something alluringly romantic. Both views lack nuance, and once again, the reason that Americans of any ethnicity are able to think of opium smoking in such simplistic terms is because the habit has so completely disappeared from our lives.

The fact is, if your ancestors lived in an urban setting in America or Canada between 80 and 150 years ago, there's a good chance they witnessed opium smoking—or at least saw its effects—firsthand. Here is a paragraph from Jack Black's memoir describing how common opium smoking was in San Francisco around 1900:

> The night life fascinated me. Grant Avenue, now filled with the best shops, was a part of the Tenderloin, and all the narrow streets or alleys off it were crowded with cribs and small saloons with a dance floor in the back room. Many of them had only the short, swinging doors, and never closed from one year's end to another. The Tenderloin was saturated with opium. The fumes of it, streaming out of the Baltimore House at the corner of Bush and Grant, struck the nostrils blocks away. Every room in it was tenanted by hop smokers. The police did not molest them. The landlord asked only that they pay their rent promptly.

As a collector, coming across a tract like this in a memoir was for me as exciting as discovering an unrecognized opium relic on a dusty shelf in an antiques shop. Yet such histories can be deceiving. One would think that San Francisco, once a center of opium smoking in the United States, would be ankle-deep in opium-smoking relics. At one time it almost certainly was, but as I had discovered in Bangkok, that was before the bonfires of the eradication campaigns had consumed them. Nowadays, most anything found on the shelves of San Francisco's antiques shops (and believe me, I made several trips to Grant Avenue to explore) had come recently from China and was usually a reproduction.

Instead of opium antiques being in the obvious places, I came across online auctions for wonderfully opulent examples of opium pipes and lamps in states such as Ohio, Kentucky, and Oklahoma. At first I thought this didn't make sense—these states had no significant Chinatowns whose inhabitants might have been able to afford impressive smoking equipment. The locales were also far from the railroads, canals, and mines of the American West that were the sites of itinerant camps of Chinese laborers.

Of course, it was possible that the pipes and lamps I was finding were the forbidden accessories of opium-smoking Americans. The authorities began shutting down opium dens in earnest after the nationwide ban on opium smoking known as the Smoking Opium Exclusion Act was passed in 1909, and many American addicts learned to prepare their own pipes and began secretly nursing their habits at home. I could imagine the great-grandchildren of these old gowsters discovering pipes and lamps boxed away in the attic along with stacks of 78 rpm records and leather-bound photo albums. It even occurred to me that some desperate, meth-addled soul may have come across the instruments of great-granddad's addiction during a frenzied search for anything that could be consigned to eBay—a sorry cycle that would have made Dr. Kane shake his head with despair.

One thing that puzzled me, however, was the fact that some of the fanciest pipes that came from these Midwestern states showed no signs of use. They were clean of dross, the black residue by-product of opium smoking whose peculiar smell continues to linger in a pipe a century or more after the last pill was vaporized.

The mystery was solved when I read an old book written by a Christian missionary in China. The missionaries' anti-opium stance was welcomed by Qing dynasty officials eager to stop the flow of opium from British India, and so they were given free rein to proselytize. These missionaries, most of whom were American or British, were supported by their congregations in their home countries. In order to raise cash for their efforts, they sometimes journeyed home and went on the lecture circuit, relating tales of their battles against heathen sin to churches packed with gasping parishioners. Opium pipes and lamps made perfect show-and-tell props, and many of these were bought new by the missionaries in China and then brought home—which explains why the paraphernalia was never used. Later—much later—the props were consigned to attics and basements and forgotten . . . only to be discovered by twenty-first-century descendants hoping to turn their keepsakes into cash.

Online auctions by sellers in the United Kingdom were another source of opium pipes. Like many of the pipes I was finding in America's Midwestern states, nearly all the pipes that I sourced in the U.K. had never been used. Some were surely missionaries' props, and some were no doubt the souvenirs of Britons who had been based in the Far East outposts of the British Empire, such as Singapore and Hong Kong. Still, it struck

me as odd that more opium pipes with signs of use weren't coming out of the U.K. After all, Victorian London, and specifically
the Limehouse district, were supposedly centers of opium smoking.

After a decade of collecting I've come to the conclusion that
Victorian London's opium-smoking reputation is nothing more
than a myth—albeit a durable one. I base this theory on the fact
that I have not once found any photographic evidence of opium
smoking in the U.K. True, there are plenty of illustrations, drawings, and etchings, but I have not seen a single photograph. This
is in marked contrast to the relatively large number of photos of
smokers—people actually smoking opium, not just posing in a
studio with the paraphernalia—taken in the United States,
France, and even Canada. I have also not been able to unearth
any news clippings from the U.K. about opium pipes and paraphernalia being heaped into piles and burned or thrown into
incinerators, as was done in America and Asia.

In 1899, under the heading "Hidden London," Arthur
Morrison—known for his Sherlock Holmes–like detective
stories—wrote a nonfiction piece describing the city's opium
smoking scene for the *Strand Magazine*. Morrison (whose
opium-related details leave little doubt in my mind that he knew
what he was talking about) admitted that there were only two
opium dens in Limehouse whose existence he was sure of, and
that one of them was little more than a "show den"—a turn-of-
the-century tourist attraction:

It was the place to which all the inquiring sightseers
were taken who insisted on seeing an opium den and
were prepared to pay for the privilege. Insomuch that if
no smokers happened to be on hand at the time of the
visit, it was the custom to send out and bring one or two,

while the visitors were delayed in a downstairs room with imaginary objections to their admission. It is said also that it was not always opium that was smoked before visitors, because a man inured to the drug might not be within call, and an attempt by another might end in violent sickness.

How then do we explain popular legend of Victorian London being cloaked in a fog of opium vapors? Surely the myth began with fictional accounts such as *The Mystery of Edwin Drood* (1870) by Charles Dickens, "The Man with the Twisted Lip" (1891) by Arthur Conan Doyle, and *The Picture of Dorian Gray* (1891) by Oscar Wilde—all fictional accounts of opium degeneracy that were meant to shock. H. H. Kane ridiculed Dickens's laughably inaccurate description of opium smoking and intoxication, yet sensationalism—not accuracy—was what readers wanted. By the early twentieth century, stories of a similar ilk were so immensely popular in Britain and America that some were even made into movies. One of these was *Broken Blossoms,* a silent film starring Lillian Gish. Released in 1919, the picture was based on a short story in Thomas Burke's 1917 book *Limehouse Nights.* Supposedly D. W. Griffith made a special trip to London in order to see the Limehouse district—including its opium dens—that he would try to re-create on film. His escort of London policemen searched the neighborhood but was unable to find a single opium den. Ironically, the director could have stayed home and witnessed opium smoking in any of America's large Chinatowns, including Los Angeles's old Chinese quarter, just a short distance from Hollywood on the present-day site of Union Station.

The fiction of widespread opium smoking in Victorian London continues to be passed on to this day. But the durability

of the myth is not what's surprising. After all, how much of
what we think we know about history is based on what we've
read in novels or seen at the movies? Perhaps the real question here is this: Why did opium smoking catch on in France
and North America but not in the United Kingdom? A large
number of Britons lived in close proximity to the vice due to
their Asian colonies, yet according to Arthur Morrison's article
in the *Strand Magazine,* it was "the rarest thing in the world to
see a European" in one of London's handful of opium dens. Why
didn't more British get hooked abroad, as the French did, and
then bring their addictions home? I suspect that the prevailing
attitude of the time had a lot to do with it—British ideas of
white prestige and nonfraternization with subject peoples were
cornerstones of their worldwide empire's success. No doubt, too,
there was a national aversion to sullying oneself with the very
poison that Britain used to choke China into economic submission. British botanist Mordecai Cubitt Cooke may have best
explained his countrymen's attitude toward opium in his pioneering book about narcotics, *The Seven Sisters of Sleep* (1860):

> Opium indulgence is, after all, very un-English, and
> never has been, nor ever will be, remarkably popular; and
> if we smoke our pipes of tobacco ourselves . . . we cannot
> forbear expressing our astonishment at the Chinese and
> others who indulge in opium. Pity them we may, perhaps,
> looking upon them as miserable wretches the while, but
> they do not obtain our sympathies.

Whenever one of my online purchases was on its way to Bangkok I felt like a kid the week before Christmas. My apartment
building has a small office on the ground floor that doubles as a

mail room, and it used to be manned by a smiling young woman who sat at a desk and snacked on slices of green mango. She got so used to me poking my head in the door and asking about parcels that I didn't have to open my mouth to get an answer. The excitement of receiving a package was always mixed with dread, however, not because the online auction sellers ever swindled me but because poor wrapping and manhandling sometimes caused pieces to break.

Before opening, I always gave the parcels a gentle shake, hoping I wouldn't be greeted by the rattle of loose shards. Then, in the privacy of my apartment, there was restrained frenzy with a knife and pair of scissors, snipping, sawing, and ripping. The layers of cardboard and Bubble Wrap fell away until finally I was holding the object before me. Sometimes my hands trembled so that I would have to immediately put the new piece on the coffee table and then sit back on the sofa and wait until I could handle it safely.

After some time examining the new object—looking at its surface with a magnifying glass and sniffing for signs of opium use—I got out my camera and photographed it from all angles. Later I would upload the images to my laptop and make notes on when I bought the piece and where it was sourced. If the new item was something very fragile I might rewrap it and store it away, but in most cases my new acquisitions were consigned to a shelf in the living room so I could casually study them over a period of weeks or months.

I printed out copies of the photos of my newly acquired pieces, and whenever I made my visits to the Bangkok antiques shops, I always took a few of these photos with me to show the merchants. I never told them where I was finding these spectacular opium pipes and lamps—I never admitted that they were coming from Cincinnati, Ohio, and Klamath Falls, Oregon, and

Portland, Maine. I certainly didn't need any competitors at the online auctions, so when the merchants asked, I kept my replies vague. The Thai language has a wonderful built-in ambiguity that allows for this without being rude. The merchants always assumed that one of their competitors had sold me the pieces, and I did nothing to discourage their assumptions.

When I first began collecting antique opium-smoking paraphernalia it was easy to feel as if I were the only person in the world who collected it. I heard a rumor that French fashion designer Yves Saint Laurent had a fabulous collection of opium pipes. His paraphernalia was said to be stored away at a secret location in Morocco—apparently not the sort of collectible that one bragged about.

It was from the antiques dealers in Bangkok that I first learned there were others looking for opium relics, and not just as an adjunct to a collection of tobacco pipes. After making a few purchases, I was on more friendly terms with a couple of the merchants, and they told me about other Westerners who made more or less regular visits to their shops to ask if there were any opium pipes or lamps in stock. One collector whom all the merchants knew and sold to was a very wealthy German who came to Bangkok annually and bought up most everything related to opium that was on offer. One of the dealers let it slip with a smirk that the German was easily fooled into buying just about anything, no matter how far-fetched the sales pitch. The German was apparently so obsessed with collecting that he would rather be cheated than chance losing out on something important.

The Bangkok antiques merchants may have admitted that other collectors were looking to buy opium pipes and lamps, but they weren't exactly keen on having these collectors know one another. On several occasions I tried to coax contact information about my fellow collectors from them, but they always played dumb, giving me a first name and perhaps a nationality but that was about all.

Then one day I happened to be at one of the upscale shops in the River City mall when a middle-aged European woman, whose deep tan and unlined face suggested a degree of wealth, walked in and greeted the Thai shopkeeper in German-accented English. I was standing before a glass display cabinet with two opium lamps—both unremarkable and overpriced—when I noticed that the woman kept glancing in my direction as she was making small talk with the shopkeeper. I was about to find out why.

When the woman asked if there was anything new, the shopkeeper's reply was as brief as it was negative. Although she was smiling and polite, the shopkeeper didn't seem to be her usual effusive self with this stranger, and this also caught my attention. I might have wandered out of the shop at that point—there was nothing in the display cabinet that I'd not already seen and asked the price of—but by then I was curious. The European woman thanked the shopkeeper and turned away, but instead of leaving the shop she walked up and stood right next to me, looking over the opium lamps. "Do you notice the price tags are always written in some sort of code?" she asked without looking at me.

"I suppose it's so the proprietor can size you up and give you a price that fits your wallet," I replied.

"Precisely!" she said, now looking at me. "My husband collects these opium objects," she continued. "He has the greatest collection in the world. Do you know Peter Lee's book? Those photos are a small sample of things in my husband's collection. He has so many others. What is shown in the book is nothing."

Now she had my full attention. As she began to describe her husband and his collection, I realized he must be the German I'd been told about—the one who was so rich and obsessed that he bought everything in sight. The Thai shopkeeper kept her distance until it was clear that the woman and I were going to have a conversation with or without her help, and then she rushed forward to introduce us. I was surprised to see the German woman's eyes widen as the shopkeeper pronounced my name. "It's you!" the woman exclaimed, her eyes flashing. "We have heard many things about you. Every antiques dealer in Bangkok is telling us about the beautiful things you are finding here. My husband very much wants to meet you. He's here in the mall, somewhere just behind me. He will be here very soon."

I have never been much for premonitions. I rarely get them and I even more rarely act upon them, but at that moment there was something inside my head telling me to flee the scene. Partly it was because I could see myself being bullied into taking these people to my nearby apartment to see my collection, but there was something else—something that I could feel but didn't have the time to think through. I simply did not want this guy anywhere near my collection. I excused myself as politely as I could and made for the door. "Wait!" the German woman called after me, and when I rushed out, calling a hurried "Nice meeting you!" over my shoulder, she, too, made for the door. "I will find my husband—he is here in the mall!" she said, heading toward the escalator in the opposite direction.

Back at my apartment I had time to sit back and think about what had happened. I took out my copy of Peter Lee's *The Big Smoke* and looked at the photographs of the collection of "Helmut P." I knew from the stories of the merchants and shopkeepers that Helmut P. had for years been passing through Bangkok and other Asian cities to buy up anything he could find. No doubt the antiques merchants of Bangkok had told him about those photocopies I was in the habit of showing around, and from what his wife had said, I knew that Helmut P. assumed I was finding these treasures in Bangkok. How would he react if we met in person? I decided I didn't want to experience his reaction firsthand.

An hour later my phone rang, and when I answered it, the pleasant voice of the young woman who worked in my building's office greeted me. In Thai she told me there was a *farang* (Western) man enquiring about my apartment number. She described him as a large man—he was standing directly in front of her apparently—and I knew who it had to be. Thinking it very unlikely that he could understand Thai, I told her to tell the man that I was not in. She said she would do this and then hung up.

The shopkeeper at River City knew that I lived in the apartment building nearby, and surely she had given Helmut P. directions. I doubted he would waste his time coming back to my apartment again, but the following morning I got another call from the woman in the office—again, the man had asked if I was in and was now waiting outside the office door, leaning against a pay phone on the wall. This sounded like something from a Raymond Chandler novel. What was his game? Did he plan to follow me to what he hoped would be my secret cache of opium relics? I wondered how long he could camp out at the building's entrance—there was no place to sit—without becoming bored or angry.

I had given some thought to my initial premonition that this guy should be avoided but could not come up with anything rational except for his connection with that shadowy character Peter Lee. There was no risk of physical danger, of course, but after a decade and a half of living in Thailand the national aversion to confrontation had certainly rubbed off on me. Mostly I think I wanted to avoid him in the same way that we all tend to give a wide berth to people who might be a bit off.

I waited a couple of hours until hunger for lunch drove me to leave my apartment—without bothering to first call the office to see if Helmut P. was still hanging around. As soon as I reached the ground floor and passed through the elevator doors, I saw him outside the office some ten yards away. He was looking right at me. There was no way to get back into the elevator without being obvious, so I pulled my mobile phone from my pocket and dialed a friend's number while setting my stride and walking almost straight toward him.

Luckily, my friend picked up after just a couple of rings and so I was talking on the phone when I strode past my odd stalker. As I walked by, I kept my eyes trained straight ahead, but through my peripheral vision I could see Helmut P.'s face following me as I passed him. He must have been unsure of himself because he made no attempt to accost or tail me. I walked out to the main street and got into a cab, having decided to lunch somewhere outside of my neighborhood. When I arrived back home a few hours later, Helmut P. was nowhere to be seen.

The following morning I got an early phone call, and in my grogginess I answered without vetting the number. "Hallo?" a German voice said thickly. He wanted to meet me that morning, saying it was his last day in Bangkok. I contemplated lying about my availability but then relented. I would see him as long as he agreed to meet somewhere outside—there was no way I was going to have him in my apartment. We settled on a place near the River City mall, a tiny open-air café up against the north wall of the Sheraton Hotel and next to the Si Phraya pier, where proximity to the river made the heat of the day bearable.

Helmut P. was a large man in his sixties, but there was nothing about his looks to differentiate him from the crowds of middle-aged European men who come to Bangkok for a good time. If I had passed him on a street near Patpong, Bangkok's tourist-oriented red-light district, I would not have given him a second look. He was already waiting for me at one of the café's tables when I arrived, sipping from a small plastic bottle of mineral water. I ordered an iced coffee, and as I was stirring the liquefied sugar into the glass, he launched into his plea.

Helmut P. said he'd been collecting for more than twenty years, making annual trips to Bangkok and other Asian cities in search of antique opium-smoking paraphernalia. He had recently been in Shanghai and told of how he distrusted the merchants there, suspecting that they were devising fakes especially for him. He talked about how he was finding less and less at his usual stops in Hong Kong, Singapore, and Bangkok, and as he said the word "Bangkok" his demeanor changed visibly.

He paused to take a breath, started to talk, and then paused again. When he finally spoke his voice cracked and he seemed to be on the verge of tears. "I have been coming here so many years, you know," he said. Again he paused to take a breath before repeating the sentence. "I have been coming here so many years."

I said nothing. He repeated the line again, like an actor trying to prompt another who is missing his cue. Finally with a sob he spat it out. "Please! Those beautiful things you are finding are meant for me! You must stop buying my things!" I didn't know how to respond. His emotions were as real as his demand was ludicrous. The guy was obsessed, but at least I could see that I had no reason to feel intimidated. It was all rather pathetic.

I could have eased his mind by admitting that my source was online auctions, but why should I invite the unwanted competition? This guy was rich and he could outbid me in any auction— and there was no reason to believe that he wouldn't buy online as voraciously as he did in the antiques shops.

I could also have placated him by saying that I would lay off buying antiques in Bangkok—just to make him happy. But for some reason I didn't want to do that, either. I tried not to gloat, but I'm embarrassed to admit that's exactly what I felt like doing. Struggling to keep a smile off my face, I drank the last of my iced coffee and watched him over the rims of my sunglasses. Helmut P. sat there panting in the heat and waiting for a reply. Then I looked him in the eyes and shook my head. "Nope," I said.

I left him sitting there with his mouth open but unable to speak. I let him see me walking into the air-conditioned River City mall. There was nothing in the entire mall worth buying, nor anywhere else in Bangkok for that matter, but Helmut P. didn't know that.

Unlike other forms of the opium-habit, that by smoking finds a special inducement in companionship, especially if the companions are congenial.

— H. H. Kane, *Opium-Smoking in America and China* (1882)

Over time, I met more aficionados of opium-smoking paraphernalia, and as my online auction bonanza continued, I was able to quickly and economically build a collection that was the envy of our tiny community. Nearly all the collectors that I got to know concentrated on acquiring opium pipes and lamps, giving little thought to the other pieces of paraphernalia that had been devised to make opium smoking convenient. I began to turn my attention to these mysterious tools of the habit.

While doing guidebook research in Laos, I spent many more hours reclining at Mister Kay's opium den. Madame Tui's had since closed. The sight of vomiting backpackers moonwalking around Vientiane eventually caused the police to pay her a visit, and from then on she smoked alone. However, nothing changed at Mister Kay's, except that my visits were not frequent enough to keep his teenaged grandson from challenging me at the door. Luckily the proprietor and regular smokers always remembered me from the times I had arrived bearing pieces of paraphernalia whose function was a mystery to me. Sometimes the skeletal old smokers would coo in amazement. "Haven't seen one of those in a long time!" they whistled through the stumps in their gums before giving me a demonstration of how the implement was used.

Mister Kay's was invaluable to me. It was the one and only place where I might learn some rare piece of opium knowledge that was otherwise lost to history. The implications of this affected me deeply. This room and its ancient habitués smoking adulterated opium with jerry-rigged paraphernalia was the last remnant of what had only a century before been a worldwide, multimillion-dollar industry. Opium smoking, a habit that had financed empires and made fortunes all over the world, was now so rare that only in this landlocked backwater could the classic Chinese vice be witnessed. Imagine the possibility that, a mere hundred years from now, the modern wine industry and the millions of people who support it could be reduced to a roomful of elderly winos swilling fortified wine from stemware held together by packing tape. This is how thoroughly opium smoking has been eradicated.

At about the same time that Mister Kay's was becoming my research lab, I again ran across the scrap of paper on which I'd written down the contact information for that friend of the author Peter Lee. Coincidentally, this person who Lee claimed could teach me much about opium smoking was based in Vientiane, so I made it a priority to contact him before my next trip to Laos.

This was how I found Wilhelm Borunoff. An expatriate Austrian who had lived in Southeast Asia since the 1980s, Willi claimed to be the progeny of Russian nobility and a long line of artists—a history that his broad Slavic forehead and precise taste in clothing seemed to confirm. He had lived in Bangkok for nearly a decade before relocating to Vientiane after the Soviets withdrew from Laos in 1991. Willi's plan was to revive a Lao coffee industry that had been established by the French before World War II, but which had all but died as a result of wars and bad politics. He had built a small coffee bean roasting facility and was one of a handful of pioneering entrepreneurs who were testing the waters of the country's fledgling market economy. When I met Willi in 2002, he was battling corrupt Lao officials to hang on to his coffee investment. "It's crazy," he explained as he gave me a tour of his operation. "Every day some new team of officials shows up to inspect and then demands a fat bribe to let me continue. I thought Bangkok was corrupt, but this place makes it look like a colony of Shakers."

Things did not look good, but that didn't stop Willi from treating me to his impeccable brand of hospitality. His home was a teakwood bungalow in a bamboo grove on the outskirts of Vientiane. The bungalow, which Willi shared with his Thai-Chinese wife, had been built using aspects of Western and Southeast Asian design, and the open spaces within suggested some tribal longhouse, with a kitchen, dining area, and room for relaxing and receiving guests situated in a row. Off the living room was a wide verandah where Willi spent long mornings sipping oolong tea and contemplating a Zen garden that he had planted below. Under the house was a basement he told me was used for storage, and behind it was a wooden pavilion built up over the edge of a lotus pond.

Willi had decorated the house with objects that he'd collected all over Asia, but with an emphasis on Chinese tea-drinking accoutrements—wood and glass display cases were filled with diminutive teapots fashioned from Yixing clay. Taking in the room on that first visit, I soon spotted a bamboo opium pipe whose saddle was adorned in the Yunnanese style with a row of semiprecious stones. A mutual friend had told me that Willi owned two antique opium pipes, and when I emailed him I used this as an excuse to propose a visit, expressing an interest in photographing them.

After I had examined the pipes, Willi invited me to join him for tea on the verandah. I was interested to know if he had had any experience with smoking opium, but Willi was prudently guarded on the subject. He admitted to having smoked in the hills with the Hmong years before, and only after I had related tales of my trips to the rustic Vientiane dens did his enthusiasm get the better of him and he began to tell some stories of his own.

"When I first came to Vientiane there were still a few members of the Corsican mob who had controlled the opium trade in Indochina before the Communists took over," he told me. "One ran a restaurant called Erawan down near Kilometer Three." Erawan is a three-headed elephant, the Lao name for the mount of the Hindu god Indra, and the symbol of the Lao monarchy. "That crazy Corsican managed to stay in Laos after the revolution, and somehow the Communists let him keep the restaurant and never even made him change its name. He's gone now. His half-Lao son got involved in heroin and committed suicide right there in front of the restaurant."

Willi claimed to have learned English as a young man in New York City while working for an old European Jew whose Yiddish accent Willi had absorbed and could turn on and off at will, an affectation that gave a playful yet cynical tone to his stories. Willi knew Mister Kay but scrunched his nose in mock disgust when I suggested that we visit the den together. "Oy! Dross smokers!" he snorted.

Later that evening, after the sun had set, I came to understand the significance of that remark. We talked far beyond the hour that I had expected the visit to last, and Willi asked me to stay for dinner. After the meal he said he had something to show me. Willi led me to the basement, and there a modest opium layout tray was being assembled by an old Vietnamese manservant dressed in what was once the fashion of the Chinese in Southeast Asia: a mandarin-collar shirt and baggy trousers that were a matching color of indigo. The layout tray was set down on a mat spread out on the concrete floor between crates and boxes in the basement storage room. I could tell by the servant's fluency in arranging the utensils on the tray that this was not the first time he had performed the duty.

Willi and I wordlessly smiled at each other as the servant lit the diminutive lamp and then bowed out of the room. As always when I was about to smoke opium I felt gripped by a giddy excitement, and I could tell that Willi felt the same. Without having to be told, I also knew that he was bestowing upon me a grand honor that he rarely extended to others. I could sense in Willi's actions a restrained graciousness that said he did not take the act of opium smoking lightly, and would not have invited me to share a pipe had he thought I wouldn't appreciate the experience.

Willi and I positioned ourselves on the mat, reclining on either side of the tray and facing each other over it. He produced a small brown bottle with a dropper, unscrewed the lid, and invited me to sniff the contents. It was opium, but in liquid form and with a surprisingly complex bouquet, as though it had fermented—it smelled something like loam drenched with red wine. He placed a few drops in a miniature copper wok perched on the opium lamp's chimney, and as the liquid began to sizzle and evaporate, a rich scent filled the air—like roasted peanuts but with a hint of animal musk.

"Picasso once said that opium is the world's most intelligent smell," Willi remarked while holding a skewer-like opium needle at the ready and without taking his eyes off the boiling opium. "Or perhaps he said it's the world's least stupid smell," he continued as he brushed the now gummy opium from the wok with the tip of the needle. "I've seen the remark quoted both ways in English. I need to find it in the original French. Depending on what Picasso really said, it's either a compliment to opium's uniqueness or a comment on Picasso's jadedness."

Willi looked at me over the tray and held my eyes, and I realized that I hadn't acknowledged his remark. I was hardly listening. Instead I was mesmerized by what I had been witnessing. Still reclining next to the tray, Willi was deftly "rolling"—the complex process of preparing a dose of opium for the pipe. It was the first time I had ever seen a non-Asian prepare opium—and he did so with unparalleled grace.

Willi's accoutrements were few, simple, and unadorned—similar to what I had seen being used in the opium dens of Vientiane—but the quality of opium that he had somehow obtained was like nothing I had ever experienced. Here finally I would taste *chandu,* that rarefied form of smoking opium I had only read about in old books. *Chandu,* a Malay word that originated with the Hindi *caṇḍū,* was once the preferred poison of sophisticated opium smokers from Peking to Paris. *Chandu* of this grade had not been produced for decades, simply because there was no longer any demand for high-quality smoking opium.

The acres of opium poppies being cultivated in Afghanistan and Burma invariably supply clandestine heroin refineries whose deadly but lucrative product is then sent all over the world. Such operations are, of course, carefully guarded at all stages. In the case of Burma, much of the opium under cultivation is watched over by the Wa, a fierce tribal people whose head-hunting made them the bane of the British during the colonial era. In modern times the Wa have traded in their spears and long knives for Chinese-made Kalashnikovs, hiring themselves out to fill the ranks of the private armies of Burma's drug-lord generals.

Obtaining raw opium in large enough quantities to produce *chandu* is dangerous and thus expensive. If someone could manage to buy enough raw opium—and if that opium were real and reasonably pure—then there was the task of boiling and filtering the crude sap, followed by hours of allowing the concoction to settle before more filtering and settling. A dash of some fragrant liqueur would be added to the elixir to kill spores that could cause mold, and the *chandu* would then be sealed up in earthenware jars capped with beeswax and allowed to age.

Willi paid dearly to obtain genuine and pure raw opium, I would learn, and then did this refining himself using a collection of copper pots, his process constantly evolving as he experimented with new techniques. Meeting Willi was for me like discovering the key that opened the long-locked door to a room full of knowledge. How many people remained in the world who, in the twenty-first century, could obtain good opium in the quantities needed to produce premium *chandu,* and who were then able to prepare and smoke that *chandu* in the classic Chinese manner? I was convinced that Willi was one of the last of an all but extinct breed.

※

The effects of opium intoxication—the quality of the high—depend on the quality and purity of the blend being smoked. In the drug's heyday, raw opium arriving in China passed through a series of brokers and merchants who had methods of diluting it in order to maximize profits. The easiest and most effective way was to add a quantity of boiled dross. Because of the high morphine content found in dross, adding it to opium changed the nature of the high. The more dross added, the more stupefying the intoxication.

The poorest users smoked pure dross, which is why descriptions in travelers' accounts of the lowliest opium dens in old China inevitably feature cramped rooms full of seemingly comatose opium smokers lying about in various stages of mental and physical decay. By contrast, Willi's *chandu* was enlightening, markedly different from what I had previously experienced while smoking the dross-laced opium on offer in the dens of Vientiane.

How did it feel? Physically, opium was energy. A few pipes and I was enveloped in an electric skin. As time passed after the initial pipes were smoked, the intensity of the high waxed and waned depending on such matters as whether I was lying down or sitting up, or whether my eyes were open or closed. Unlike the opium I had smoked previously, Willi's *chandu* allowed me to move about without any loss of physical coordination—there was no staggering or moonwalking. I also noted that throughout the session, Willi's meticulous rolling never faltered.

Mentally, opium was a welling euphoria followed by a serene sense of well-being. The effects of the *chandu* were gradual and subtle, washing over me like a succession of tender caresses. A juvenile lust for kicks would not likely be satisfied by *chandu*'s leisurely and deliciously nuanced mental banquet. This perhaps explains why, in China's past, high-quality opium was considered an intellectual pursuit and not recommended for young people or the mentally immature.

Contrary to opium's popular reputation, my own experiences indicated that the drug was not hallucinatory. Rudyard Kipling's short story "The Gate of the Hundred Sorrows" (1884)

features an opium addict who watches two dragons on a brocaded pillow become animated and begin dueling as the character smokes pipe after pipe. A memorable scene perhaps, but
Kipling's portrayal strikes me as the fantasies of someone who
had no firsthand experience.

The so-called opium dreams—at least in the primary stages
of opium use—are not waking dreams or hallucinations. In fact,
a bit of vintage slang still in use today best illustrates opium's
most prominent mental kick: "pipe dream." This term meant
the same then as it does today, a way of describing an irrational
sense of optimism. Irrational or not, this is opium's greatest gift
to the smoker: boundless optimism—the kind that one rarely
experiences beyond childhood. All good things seem possible;
problems are easily solvable; obstacles are always surmountable.

For me, smoking opium in those early, heady days of experimentation was like donning a custom-made pair of rose-tinted
glasses. Besides the optimism, a few pipes made me feel as though
I could recapture a childlike wonder at the world. I also felt a
renewed sense of excitement—again, the pure emotions from
childhood. Yet these feelings of wonder and excitement were
applied to an adult's sophisticated sense of appreciation. Watching a dragonfly hover above the jade-hued surface of the lotus
pond behind Willi's house was not merely captivating but joy-
inducing. Opium did not alter the landscape; it merely made me
wondrously aware of the world's beauty, giving me the sense that
I was seeing it all for the first time. Transported to such a place,
who needed dueling dragons on pillows?

❧

Sometime during that first session I had an idea. Willi had access
to a grade of opium that was all but impossible to find and, even
more important, a safe place in which to enjoy it. I had in my

collection pieces of paraphernalia that were of an opulence and richness that could no longer be reproduced. Some were missionaries' trophies and had never been used. Although more than a century old, these pieces were in near pristine condition. What if Willi and I were to combine these rare aspects of opium smoking—his incomparable *chandu* and my antique paraphernalia? Over the next few years that is precisely what we did. Our goal was to put together a layout tray with all the requisite pieces that, when finished, would comprise dozens of rare items crafted specifically to assist in the ingestion of opium. It would be a complete layout the likes of which hadn't been seen since the People's Liberation Army marched into Shanghai. The pieces of paraphernalia would, of course, have to match, and that was the real challenge: to find accoutrements that matched as closely as possible and assemble them into a stunning whole.

Visiting Willi once a month, I would take the night train from Bangkok and disembark in the cool of the morning, transferring to a bus in order to cross the bridge over the Mekong River into Laos. With each trip I brought with me a rare piece of antique opium paraphernalia, having spent the time between visits feverishly seeking the next piece. My research would begin with my photo archive—a part of which was devoted to historical photographs of opium smokers.

Images of people smoking opium are not exactly plentiful. By the time photography was invented there was a social stigma attached to the vice even in those places where the drug was not illegal. The photographs that do exist can be divided into two groups: people smoking opium and people simply posing and pretending to smoke. As usually happens in life, the posers were easier to find, but fortunately they were also very useful to me. With the boom in popularity of postcards in the early 1900s, photographers began looking for subjects that would sell. In places where opium was known to be smoked, a postcard depicting the act was a popular souvenir with visitors. China was, of course, known for its prodigious opium consumption, but going into an opium den or the smoking room of a private residence and taking a photograph was usually out of the question.

To solve the matter, photographers in cities such as Hong Kong and Shanghai re-created such scenes in their own studios, complete with layout trays and at least two smokers posing on either side. Sometimes the scene included an elaborate set of hardwood furniture—including an opium bed, a pair of stools, and perhaps a chair or two—and a party of Chinese onlookers waiting their turn at the pipe. Despite the fact that the subjects were merely going through the motions, the images were important to me for the lavish paraphernalia on display. If I scanned and enlarged the images I could sometimes obtain a clear view of complete opium layouts with all the accoutrements beautifully arranged in the symmetrical way that was so popular among the Chinese.

Photos of people actually smoking opium are rare—especially those captured in China. More common are photographs of people indulging in the vice in French Indochina and the United States. Some of the postcard images from France's Southeast Asian colony look to have been taken in studios, albeit with smokers actually in the act of smoking. Others are in rustic settings that suggest the photographers searched villages or the "native quarters" of towns until they found a smoker willing to pose with his layout.

In San Francisco's Chinatown there were dozens of photographs taken, including a handful of images that were reproduced thousands of times on postcards. These, too, look as though the subjects were actually smoking, and there are even photos dating to the late nineteenth century that seem to have been taken on the sly—the photographer sneaking into a dimly lit opium den before tripping the shutter, igniting the flash powder, and then fleeing the scene.

While these more genuine depictions are probably more important historically, most were of little use to me because the smokers captured were poor and had paraphernalia that reflected their poverty. As in China, it would have been all but impossible for a photographer to gain access to an upscale opium den or a private smoking room in San Francisco's Chinatown. A notable exception that I found and was able to study was a unique portrait taken in 1886 by famed California photographer I.W. Taber. The photo shows two Chinese men smoking opium in what looks to be a lavish room just for that purpose, complete with an ornately carved hardwood opium bed and a layout tray inlaid with mother-of-pearl.

So with the help of my selection of photos, all scanned, enlarged, and cropped, I made a list of what pieces of paraphernalia I would need and then set out to find them. In searching for these tools I had even more of a challenge than I did in looking for opium pipes and lamps. Because the uses of most of the smaller pieces of paraphernalia had been long forgotten, antiques dealers—even the ones who sold the occasional opium pipe or lamp—never carried them in their shops. Merchants are wary of buying something they might have trouble reselling, and knowing nothing about an item is good reason not to invest in it. I showed pictures to the shopkeepers in Bangkok, all of whom got their antiques from hunters roving around China and Southeast Asia. None showed much enthusiasm for passing on a search order to their hunters. I couldn't really blame them—I was the only customer interested, and if by chance the hunters brought

Opium smokers in an opulent private smoking room in San Francisco's China-town, photographed by I. W. Taber in 1886. These men are reclining on a "bed" especially made for the purpose of opium smoking. (Courtesy of the California History Room, California State Library, Sacramento, California)

back some item that I didn't want, the antiques dealers would likely be stuck with it.

The online auction sites were my next stop. There I found much the same problem that I had with the Bangkok antiques shops—how would a seller list something if he or she didn't know what it was? Adopting the tactic I had used to find antique opium pipes and lamps on eBay, I thought up a series of searches designed to ferret out any opium paraphernalia that had been misidentified.

My success was limited, but I did manage to find a bowl scraper with a water-buffalo horn handle and iron blade (in Chicago, listed as a "Japanese tool"), a pewter dross box with an openwork brass lid that spelled out the characters for "double happiness" (in Washington State, listed as a "cricket cage"), and a *paktong* needle rest in the likeness of one of the auspicious Hoho Twins reclining on his belly (in California, listed as a "chopstick rest").

The problem was that my searches were time consuming, and they turned up maybe one piece of arcane paraphernalia a month. It was a slow way to build a collection—especially since I wanted accoutrements that matched as closely as possible so that the finished layout would look as though each piece had been crafted specifically for it. I needed a better system.

By chance while doing my online searches I ran across a seller based in Beijing who had an opium-needle cleaner on offer but didn't know what it was, labeling it a "scholar tool." I decided to email him with a wish list in the hopes that he could find other pieces of paraphernalia to sell me.

It was a calculated risk. I had already tried this approach with dealers in China and gotten less than satisfactory results. Once, I spent a week getting to know a merchant in Hong Kong via email who had listed an opium lamp on eBay. He said he was open to looking for more lamps for me, and I emailed him photographs of lamps from my collection to educate him about how opium lamps differed from other types of oil lamps. The merchant soon began to find opium lamps, but the prices he attached to them for resale were way beyond my means. I managed to haggle his prices down a bit and bought the best ones.

The merchant then asked me to be patient and said he would contact his dealer friends on the mainland to see if they could source more opium lamps. I thought I might start acquiring some decent items through this network, but when the merchant finally emailed photos of opium lamps he claimed to have found in China, I was surprised to see that they were all fakes whose designs were based on my own lamps—the ones in the photos I had sent him. It had taken the Hong Kong merchant mere weeks to have the reproductions made, and although I had managed to spot them, they were very good fakes. The thought was frightening.

The experience was an education, and I was to learn over time that antiques merchants in China are a particularly shrewd breed. My dealings with them seemed to follow a familiar arc: I would buy a couple of items from a merchant, and he or she would, in turn, look for more to sell me. Because there were so few authentic opium artifacts out there, the pickings soon got slim and the merchant looked for ways to cheat, substituting pastiches or out-and-out fakes. Once this began to happen, it was time to look for a new dealer.

Despite the hassles, it made sense that China would be the best place to look for the lesser-known bits of paraphernalia that I would need to build a complete working layout. More people had smoked opium there, percentage-wise and in sheer numbers, than anywhere else in the world, and the huge quantity of paraphernalia once in use there surely meant that many of these items would have escaped the bonfires of the eradication campaigns. It also stood to reason that officials in charge would have focused on destroying the easily recognizable opium pipes and lamps, and that the esoteric tools I was looking for were more likely to have survived.

Traveling to China to hunt for paraphernalia might seem like a logical move, but I knew from my forays in the antiques shops in the cities of Southeast Asia—the vast majority of which are owned by ethnic Chinese—that antiques hunting in China would be a slog, and a really expensive one at that. Shopping for Chinese antiques is a ritualized process, and not being Chinese is a distinct disadvantage. Most antiques merchants there are older men who have been in the business for years and consider themselves experts in their field. The thought that a non-Chinese might be able to discern or even appreciate the finer points of their art is laughable to them. Too many tourists have walked into their shops and balked at the prices of their treasures; too many others have allowed themselves to be fleeced. So it should come as no surprise that a non-Chinese customer walking in for the first time will be shown the worst items on offer, not the best. To get past this takes time. Assuming the proprietor will talk to you (I have set foot in Chinese antiques shops and been pointedly ignored), you must convince him that you are worthy of his time. Dress is important. The instant you walk in he will look you over and decide whether you are worth talking to. His ultimate goal is to make lots of money, and if you dress as though you have little, the proprietor will treat you accordingly.

If you manage to catch the merchant's attention you will need to present yourself in a way that lets him know you are not a rube. It is a very good sign if he offers you tea. Sip it slowly and talk for a while of matters totally unrelated to the reason you are there. If there happens to be a piece of opium paraphernalia on display, an old lamp or pipe, ignore the item until sufficient pleasantries have been exchanged. After complimenting a few unrelated items, let your eyes rest on the piece of paraphernalia and inquire about it. Never be in a rush to ask its price, no matter how much you want it. Instead, get a sense of how much he knows about it and if he has more stashed out of sight. Often it takes more than one trip to get such information, so imagine the investment of time and money involved in going to China and following this routine at each and every antiques shop.

Shopping online still seemed to me a way to more quickly and efficiently get at what I was looking for. I had developed an eye for spotting fakes, pastiches, and extensive repair work so I wasn't put off by the idea of buying without examining items in person. All I needed was a dealer in China whom I could trust not to bolt with my information and use it to mass-produce fakes.

I decided to try my luck with the guy in Beijing who had listed the "scholar tool" on eBay. Immediately after my initial email to him I got a reply. As eBay is loath for its users to do, we began a relationship outside of the site's confines. The seller went by the name Alex and had only recently begun selling on-line. Alex was my age and had been trading in Chinese antiques on a small scale for a couple of years. He had no shop but instead had set himself up as a middleman—buying antiques at flea markets and then reselling to the owners of Beijing's high-end antiques shops.

At first I was reluctant to let Alex know the real use for his "scholar tool," but it soon became apparent that if I was unwilling to trust him with my knowledge there would be a real limit on what he could do for me. I proposed a trade—an education for the opportunity to have the first look at anything he found. I would also supply the contact information for a handful of other collectors who I knew would be interested in buying the items I had passed on. I was fortunate that Alex saw the opportunity for what it was—a way for him to corner the market before anyone else in China knew that a market even existed, giving him an advantage over all the other hunters and dealers who were out there looking for the next big collectible.

Over two years I fed Alex a steady stream of photos and requests. Once he had scoured Beijing's flea markets and sidewalk stalls, he began making trips to explore other cities. The result was a bountiful harvest that wildly exceeded my expectations. Alex took a keen interest in the workings of the paraphernalia and its ornamentation, and seemed genuinely excited whenever he discovered a particularly well-crafted item. Unlike other Chinese merchants I had dealt with, he never feigned excitement in order to justify slapping exorbitant prices on his finds. No matter what Alex discovered, his prices always remained fair. With his help, I was able to acquire those pieces of paraphernalia that I'd previously seen only in historical photographs, and the complete working layout that Willi and I had dreamed of assembling became a reality.

Willi and I liked to think of ourselves as heirs to the lifestyle of wealthy, old-time smokers whose only limitations were their own imaginations. Not content with a single opium pipe, we amassed a small selection of pipes to choose from, each a favorite because of some unique detail in its design or ornamentation. Some were the aforementioned spoils of missionaries, long unused but finally put to the test by the two of us.

One pipe had once belonged to a Lao prince, its stem of knotty wood and mouthpiece of polished horn so heavily impregnated with opium resins that you might think they were carved from stone. Another cherished pipe was a standard model of which there had once been millions. Its mottled bamboo stem came from the forests of China's Hunan Province. The stem was fitted with ivory end pieces—de rigueur on all but the most modest pipes—and on the *paktong* saddle was the pipe's only adornment: a fiery red stone whose color was the yang meant to balance out the yin of the opium being smoked.

One of our pipes was of recent manufacture. Madame Tui's husband, Vientiane's maker of opium pipes, had apprenticed his only son to the craft at the age of thirteen. The old pipe maker had died in the late 1990s, but by that time he had also passed on his Vietnamese love for chased-silver depictions of muscular dragons to his son, Kai. By chance I met Kai, by then in his thirties, during a visit to Vientiane after the city's opium dens had been shut down in 2002. Since their closure he had carried on as a silversmith, busying himself making jewelry and a few reproduction opium pipes for tourists.

A rare opportunity became clear to me as Kai told me his father's story. The old pipe maker had learned his craft from an elderly Chinese who'd fled to Hanoi, in what was then French Indochina, just before the 1949 Communist victory in China. Less than a decade later, both men found themselves living under another opium-hostile Communist state—this time Ho Chi Minh's Democratic Republic of Vietnam. Madame Tui and her husband fled to Laos, then still a Buddhist kingdom, and set up shop in Vientiane. It was the right choice, given the country's tolerance of the vice outlasted everyplace else on earth—the old pipe maker was able to carry on with his trade until shortly before his death.

By the end of Kai's story I realized who I had standing in front of me: a classically trained opium pipe maker whose techniques were based on knowledge stretching all the way back to pre-Communist China. He was perhaps the very last of his kind, and there he was making trinkets for tourists! I asked him if I could commission the finest opium pipe he was capable of making. Kai was more than open to the idea of crafting a custom-made opium pipe—it clearly excited him. He had been using substandard materials—substituting brass for silver—to make cheap pipes for tourists because the relatively pricy examples that he had produced based on his father's teachings sat unsold on the shelves of Vientiane's souvenir shops. I asked Kai how much he would charge for his best work, and he estimated a price of no more than $200.

My self-designed pipe took nearly a year to finish. After

finding a suitable piece of bamboo in the jungle, Kai had to cure the stem to ensure it would not split—a process that in itself took many months—before fashioning the silver fittings to my specifications. Ivory end pieces were essential but, of course, using new elephant tusks was out of the question. Instead, I picked through the antiques shops of Bangkok, Penang, and Singapore until I happened upon the perfect mouthpiece: It was a five-inch length of ivory that had begun its life as a sword handle. At some time in the distant past it had been detached from its blade and a hole had been carefully drilled through its center so the ivory handle could be used as an opium pipe's mouthpiece. The idea was rather ghoulish—had the sword ever been used to kill anyone?—but my fondness for the rich, amber-colored patina of the ivory outweighed any qualms I had about inhaling opium vapors through it.

I took the ivory to Vientiane and left it with Kai along with hand-drawn schematics of what I felt would be the perfectly balanced pipe. When finally finished, the pipe would have a blond bamboo stem with silver fittings featuring painstakingly hammered motifs that included stalks of bamboo and lush leaves. It took several trips and many modifications before the pipe was right—Kai had never undertaken the crafting of a pipe of such expense and seemed anxious he might make an error that would ruin it. When he reached a step about which he had questions, there was no choice but to put the project away until I had the time to go to Vientiane and have a look. This was, of course, not a problem—every three months I had to leave Thailand and get a fresh tourist visa.

Once the pipe was completed I gave it a name: the "Dream Stick"—an American slang term dating to the Roaring Twenties. The Dream Stick was one of six pipes from which Willi and I could choose at the start of each session—always after much enthusiastic deliberation over the merits of each pipe. I was drawn to the most ornate pipes, but Willi preferred the more streamlined examples. Usually, however, the pipe that needed the least amount of preparatory maintenance won out. Here I discovered yet another reason why opium smoking was relatively easy to eradicate: Opium pipes required constant and meticulous upkeep. They expanded and contracted with rising and falling temperatures and humidity. Pipes were mixed media, made up of parts crafted from different materials—bamboo, ivory, silver, *paktong*, clay—and these parts reacted differently to the surrounding atmosphere. Because of this, they always needed an inspection and some minor repairs before each smoking session. Most important, opium pipes had to be airtight before they could be used—if not, the complex vaporization process would not work.

Of all the pipe's parts, the distinctive ceramic bowl was the most crucial to this process. Functional pipe bowls were also the most difficult items for me to acquire. I would look at hundreds before I found one that was still in good enough condition to actually use for smoking. Usually the tiny needle hole had widened during the countless times in the past that opium needles had been thrust into it. This widening, almost imperceptible to the untrained eye, meant that precious *chandu* would be wasted during smoking—making the bowl useless.

Fortunately I found a pair of pipe bowls on eBay that were at least a century old, unused, and still in their original box. Made from Yixing, the porous clay prized by Chinese as the perfect material for teapots, the bowls were part of a cache of opium paraphernalia discovered behind a false wall in a store in Vancouver's old Chinatown—no doubt illicit inventory that was to have been smuggled into the United States. I paid twenty-five dollars for the pair of bowls on eBay. The seller knew what they were, listing them correctly as opium pipe bowls but foolishly giving prospective buyers a "buy-it-now" option. Were there others who would have bid on these relics? Perhaps, but according to the counter at the bottom of the webpage, I was the first to view the lot. I bought them immediately. To me these pristine bowls were priceless—I would have happily paid ten times that price.

Normally, if I came across something extraordinary online, I would email Willi a link, but this time I waited to tell him anything until the pipe bowls had arrived in Bangkok by airmail. I photographed the pair still in their original box, and emailed the image with a simple note confirming that they were in my possession. Almost immediately the telephone rang and Willi exclaimed over the line, "You must come up at once! Please stop whatever you are doing and board the train now!"

It was exactly the response I was hoping for. I will never forget the feeling of excitement as I arrived after a night on the train. I was carrying the small cardboard box enveloped in a bolt of silk, and Willi and I unwrapped and examined the bowls with the deliberation and respect befitting such prized objects. Willi selected one of them and then we readied it for use with one of the trophy pipes that had belonged to a China-based Christian missionary. After a century suspended in time, this pipe bowl would be used as the artisan who crafted it had originally intended.

The scene that day reminded me of a Jacques Cousteau program that I had watched on television as a child. The underwater archaeologists had found a cache of centuries-old wine cradled in some shipwreck and, being Frenchmen, they brought the bottles aboard the *Calypso* and drunk their contents with gusto. Willi and I inhaled the first pills of opium through our newly acquired relic with the same enthusiasm. The pipe bowl performed as though it were rewarding us for our efforts in bringing it to life. There were no burned pills that night, and not a single drop of *chandu* was wasted. After smoking his tenth pill, Willi exhaled a column of near invisible vapors toward the ceiling and fixed me with an impish grin and a gleam in his eyes that told me his next utterance would be inflected with Yiddish. Even in the dim lamplight I could see that his pupils were dots as tiny as the eyes of a shrimp. He smacked his lips with satisfaction and lisped, "Isssss qvality!"

❧

"There's nothing like a complete opium set to grab peoples' attention," an old German who ran a high-end antiques shop in the River City mall once told me. "I one time had a full opium set on a tray in my display window, and I watched the people walking past my shop stop suddenly to point and stare."

Opium pipes are the old masters of opium antiques collecting. Pipes have broad appeal and are more readily recognized and appreciated by noncollectors than lamps and other accoutrements. But nothing impresses like a complete layout, especially one as opulent as Willi and I had assembled. In all, there were nearly two dozen separate pieces of paraphernalia on our tray. Each item was crafted from either brass, copper, *paktong,* or a combination of the three metals, and kept polished to a high shine by Willi's servant. Many of our pieces were meticulously decorated with delicate openwork that an artisan had cut into the metal with the tiniest of saw blades.

Because Buddhism was important in old China, swastikas were a common motif adorning Chinese artworks—and opium paraphernalia was no exception. The swastika is an ancient Hindu and Buddhist symbol, and for the Chinese and other Buddhist cultures, the swastika carries none of the dark historical associations that it does for most Westerners. I had been so long in Asia, and had so many times seen the swastika as a decorative component of these religions—as adornment on Buddhist temples as well as on Indian, Chinese, and Vietnamese art—that Nazi associations no longer sprang to mind upon seeing swastikas in this context. So I decided not to shun paraphernalia with the ubiquitous swastika but instead to celebrate the symbol as adherents of Hinduism and Buddhism have for millennia. By doing so I felt I was taking back this mysterious spiritual motif from the monsters who had so recently hijacked it.

The opium lamp that Willi and I used was a model from China's Yunnan Province. Minute openwork had been cut into its octagonal base of tricolored metals, allowing air to feed the flame while providing hundreds of facets on which the glow of the lamp could reflect. Although the light produced by the lamp was feeble, when coupled with the effects of a few pipes of opium, its reflection upon the layout's gleaming surfaces seemed to tickle my eyelashes like a faint breeze.

Our lamp was fitted with cotton wick that I had sourced at a shop in Bangkok's Chinatown. At the start of each session, Willi would push its long tail deep into the lamp's reservoir, which he kept filled with a fragrant brand of coconut oil from India. Then he would fastidiously trim the wick with a dainty pair of brass scissors—barely two inches in length—that had been specially made for the task. He used a matching pair of tweezers to gently advance the wick when necessary. Both tools were kept in a deep brass tray that supported the lamp and contained any oil that might be spilled while filling it. Also on this deep tray was the miniature wok for evaporating the liquid *chandu* as well as various tools to assist with the rolling process.

The lamp tray sat centered on a much larger brass layout tray that was crowded with engraved brass and copper boxes for storing dross, gee-rags, and lamp wick, as well as a trash receptacle shaped like a miniature spittoon. Brass tools for scraping dross from the inside of pipe bowls leaned against their own matching stand, next to a rest for the all-important opium needle.

All these rare and wonderful things were upstaged by what in my opinion is the holy grail of antique opium paraphernalia collecting: a shade for the opium lamp—in this case a silver cicada whose eyes were set with rubies. To smokers of yore, the burbling sound of an opium pipe was said to echo certain sounds found in nature—particularly the mating calls of cicadas, frogs, and a species of freshwater crab. Thus these three creatures became opium smokers' mascots, and to honor them as such, artisans crafted their images onto paraphernalia. Our cicada lampshade hung from the lip of the lamp's glass chimney, blocking the glare just so—a whimsical remedy for the opium smoker's heightened visual sensitivity.

"These old-time smokers were like children with their toys," Willi once remarked to me during a session. This, I theorize, was what kept the makers of fine paraphernalia in business. Just like kids, the smokers would have tried to outdo one another, always competing to be the one with the coolest playthings.

The more we used the antique paraphernalia, the more evident it was to us that many of the finest smoking accoutrements were created with the heightened senses of opium smokers in mind. The astounding attention to detail—the filigree-like openwork, the ornately ornamented surfaces etched with lines as light and tight as a feather's—all of it was meant to catch and dazzle the opium-thrilled eye. To prop myself up on one elbow and behold our gleaming layout in the darkened room made me feel like a storybook giant who had stumbled upon a miniature city of gold—a shining El Dorado in some lost valley, banishing gloom with its magical radiance.

Likewise, the textured surfaces on the handles of the tools, lids, and other bits meant to be touched were there to titillate those millions of hypersensitive nerve endings on a smoker's fingertips. The full genius of the artisans' efforts to create pleasing textures was most abundantly experienced by the lips. No kiss has ever been sweeter, more supple, or more enchanting, than that of an ivory mouthpiece upon the lips of an opium smoker.

In the most basic sense, the huge layout—the pipe and lamp and sundry tools spread out upon their respective trays—was a system for keeping the involved and messy process of opium smoking as organized and tidy as possible. But to Willi and me, it seemed much more significant. Many pieces of our paraphernalia had been handled by long-departed souls who were adept at spinning the sap of poppies into dreams. We came to believe that the accumulated knowledge of this escapism was trapped within the paraphernalia itself, and that by using it, Willi and I were somehow learning important truths that had been long lost. Our sessions, progressively more blissful with each meeting, seemed to bear this theory out.

Once the layout seemed perfect, Willi and I turned our attention to the space that hosted our sessions. After Willi had arranged for the basement storage room to be emptied, we gradually introduced decorative objects and period furniture from old China. Neither of us had the means to complete the embellishment of our smoking room all at once, but we felt that our inability to instantly transform the space made us more selective and gave us time to appreciate each new addition.

Our decorative theme evolved in a way that made the room seem as though it, too, had gone through several permutations over time. Originally we conceived of the space as a classical

Chinese study—a place of solitude that might have been used by some bespectacled student preparing for the imperial examinations. Later, as the nineteenth century gave way to the twentieth and the Qing dynasty fell to Sun Yat-sen's republic, our room, as did all of China, came under the influence of Western ideas. This could be seen in the English-made pendulum clock we positioned prominently on the wall, as well as the framed American sheet music covers that hung between scrolls of calligraphic poetry on rice paper. But our march of time had stopped in Jazz Age Shanghai—in the 1930s—when the Japanese invasion of Manchuria had given China a fatalistic, devil-may-care attitude that the invaders encouraged by making opium more plentiful than ever before. At some point during the transformation, Willi christened the room: "the Chamber of Fragrant Mists."

It was in this safe haven that Willi and I smoked opium on a regular basis from 2002 to 2006. Upon my arrival—usually at mid-morning in a three-wheeled motorcycle taxi—Willi would be waiting on the verandah and, after a hearty greeting, would direct me to the shower where I could scrub off the grime of a night's worth of tropical train travel. Then I exchanged my modern clothes for loose-fitting Chinese pantaloons, black cloth slippers, a white silk singlet, and a smoking jacket of brocaded indigo silk. This latter garment was also an online purchase— a relic with tags stitched into the lining indicating that it had been tailor-made by a shop on Yates Road in old Shanghai's International Settlement. Perhaps it had been worn by Silas Aaron Hardoon himself—called the "Baghdad Jew"—who amassed a fortune trading opium in what was then known as the "Wickedest City in the World."

Once Willi and I were properly outfitted in period clothing, it was time to conduct the many pre-smoking rituals that we performed before the start of each session, descending into the dark and shuttered Chamber after weeks of absence. The old pendulum clock was set and wound only when the Chamber was in use—kick-starting time in our Chinese Brigadoon. I usually did the honor myself, fingering the pendulum into action and twirling the minute hand round and round until the clock caught up with time, the lost hours bonging away frantically.

Then, once the clock was in motion, I gave my attention to the calendar. The number prominently displayed on the hanging pad of pages indicated the last date we had filled the Chamber with the sweetish scent of opium. One at a time I tore away pages until the present date appeared, making sure the sound of each one being ripped from the pad was clear and distinct. When the pages to be torn away were many, we lamented the time lost to mundane activities—how could we have squandered so many days without a visit to our beloved Chamber? If the pages were few we congratulated ourselves on having so soon found time to indulge.

After the clock and calendar had been adjusted, I then made offerings of candles and incense to the Den God, an image of a nameless Chinese deity that I had rescued from a dusty stall at a flea market in Bangkok. Willi had converted an empty corner of the room into an elaborately gated shrine for the deity, framing it with decorative wooden panels that were salvaged from the interior of a demolished Chinese mansion. Upon the altar were smoldering sticks of incense and thick red candles whose tall flames softly illuminated the benevolent face of the Den God. Ribbons of smoke rose from the glowing tips of the joss sticks, stretching upward through the breezeless air in slender columns that billowed against the red lacquered ceiling. After countless sessions, the room's surfaces became coated with the oily smoke of incense and opium, bestowing upon everything the glossy sheen of antiquity.

Dominating one wall of the room was a huge old Chinese shophouse sign that I had bought at an antiques shop in Penang while updating a chapter of a guidebook about Malaysia. Made long ago from a single block of black lacquered wood, the sign consisted of two Chinese characters deeply carved and detailed with gold leaf. During our sessions, the faintest candlelight would reflect in the sign's gilt recesses, causing the characters to shimmer softly above the room. When I first saw the sign in the antiques shop, I was only making conversation when I asked the proprietor to translate it for me. The sign read "Doctor with Peerless Hands." I immediately bought it for the Chamber and in so doing, Willi gained a new nickname: "The Doctor."

On a long, narrow Chinese table positioned against another wall, Willi had arranged two wooden racks to display our pipes. Hanging above this was a wood and glass curio cabinet with our precious hoard of pipe bowls stored under lock and key.

Over the years we covered nearly every inch of the Chamber's brick walls with vintage Chinese advertising, old photos, and obscure, opium-related ephemera. My contribution was our collection of American sheet music covers—reminders of a time when opium smoking in America was so commonplace that it was the subject of popular songs. The oldest was Will Rossiter's "I Don't Care If I Never Wake Up" from 1899. There was also "Roll a Little Pill For Me" by Norma Gray from 1911, and Byron Gay's "Fast Asleep in Poppyland" from 1919 (chorus: "Lights burn low / dreams come and go / dreams of happy hours / spent among the flowers").

Our favorite for cover art was Ole Olsen and Isham Jones's "Frisco's Chinatown" from 1917, which featured a depiction of an opium den with four pigtailed Chinese slumbering snugly in the tiered bunks that were a common space-saving arrangement in American "hop joints."

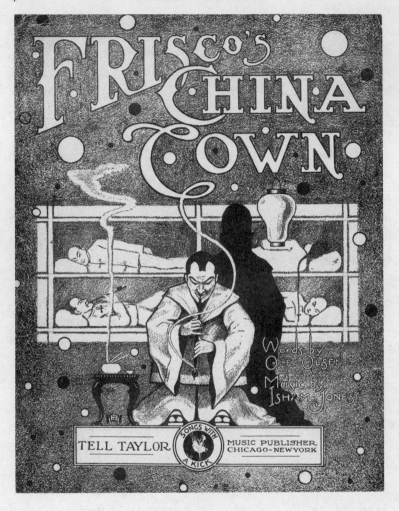

Sheet music cover from 1917 with a depiction of a typical "hop joint" in San Francisco's Chinatown. Between the 1890s and the 1930s, opium smoking was so well known in America that it was mentioned in popular songs, many of which also reflected the association of the habit with Chinese immigrants, who introduced it from China in the 1850s. (From the author's collection)

The old song sheets notwithstanding, Willi and I preferred silence over music while smoking. Any loud, sustained noise—

any sound other than the steady tick-tock of the pendulum clock—would mask the gentle burbling sound of the pipe. If a smoker cannot hear his pipe, the sound of which resembles the dregs of a milkshake being lightly sucked through a straw, he can't tell if the opium is properly vaporizing, especially since the vapors of good *chandu* do not burn the throat or lungs like tobacco smoke.

The all-important opium bed, the room's centerpiece, was a heavy, baroquely carved rectangular hardwood platform. Unlike a traditional bed, the two long sides of an opium bed are its head and foot. Ours was positioned with one long side—the bed's head—against a wall. The head and sides of the bed were enclosed with wooden panels about two feet high, meaning that it could only be mounted from the foot. This was designed to afford privacy to the bed's occupants, keeping out any unwanted distractions and helping to cut down on drafts that might make the opium lamp flicker. Our opium bed was additionally sheltered from the rest of the room by a low-hanging canopy of silken brocade woven with elegant floral motifs that were just faintly visible through the smoky gloom. The result was a womblike space within a space, enveloped by darkness and quiet, a willful cocooning against the world.

I always looked forward to my weekends away from Bangkok with its gridlocked thoroughfares and ubiquitous construction sites towering above gouged and pummeled earth. In my mind it wasn't the opium that I missed—it wasn't the high that I craved. What I longed for was sanctuary from the modern world. Life outside the Chamber seemed increasingly cruel. Out there were the twenty-first century, war, and terror. A relentless feed of information made far-off events difficult to ignore, but even if I could turn my back on the larger world, the situation around me was just as disturbing.

The Southeast Asia that Willi and I had both gravitated to in our respective youths had grown modern and materialistic. We both watched in dismay as many of the quaint traditions and customs that had attracted us to the region in the first place vanished before our eyes. Westernization is the bugbear most often cited as causing the demise of old Southeast Asia, but, in fact, the majority of changes we saw were brought about by the relentless rise of new China.

The behemoth's influence could be seen everywhere, but most noticeably in the region's largest cities. During the 1990s, Southeast Asia began giving up its traditional architecture of teak and brick and stucco for modern Chinese-inspired concrete boxes clad in glazed tiles and tinted glass. Local craftsmen were squeezed out by a flood of impossibly cheap Chinese goods. Most affected were the ethnic Chinese themselves, descendants of a nineteenth-century exodus from the country's turbulent past. Generations of living in Southeast Asia had bestowed upon the great-grandchildren of that first wave the easy habits common to people who live in tropical lands of plenty. They were no match for these new Chinese—famished after decades of austere Maoism and accustomed to using sharp elbows to push to the head of the line. When in 1992 Deng Xiaoping declared "To get rich is glorious," his mantra soon carried his countrymen on a renewed push for China's traditional southward expansion. As the century turned, the pace of modernization quickened as China became richer, and billions were invested in Southeast Asia. The swiftness of change was astonishing.

If Willi and I had allowed outsiders into the Chamber to gaze upon our meticulously re-created surroundings and to witness our cryptic rituals, most would have concluded that we were a couple of eccentric Sinophiles. But such assumptions would have missed the point. Willi and I were fans of the old, inscrutable China, its mysteries and idiosyncrasies an essential part of its charm. Opium was our time travel back to that simpler era before China—and the whole of East Asia—became known for karaoke-caterwauling and crassness.

While under the narcotic's optimistic influence, Willi and I strove to re-create that romantic period in Chinese history when a poet might spend the day flying a kite while drinking rice wine spiced with chrysanthemum petals. New China, as well as the rest of the modern world, was a horror to us, and we went to great lengths to ensure that it ceased to exist the moment we entered the Chamber of Fragrant Mists. There were no telephones or other ways of communicating with the outside world allowed in the Chamber, and while there ensconced we never discussed current events.

Instead, we might try to identify the calls of wild birds that inhabited the thickets of bamboo on the far side of the lotus pond. We might discuss the merits of a Tibetan rug—shaped and patterned like a tiger skin—that Willi had bought from the estate of a long-dead British civil servant who had once maintained a bungalow near Mandalay. Willi and I might take turns reading aloud passages from some of our favorite books (David Kidd's *Peking Story* and John Blofeld's *City of Lingering Splendour* were always at hand), and at least once during each session Willi's wife would come down to the Chamber to say hello and recline for a pipe or two.

Willi and I spent hours in each other's company, but flagging conversation is never a problem with opium smokers. As the hours passed and the number of pipes smoked increased, we found ourselves in the Land of the Gentle Nod, a state somewhere between slumber and wakefulness, like that last second of consciousness before one drifts off to sleep. Here the clock would slow to such a crawl that lifetimes seemed to pass during the pauses in our conversation. Opium is its own timekeeper, as every smoker soon learns. At that time, when I was but a novice to smoking and enjoyed a nightlong session perhaps once a month, a single night on opium left me feeling that I knew the true meaning behind the title of Gabriel García Márquez's first novel. Years later, after I had begun rolling my own pipes and smoking alone, hours could pass in three nods of my poppy-fogged head. I would light the lamp just before midnight and then, seemingly within minutes, an unwelcome dawn was worrying the curtains.

Over time, a single night in the Chamber seemed inadequate and my one-night trips to visit Willi became long weekends. These two- and three-day sessions, when we could manage them, were sublime. Willi had a talent for Old World hospitality and he often spent a whole week preparing for one of my visits, ensuring that arrangements were perfect in every detail.

Food may not seem to be compatible with opium smoking, but in fact the high-quality blend, when used in moderation, produces in the smoker both the desire and the ability to enjoy food. Our fabulously rare *chandu* heightened all senses of perception, including taste. Once we had discovered this, Willi and I added an aspect of culinary adventure to the opium equation.

Like everything else in the cosmos, Chinese foods can be divided into two groups, depending on whether they possess cooling yin or heating yang properties. Since opium is female—or yin—smokers favored masculine yang foods to keep things in balance. During its nineteenth-century heyday, opium smoking gave rise to a complementary cuisine. But, like just about every-thing else pertaining to opium culture, the knowledge, if not altogether lost, had been hidden away and forgotten. It wouldn't be a matter of searching Amazon for a cookbook.

Instead, I was in charge of poring through my books in hopes of running across a reference to some opium smoker's favorite recipe that we might resurrect. Willi might then drive his pickup truck to northern Thailand just to buy smoked boar's meat sau-sages from a butcher at some Kuomintang village that he had passed through and noted years before. Back in Vientiane, Willi would seek out elderly members of the Chinese community and then, with uncommon ingredients in hand, talk them into pre-paring morsels that hadn't been attempted since mid-century revolutions and migrations had made them unthinkable luxu-ries.

The result of all these preparations were halcyon days spent gently padding back and forth between the incense-scented coolness of the Chamber and the warmth of the sun-soothed pavilion over the lotus pond. In the shade provided by the pavil-ion's roof, its thick wooden shingles covered with feathery moss, sat a low teakwood table. By mid-morning Willi's servant was busy arranging the tabletop with rows of porcelain bowls, each containing some delicacy that Willi had spent the previous days procuring. There was pickled ginger dyed a lurid pink that seemed to match its spicy tang; flaky Chinese pastries whose waxy red and yellow markings codified sweet and savory fillings; spongy buns from which escaped a sigh of steam when torn in half—and all of it washed down with countless thimble-sized cups of slightly bitter, palate-cleansing tea. Willi directed that our banquets be served in leisurely, unhurried courses that punctu-ated our smoking sessions and lasted well into the night. Once the old servant had cleared away the crumbs and dregs, applause for Willi's efforts took the form of creaking wicker as our satiated bodies sank deep into rattan chairs.

When the echoing calls of night birds became more urgent, and the fireflies' luminous signals began to wane, we took them as signs to leave the rapidly cooling outside air for the warmth indoors. We might continue to smoke until midnight, and Willi would then roll us a nightcap—a last pipe or two—before blowing out the lamp and retiring to his room upstairs, leaving me to lounge away the sweetened night alone in the Chamber.

Opium puts one on the verge of sleep, but if smoked to excess the threshold of sleep cannot be passed. I *always* smoked too much and could never fall asleep. Yet far from feeling the frustration of insomnia, I savored these hours of drifting in limbo. I would pass the night lying on my back with my fingers laced upon my chest, my eyes closed so their inner membranes could serve as screens upon which deeply buried memories were projected. The clarity of these visions delighted me, and the rush of love that I felt upon seeing a family member or a childhood friend sometimes brought me to tears.

These might be termed "opium dreams" by some, but they were really no more than memories that opium had made more vivid—fragile images that vanished as readily as dust blown from the cover of an old book. As long as I focused on the memories they were there, but opium in excess works against concentration, and the encounters were fleeting. Between these images were playbacks of conversations that Willi and I had had earlier that day. One exchange in particular came back to me. It was based on a nagging question that of late had made even my most rapturous moments bittersweet: Must this end?

"Willi, you know, every time I think to myself that this simply cannot get any better, I also can't help but wonder how long we can keep it up."

Willi had raised himself up from the bamboo mat in order to best use a wooden back scratcher to dig at the small of his back. He looked at me with bliss-heavy eyes and then turned to address the Den God in its little cove of drippy candles. "I don't see any reason we can't keep this up forever as long as we're disciplined about it," he said. "Obviously the dangers of becoming addicted have been exaggerated. Look how long we've been doing this." Willi paused and then asked, "After you've gone back to Bangkok do you find your cravings for opium unbearable?"

"Mondays I usually sleep most of the day. Tuesdays I often have a yen," I said, purposely using some vintage slang to amuse Willi.

Willi chuckled and rose to the occasion—the Chamber library included an old book with an extensive list of dated American underworld slang. Slipping examples into conversations was one of our favorite Chamber pastimes. "You're just a joy-popper with an ice cream habit," Willi quipped. He then said with some seriousness: "As long as we keep to once a month or so, we can't get hooked."

"Well, as long as kicking the gong is a train ride away, I guess I don't have to worry. I don't know how you do it, though. If the Chamber were as close to me as it is to you, I'd be on the mat every day."

Willi shrugged. "I have other poisons. I drink a bottle of Prosecco nearly every day. Of course, alcohol is a crude substitute for *chandu,* but I can't afford to become hooked. This stuff costs more per ounce than gold. If somehow things got out of hand, it would bankrupt me."

"So how do people maintain habits?"

"Do you mean those dross-smoking skeletons puffing away down at Kay's?" Willi winced. "Where's the joy in that?"

Then Willi broke into a smile as a thought came into his head. "There *is* someone who maintains an old-fashioned habit. I've never told you about her, but it's her patronage that makes it possible for me to keep the Chamber stocked with *chandu*. She's a real old hand—an American left over from the war in Indochina. And as it happens, she's due for her annual visit next month. Would you like to meet her?"

Once a woman has started on the trail of the poppy, the sledding is very easy and downgrade all the way.

—Judge Emily F. Murphy, *The Black Candle* (1922)

I'm not a Christian by anybody's measure. My father's family was supposedly Episcopalian; my mother's Baptist. I once asked why we as a family never went to church, and my father replied that he'd be damned if he was going to waste his only day off listening to a sermon. On the rare occasion that I set foot inside a church while growing up, it was always with some churchgoing neighbor family who had coached their children to invite me along to a Sunday service. The only aspect of these outings that impressed me were the pastry feasts that followed the services of certain Protestant denominations. The Catholic masses that I attended were interesting for their rituals, but the after-service refreshments were stingy affairs. In the end, neither the colorful rites of the Catholics nor the sugar highs of the Protestants were able to inspire any spiritual yearnings in me.

From 1990 until 1995, I lived in Chiang Mai, and this brought Christians to my attention once again. Northern Thailand's principal city has long been a base for Christian missionaries. The first one, a Presbyterian from North Carolina, arrived in 1867 when Chiang Mai was still a separate kingdom from Siam (which has officially been known as Thailand since 1949), and made his first convert two years later by using astronomical tables to predict an eclipse of the sun.

As the missionaries' "vision" for pursuing converts spread beyond Chiang Mai, the Presbyterians began to clash with American Baptists who were competing to harvest the region's souls. An agreement between the two denominations eventually kept the Baptists within the borders of neighboring Burma and the Presbyterians in what is now northern Thailand.

Living in Chiang Mai in the early 1990s, I at first found the city's missionaries a curiosity, but the better I got to know them, the less I was able to smile through my encounters with them. Their inflexible ways and blinkered outlook on life were astounding. These were people who had traveled far from home and settled in the most exotic surroundings they could find, and then devoted their lives to making the locals dress, act, and believe exactly as they did. In Chiang Mai I met a middle-aged couple from America's Midwest, overdressed in the tropical heat, who chirpily told of how they were able to convince whole villages in Burma to give up their traditional clothing and festivals. Being oblivious to their own arrogance was a trait that they all seemed to share.

More interesting to me, though, than the proselytizers themselves were their own lapsed children, living as natives in lands that their parents had dedicated entire lives to Christianizing. Some missionary families had spent generations in Southeast Asia, and it was not unheard of for their offspring to leave the fold or find more adventurous callings. Bill Young was one I heard about and wanted to meet. Born in Burma to Baptist missionary parents, Young was raised in tribal villages and was said to speak fluent Hmong and Lahu, as well as Shan. As a young man in the 1960s he had been recruited by the CIA to run espionage operations into southern China from northwestern Laos. Among other activities, Young arranged for Golden Triangle opium caravans returning from Thailand to transport radios and other espionage equipment to CIA listening posts inside the Chinese border. Young's understanding of the terrain and the people who inhabited it resulted in his being possibly the most effective CIA agent who served in the Indochina War. But when he demurred at instituting policies that he thought would adversely affect the tribal peoples under his charge, he was replaced by a ruthless operative called Tony Poe—who is said to have been the inspiration for Marlon Brando's commander-gone-mad character in the film *Apocalypse Now.*

Young's story intrigued me, but he was reclusive. As one British resident of Chiang Mai told me, Young's CIA past had been "exposed" in a book called *The Politics of Heroin in Southeast Asia,* and he had since refused all interviews. At the time I had not yet tried my hand at journalism or had anything published— I simply had a personal interest in hearing the stories of the region's Western old-timers. Young had retired in Chiang Mai and become a member of the city's large expatriate community, a colorful group that included a number of Vietnam vets (a few of them spectacularly unhinged) who had been discharged stateside before drifting back to Southeast Asia. There was also a commune of aging hippies who had reinvented themselves as New Age gurus; a colony of artists attired in a patchwork of tribal costumes and jewelry; a smattering of mildly pompous academics and experts on local arcana; even a group of Western monks cloistered at one of the city's Buddhist monasteries.

Among these expats were a few genuine old Asia hands, real long-termers who had arrived in the 1950s or '60s. They remembered when it was possible to ride a pedicab from one end of Thapae Road to the other without being passed by a single automobile. Length of stay was not the only criterion that made an old Asia hand—the genuine article had a certain attitude, an air of unflappability. They were never jaded or cynical. On a continent that turns some long-term Westerners into haters, whiners, and grumblers, they remained interested and engaged. Bill Young undoubtedly epitomized the persona, but I was having difficulty tracking him down. My asking around eventually led me to Roxanna Brown.

Roxanna ran a bar not far from Chiang Mai's famous Night Bazaar. It was an unlicensed Hard Rock Café—the sort of knockoff that raised no eyebrows in the days before any international chains had reached the city. The bar's interior walls were lined with dusty album covers, and there were faded and threadbare concert T-shirts tightly stretched and pinned to the ceiling with thumbtacks like the skins of oversized rodents. Roxanna's bar was not yet open for business when I rapped on the door one day, but she answered and waved me in out of the sun.

Roxanna was small in stature, friendly, and about my mother's age—not the type you would expect to see running a bar in Thailand, where the majority of Western barkeeps seem to be male, argumentative, and British. She wore a gauzy beige outfit that appeared to be patterned after a Vietnamese *ao dai,* and her short, reddish hair was tight around her head as if she had been wearing a cloche hat. I also noted a pronounced limp, but other than these facile observations, I failed to see anything remarkable about her. I scribbled some names and phone numbers into my notebook as Roxanna listed people who would know how to contact Bill Young. Five minutes later I was back on the street and thinking about my next move. Soon I'd forgotten all about Roxanna Brown.

In the end I never got to meet Bill Young in person. We talked on the telephone, but he apologetically explained that he was in ill health and unable to receive visitors. It would be a decade before I would meet Roxanna again.

❦

A few weeks after Willi had promised to introduce me to that mysterious American with an old-time opium habit, I was back at the Chamber. It was late March and the day was brutally hot. Whenever I visited during Vientiane's oppressive summer, Willi and I spent a significant portion of the session debating the merits of installing air-conditioning. Being a purist, I resisted. How could we have an authentic experience with an air conditioner droning in the background?

I had arrived mid-morning and by late afternoon both Willi and I were half-cooked. Through heavy lids I watched Willi holding a needle poised over the tiny wok of bubbling *chandu,* the yellow glare of the opium lamp reflecting in the beads of sweat that speckled his forehead and upper lip. My silk singlet was clammy with perspiration and clung to my back, but the porcelain pillow felt blessedly cool against my cheek. Willi finished preparing the pill, inhaled it with a series of short, gulping draws he called a "De Niro hit" (from the opium den scenes in *Once Upon a Time in America*), and let out a satisfied sigh as he blew the vapors toward the ceiling. He then announced a break by calling for the servant to bring iced coffee in the Vietnamese style—with generous dollops of sweetened condensed milk and chasers of hot tea. The coffee arrived with a plate of crumbly almond cookies, but these went untouched—it was simply too hot to eat. I sat upright on the opium bed just long enough to drink my coffee and then I let my eyelids slide shut and allowed my mind to drift, the heat and humidity forgotten. Willi and I lapsed into a comfortable silence and didn't speak again until the sound of a three-wheeled motorcycle taxi puttering up the gravel drive made us suddenly alert. "It's Rox," Willi said, sliding off the bed and making his way out to greet her.

I could hear their conversation through the vents in the walls up along the Chamber ceiling. Willi paid the taxi driver to save Roxanna the trouble, and then I could hear her steps—an unsteady crunch on the gravel—as Willi led her around to the back of the house so she didn't have to climb any stairs.

"Oh my, it's dark in here!" Roxanna said as Willi guided her through the back door. She stood just inside the Chamber, letting her eyes adjust. I recognized her and noted that she had not changed at all in the ten years since I met her in Chiang Mai. Willi made introductions, but Roxanna didn't remember me. No matter—there are no strangers in an opium den. Her pleasure and excitement at being with us was obvious, and it made me want the visit to live up to her expectations in every way. I cleared a place on the opium bed for her, moving the layout tray toward Willi's side of the bed and putting away the picture books that he and I had been leafing through.

Roxanna complimented Willi on the Chamber's décor—it had been more than a year since she'd seen it last and there were many new items on display. Willi graciously pointed out that much of it was my doing and asked me to field Roxanna's queries about the provenance of each new piece. She was most interested in some ceramic pipe bowls that had been crafted a century before in the town of Jianshui in China's Yunnan Province. The small town was famed for an ingenious inlay technique that used clays of contrasting colors to make designs on the surfaces of ceramics such as opium pipe bowls. The breakthrough caused a sensation among opium smokers in the nineteenth century: Here were bowls that could be intricately adorned with any design imaginable—bucolic landscapes, charming still lifes, scenes from legends, poetry in characters that mimicked brushstrokes, even personalized dedications—and yet the decorated surface was perfectly smooth for rolling and impervious to heat.

"Do you use these?" Roxanna asked, gently lifting one of the inlaid bowls from its shelf.

"Of course," Willi replied. "Pick a pipe stem from the rack and any bowl from the cabinet. Steven here is my pipe boy. He doesn't yet know how to roll, but he can do just about everything else."

Roxanna laughed at the reference to a long-dead custom. In old China, overseas Chinatowns, and everywhere else that old Chinese culture was transplanted and took root, wealthy opium smokers employed the equivalent of a personal valet specially trained in the maintenance of opium accoutrements and, most important, in the art of preparing pipes. The pipe boy usually apprenticed in his early teens, when sharp eyesight and nimble fingers made training less of a challenge. Besides rolling, duties might also include ensuring that enough *chandu* was on hand in case a guest arrived unexpectedly; tending a charcoal fire during winter months to boil water for tea as well as to keep the oil for the opium lamp from congealing in the cold; scraping opium ash from pipe bowls and then collecting and storing the dross until there was a sizable enough quantity to resell to the local opium merchant for recycling. An accomplished pipe boy might also be able to play a repertoire of soothing ballads on a musical instrument such as the moon guitar.

Some smokers prohibited their pipe boys from using opium, lest they become addicted and lackadaisical in their tasks, but secondhand vapors usually ensured that nonsmoking pipe boys in the employ of heavy smokers developed a habit over time. If a boy turned to thievery to pay for clandestine trips to public dens or began to pilfer opium from his master's stash, it was time to apprentice a new pipe boy. On the other hand, if after years of service a smoker became attached to his valet's skills, he might purposely get the young man addicted to preempt him from thinking seriously about looking for a wife and starting a family.

In France's colonies in Indochina, the practice of employing a pipe boy was such a status symbol among French opium smokers—the addicted colonials seemingly always reclining in the cool shadows alongside shirtless Vietnamese boys—that non-smoking colonials became convinced opium could turn any virile Frenchman into a keeper of catamites.

Roxanna chose a pipe stem from the rack of six: a lady's pipe crafted from a gracefully slim length of bamboo and fitted with a layered Yunnanese saddle and jade end pieces. She took her time in choosing a bowl from the cabinet, holding up each to a candle as she examined the inlaid designs and chop marks. I used the delay to pass a ramrod through the pipe stem and buff its surfaces with a damp cloth.

Roxanna's final choice was telling: It was the obvious pick of a confirmed smoker. The bowl was from northern China, short on decorative frills but made from the absorbent Yixing clay that to this day is favored for making fine teapots—due to its purported ability to produce a more flavorful tea with each successive serving. Such pots are never washed with soap as this would strip away the delicate residue of countless teas that have steeped within them. Opium pipe bowls made from Yixing were thought to possess this same quality. As long as the bowl absorbed vapors of only the best *chandu,* its porous interior surface would retain a trace of the rich flavors that passed through it. With each and every pipe inhaled, the user of such a bowl came ever closer to having the perfect smoke. However, if the bowl was exposed to a single hit of oily smoke from inferior dross-laden opium, the mellow taste that it once imparted would be lost forever.

"I'm not particularly fond of jade," Roxanna said while wiping the end of the pipe's mouthpiece with a crooked thumb, "But I haven't used a lady's pipe since the war, and something tells me this one doesn't get much use."

"Then let's breathe some life into it," I said, taking the pipe from Roxanna and firmly pushing the bowl into the saddle's socket. She made her way across the room and I noticed for the first time that she was using a cane. She propped it against the opium bed and sat down, the bed's walled configuration necessitating that she slowly pull herself backward onto it. It was then I realized that one of her legs was a prosthetic.

Willi switched on a gooseneck desk lamp that beamed down on the layout tray. I handed him the pipe and he inspected it under the lamp. Roxanna was reclining on her right hip and examining the contents of the tray. She was wearing a sleeveless smock of Khmer silk in burgundy tones that matched her short-cropped, henna-rinsed hair. Again the mother image came into my mind. Perhaps it was just that her age and petite size reminded me of my own mom. Yet I was about to discover that behind her unassuming façade—the frail gait and amused smile—was an eccentric character whose past was more complex and fascinating than that of any other Westerner I had met in Asia. My search for an authentic old Asia hand in Chiang Mai had been wildly successful—it just took me a decade to realize it.

I moved one of the two drum-shaped porcelain stools at the foot of the opium bed and positioned it so that I sat between Willi and Roxanna, giving me an intimate view of them facing each other over the layout tray. Willi used an eyedropper to count seven drops of *chandu* into the tiny copper wok and then, pinching its ivory handle between thumb and forefinger, he perched the wok on the chimney of the opium lamp. We all watched in silence. After the first pill had been rolled Willi handed the slender pipe to Roxanna mouthpiece first, keeping hold of the end piece so he could guide the pipe bowl over the flame as she inhaled deeply. Save for the sound of the pendulum clock and the burbling of the bowl, the room was silent. Roxanna exhaled slowly with her eyes closed, and a gentle smile crossed her face. Willi began rolling another pill. "You have some catching up to do. Steven and I are way ahead of you."

Willi rolled five pills for Roxanna over a period of twenty minutes, and during that time I sat and listened as they talked themselves up to date. When there was finally a lull in their conversation I jumped in with a question I had been eagerly awaiting a chance to ask: "So you were in Vietnam during the war?"

"Yes, there and Cambodia and Laos."

"You were in the military?" I asked.

"I was a journalist. Freelance."

Roxanna took the mouthpiece of the pipe in her left hand and held it to her lips, again letting Willi steady the pipe bowl over the lamp. I noticed that she did not hold the vapors in her lungs as Willi and I habitually did—she immediately exhaled and did so with her eyes closed. When she opened them again she looked up at me and smiled, which I took as encouragement to ask another question.

"Did you know Michael Herr?"

"I knew friends of his." Again, a short answer followed by a smile that I was having trouble reading. Opium makes one hypersensitive to everything, including the feelings of others. In this matter it has nearly the opposite effect of alcohol. Booze shatters inhibitions; opium fosters empathy. I wasn't sure whether Roxanna's reaction to my questions was a soft rebuke. I decided to make one more attempt before dropping it.

"Tell me about somebody I might have heard of."

Roxanna took another draw from the pipe and then carefully shifted onto her back, rolling her head on the porcelain pillow until she faced the ceiling. Her eyes were shut and her features seemed to soften as the opium caused her facial muscles to relax. I was sure she would decline to continue the conversation—maybe even refuse to talk to me again. Willi shot me a look that said, *Let her be,* and just as he did, she opened her eyes and began to tell a story.

"I was with my friends. There were about six of us, all journalists and photographers. Saigon was expected to fall that week and we were all of us there in the city. There wasn't any need to fly out of Saigon to look for the war. The fighting was all around us."

Roxanna's smile was in evidence again and I found it baffling. Later—much later—I understood her smile to be a manifestation of her acute shyness.

"We were all at the bar of the Continental Hotel. Not the famous bar on the terrace—that was closed for fear of rocket attacks. I wasn't much of a drinker, but the bar at the Continental was the place to go to catch news or at least rumors. I remember we were talking about the best way to cover the fall, and how we were going to get out of South Vietnam after it fell, and when. And then this stranger walked in and looked around the room like he was expecting to find somebody."

Willi quietly began preparing another pipe for Roxanna, his movements concise and understated so as not to distract from her story.

"There was something about this man that made him stand out. He was very ordinary looking, and at first I couldn't put my finger on it. He stood there between the tables looking around, and then he accidentally dropped his notebook on the floor, and when he bent down to pick it up, some other things like a pen and a pair of sunglasses fell out of his shirt pocket and hit the floor, too. The guy stooped down to get his things, and two Vietnamese waiters were also down on the floor trying to help him, giggling in that way Vietnamese do when somebody embarrasses themselves. By then we were all watching, and one of my friends said, 'Who is that asshole?' and right away I answered, 'That's Hunter Thompson.'"

I sat straight up on the porcelain stool and asked, "Hunter S. Thompson?"

"Well, yes. *Rolling Stone* sent him to cover the fall of Saigon. At the time I happened to be reading *Fear and Loathing in Las Vegas,* and I must have recognized him from the author photo. I don't remember now how I knew, but in that instant I just knew who he was."

"Did you get to meet him?"

"Oh, yes. We invited him to sit with us and he did. Every one of us was very much in awe. Here we were a bunch of journalists, most of us freelancers or stringers, and in walks this famous writer on assignment for a magazine that we all admired. He ordered a drink, and the others were kind of stunned into silence, and since I was reading his book, I ended up doing most of the talking."

Willi had finished rolling. The pill of opium was stuck to the bowl and just waiting to be reheated. Roxanna noticed this and reached across the tray, prompting Willi to hand her the pipe. She didn't speak as she took the pipe into both hands, this time holding it over the flame without any assistance. It was a long, sustained draw on a pill flawlessly rolled and perfectly vaporized. Roxanna closed her eyes and slowly exhaled with a sigh that concluded in a barely audible coo of bliss. For long seconds she lay silent, and I guessed that her opium-rushed memories were becoming vivid.

"Hunter offered to buy me a drink, but instead I asked him

if he wanted to go back to the apartment to smoke opium," Roxanna said with a chuckle. "He said he'd never tried it and he didn't seem too keen, but the others were excited at the idea of having Hunter Thompson as a guest at the apartment, and everyone was saying, 'Come on! It's just down the street!' so he finally agreed."

"Was the apartment on Tu Do Street?" I asked.

"I don't remember exactly. It was so long ago. It wasn't my place—I lived with a Vietnamese family in another part of town. The apartment was rented by some friends, and it was where we used to hang out whenever we were in Saigon."

Saigon! Hearing that city's former name always gave me a thrill. I had visited Ho Chi Minh City for the first time in April 1993. Vietnam had just opened its doors to unrestricted tourism the week before I arrived. No longer was it necessary to hire a government guide—really an official babysitter—at an exorbitant rate. No longer was most of the country off-limits. Except for Russians, Ho Chi Minh City had hosted very few Westerners since 1975 and the city still had an occupied feel about it. Vietnamese men and women approached me constantly during my stay, stopping me with a tap on my shoulder or by clasping my arm—alarming to somebody who has grown accustomed to Thailand where grabbing at strangers is considered rude. The Vietnamese wanted to know if I was American, and then they grilled me about lost relatives who had fled to California or Texas or some state they couldn't remember how to pronounce.

In Ho Chi Minh City at the time, one of the only sites being actively promoted by the national tourism authority was the Museum of American War Crimes, a hall in which the walls were covered with greatly enlarged photographs of Vietnamese civilians with horrific wounds, and the display shelves were crowded with ghastly jars of pickled fetuses said to be victims of

Agent Orange. Partly to assuage my guilt after emerging from this chamber of horrors, I lingered at the museum gift shop and ended up buying a green pith helmet of the type the North Vietnamese Army had worn during the war. While riding in a pedicab back to my hotel I unthinkingly put the hat on, but not more than a few seconds passed before the pedicab driver leaned into my ear and whispered with real anger, "VC no good!" The helmet, of course, immediately came off.

On a subsequent visit to Ho Chi Minh City a mere two years later, I found that the mood of the former capital of South Vietnam had changed. Those intimations that old Saigon was an occupied city—displaying all those Uncle Ho portraits against its will—were gone, and I walked the streets alongside crowds of backpackers, eliciting no more attention from the locals than anyone else.

I tried to imagine the Saigon that Roxanna had known, a desperate place that I could detect only hints of during my first trip in 1993. What I hadn't seen were any signs of the decadence and hedonism for which the city was known back when it was a springboard to war. In Ho Chi Minh City of the 1990s there were no prostitutes on Hondas yelling bawdy offers in pidgin English. There were no bars with names meant to elicit home-sickness in young American soldiers. There were certainly no longer any opium dens to be found. I envied Roxanna her ex-citing past—the Southeast Asia she had seen and lived.

"Opium was illegal at the time but then so was prostitution and gambling and everything else Saigon was known for," Rox-anna continued. Willi was unhurriedly preparing another pipe, pausing between steps to give full attention to her story. "There was one opium den we used to go to, but we couldn't go as a big group because there just wasn't enough room and it would have been too disturbing for the other patrons. I often used to go by myself, sometimes with one other person, but if there were more than two wanting to smoke, the apartment was much more comfortable."

"Did you roll your own pipes?" I asked.

"I could roll for myself and maybe one other person, but if there was a crowd I wasn't fast enough to keep people from getting impatient. So whenever a bunch of us wanted to smoke at the apartment we used to telephone the opium den and ask them to send over one of their attendants to roll for us. Half an hour later he would show up on his bicycle with a pipe and lamp in a wooden carrying case. Inside was a kit full of little drawers and everything you needed to smoke opium—all the tools, oil for the lamp, all of it was there."

Details like this set my head spinning. I would have given anything to be able to go back in time and see an opium smoker's travel kit being used. I had a number of such kits in my collection but the function of some of the components was a mystery to me. Not wanting to interrupt her story, I made a mental note to ask Roxanna about the kit later that evening.

"So when the guy from the opium den arrived, we spread out some mats on the floor of the apartment. I remember giving Hunter instructions on how to inhale. Beginners are always surprised at how hard you have to huff to get the opium to vaporize. Since he was the guest of honor, we offered Hunter the first pipe. We were all pretty thrilled by the whole scene. Imagine, Saigon was surrounded by North Vietnamese, everyone was terrified and the city was descending into chaos, and there we were smoking opium with Hunter Thompson."

Willi handed the pipe to Roxanna and again she took a long draw. Despite the excitement she described, her voice had become far-off and flat, almost like the intonations of somebody under a hypnotist's spell.

"Then something strange happened. After his very first pipe Hunter began hyperventilating. At first I thought he was joking with us, but it was real. It was like he was freaking out. He was pulling at his shirt like he was trying to rip it off, like he couldn't breathe. And his eyes were huge and rolling around. It was really scary."

Roxanna looked toward the shrine as though the scene were unfolding within the clouds of incense that enveloped the Den God. I thought I detected a hint of concern on her face as she relived the emotions of that day long ago.

"The guy from the opium den told us to get hot and cold towels and apply them to Hunter, so we hurried to the kitchen, putting one towel under the tap and pouring hot water on another. Then we rushed back and began rubbing his face and chest with this succession of hot and cold towels. And it worked. Hunter started to calm down and finally he seemed okay. We asked him what happened and he said he didn't know. He looked sheepish and then excused himself and quickly left the apartment. It was really odd."

Roxanna paused and her face creased into a puckish smile, as though she was recalling the punch line of an old joke she hadn't heard in a while.

"So we had the guy from the den roll us some pipes, and we started talking about what just happened. Some of my friends were really down on Hunter. Maybe they were just really disappointed. You know, his reputation and all . . . we were expecting to turn him on and have this experience right out of his book. But to see him panic like that, well . . ."

Roxanna interrupted herself to ask Willi how many pipes she had smoked. He looked at me. "Ask the pipe boy."

"It's been nine so far," I said, grateful that I'd remembered to keep track.

"Oh dear, maybe it's time for a break."

Roxanna began fossicking through her handbag and finally produced a pack of Thai cigarettes and a plastic disposable lighter. Willi invited her to try one of his local cheroots instead. Roxanna took one, sniffed at the cheroot's banana-leaf wrapper, and smilingly consented as Willi struck a match and cupped it in his hands. Roxanna held the cheroot to her lips and leaned it forward into the flame. After Willi blew out the match he said, "Disposable lighters are on the list of banned items in the Chamber."

"As they should be," Roxanna concurred. "How much style have we abandoned for the sake of a little convenience? I remember when a Zippo lighter was one of those accessories you didn't feel complete without."

If old studio portraits of opium smokers are to be believed, tobacco smoking was an indispensable part of a typical opium-smoking session—even long after the Chinese discovered the secrets of vaporization and had dispensed with the tobacco and opium blend. Tobacco was most often smoked in an upright metal water pipe with a tall, gracefully curved stem. Perhaps due to lingering associations, these metal tobacco pipes are commonly sold in antiques shops as opium pipes. Stickler that I was for historical accuracy, I drew the line at smoking tobacco in the Chamber—I had tried it once but didn't like how the nicotine seemed to dampen my opium euphoria.

Roxanna and Willi had gone quiet while smoking their cheroots, but I still had questions about the encounter with Thompson. "So he left the apartment after freaking out, but you must have seen him again around town, right?"

"Well, after Hunter left the apartment some of my journalist friends hatched a plan. They decided they were going to play with his head. Maybe they felt silly for being so in awe of him

earlier. I don't know. You know how young men are. So that's
what they did over the next few days: They took turns working
on Hunter. First, two guys went to his hotel to inspect his room
and give him advice about which window was best for defending
the building. They gave him an old pistol and some ammunition
and they pointed through the window down at the street to give
him an idea of the range of the thing. Then they left him there.

"A few days later, more of my friends showed up at Hunter's
hotel room and gave him a bag of grenades. They told him the
pistol would be worthless if the hotel was overrun by the North
Vietnamese. They advised him to toss the grenades out the door
so they rolled down the stairs. Later they told me Hunter looked
very alarmed by the whole idea. The guys thought it was hilari-
ous. They planned out their next visit and somebody even found
an M–16 they could give Hunter, but when they went back to
his hotel he had already checked out. For the next few days we
looked everywhere for him, but Hunter was gone. It wasn't until
later I found out he'd flown out of Vietnam."

I sat there stunned by what I had just heard. The known version of the story about Hunter S. Thompson's Saigon gig was
that *Rolling Stone's* Jann Wenner had torpedoed the assignment,
pulling the plug after Thompson was already on his way to cover
the fall. Without an employer—and the insurance coverage that
came with the magazine assignment—Thompson had decided it
was too dangerous to stay in Saigon.

Was it possible that this accepted version was just a piece of
the larger story? Roxanna didn't linger on the subject. After asking Willi if he wanted a break from preparing pipes, she switched
places with him on the opium bed so that she was lying on her
left side and her right hand was free to roll. Roxanna prepared
pipes in the same way that she had told her war story, in a deliberate, unhurried fashion. She lacked Willi's speed and flourishes,

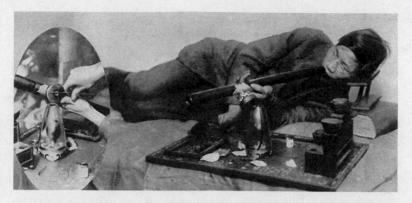

This photo of an opium smoker has an insert showing a rare close-up of a pill being rolled. The image is from a 1919 issue of the French magazine *Le Pays de France,* but the photos are two of a series believed to have been taken in New York. (From the collection of Yves Domzalski)

but instead had the cadence of someone who could roll pills in her sleep.

"Was Saigon during that time really as dangerous as your friends made out?" I asked.

"Probably not. Nobody I knew was killed covering the fall. Probably the closest call I ever had was in Cambodia. Although at the time I didn't know it was a close call."

Roxanna handed the primed pipe to Willi, who took it with both hands to show that he didn't need her to guide him over the flame.

"I had this idea to go to Phnom Penh. This was in 1970, a couple weeks after Lon Nol had replaced Prince Sihanouk in a coup. Cambodia was where the story was, and a lot of my friends were there already. Plus, there were two superb opium dens in Phnom Penh, and I was always looking for a reason to visit."

Again I sat up straight on the porcelain stool, about to interrupt and ask for details about Phnom Penh's opium dens, but Roxanna had already moved on.

"The road between Saigon and Phnom Penh was bad. Route One, it was called. On the map it looked like a highway, but a lot of Route One wasn't paved. I thought if I left Saigon early enough in the morning I could reach Phnom Penh well before dark, so I set out on my motorbike just before dawn."

"You drove a motorcycle?" I asked with surprise. "Alone?"

"There really wasn't any other way. It wasn't like in Vietnam where I could always hitch a ride just about anywhere in U.S. Army helicopters. My journalist friends were always so jealous of me. Being a young white woman I was a rarity in Southeast Asia. Those military guys almost never said no when I asked for a ride. Of course, in Cambodia there were no U.S. military flights. Not officially anyway. And I couldn't afford to charter a private plane, so the motorbike was the only alternative."

Willi handed the pipe back to Roxanna and she used a damp sponge to wipe the blackened opium residue from the pipe bowl's surface.

"I'll never forget that border crossing. The Vietnamese and Cambodian border officials were shooting at each other. It wasn't a heavy firefight, just this kind of low-key feud. The Vietnamese had a card game going, spread out on a grass mat on the floor, but every few minutes one of them would get up and fire some shots at the Cambodian border post a couple hundred yards away."

Roxanna flicked the pipe bowl with the nail of her index finger, listening to the sound it made in order to judge whether or not the bowl needed to be scraped clean of dross. I couldn't tell the difference, but she must have decided the bowl was still clear because she began counting another dose of *chandu* into the little copper wok.

"I was delayed there for hours because the Vietnamese said I had to wait until lunchtime. That was when the two sides had both agreed to stop shooting. I joined the Vietnamese officials for a lunch of *pho* and after we finished eating they stamped me out of Vietnam. By that time the sun was horribly hot, but at least the crossing was quiet. I walked the motorbike across the no-man's-land between the two border posts. When I got to the Cambodian side, I saw their little concrete post was all shot up and deserted. I thought they must all be dead, and I almost turned around and walked the motorbike back into Vietnam. Then I heard something from behind the building. It was somebody snoring. I found the Cambodian officials taking a nap in the shade. One of them got up and stamped my passport, and then I was on my way."

Like Willi, Roxanna eschewed the fancy rolling tool on the layout tray and instead rolled the pill of opium against the pipe bowl's smooth upper surface. Their techniques diverged in the way that Roxanna used the flat end of the needle to scrape the wok clean of dried *chandu* and then dipped the sticky pill into the powdery remnants. When Roxanna rolled not a speck of opium was wasted.

"The Cambodian countryside was a real contrast to Vietnam. There was no traffic on the road, nobody but me. And there wasn't anybody working the rice fields, either. Even the little villages I passed through were empty. I had been riding for an hour or so and, wouldn't you know it, I got a flat tire. It was so hot and there was no shade on that road, and I remember being afraid of the heat more than anything else. I walked the motorbike in the direction of Phnom Penh. There was nothing else I could do."

If I had been reclining I would not have been able to keep my eyes from sliding shut and letting my imagination supply the visuals, but sitting upright on the porcelain stool kept my mind sharp and allowed me to focus on both listening to Roxanna's story and observing her rolling technique. I was spellbound. After she had finished shaping the pill on the end of the needle, Roxanna had an alarming way of seating the pill on the bowl's needle hole, letting the wad of *chandu* cool for what seemed an inadequate amount of time before abruptly thrusting the needle deep into the bowl to break the pill free from the needle. Each time I saw her do this I was sure that she had botched this most difficult step in the process, but each time I was surprised to see her easily extract the needle, leaving the pill stuck fast to the bowl, and with a perfect little hole through which to inhale the vapors.

"I had been walking for only a few minutes when out of nowhere a man and a boy appeared on the road ahead of me. They were very dark skinned and were wearing the black pajamas of the Khmer Rouge. The boy had a shoulder bag full of tools and the man was carrying a bicycle pump and without even looking at me they began working on the flat tire. It was really odd. They quickly fixed the tire and pumped it back up and then without a word they walked down the road in the direction I had come. I got on the bike and started it, but when I looked back to wave at them, they were gone."

Willi slid off the opium bed and motioned for me to take his place. Roxanna stopped telling her story until I was comfortably reclining on my right side and facing her over the tray. She handed me the slender pipe, guiding it over the lamp while I inhaled, but she didn't resume speaking until my lips had left the jade mouthpiece.

"I didn't see another soul until I got to the ferry crossing hours later, but by then I was only an hour away from Phnom Penh. Just after I arrived in the city, I ran into a couple of friends including Sean Flynn. He was Errol Flynn's son. The famous actor."

"Sure, I've heard of Errol Flynn," I said while letting the opium vapors slowly escape from my lungs.

"Well, if you know who Errol Flynn was then you'll know how handsome he was. His son, Sean, was even better looking. He had the type of face that if you walked into a room full of people, he was the first person you noticed. But he was one of those rare people who don't seem to realize how attractive they are. There was nothing vain about Sean."

Roxanna took the pipe from me and removed the bowl to scrape it clean of ash. Her fingertips were so calloused that she was able to handle the hot bowl with her bare hands. She held the doorknob-sized bowl in her left hand while gripping the scraper—about the length of a household screwdriver—in her right, winding the scraper's curved blade around the inside of the bowl. Sand-like dross poured from the bowl's open end as Roxanna shook it over a cylindrical container, creating what looked like a small pile of ground-up pencil leads.

"When I told Sean where I'd just come from he thought I was joking. The news in Phnom Penh was that Route One was too dangerous to travel. I told him my story about the flat tire, and he was sure that who I met were Khmer Rouge. The fact that they'd helped me really excited him. It wasn't long after that I heard he and photojournalist Dana Stone rode some motorbikes back in the direction of Saigon and were captured. They were never seen alive again."

By now there was no emotion in her voice or on her face. Had I known nothing about opium, I might have taken her reaction—or the lack of one—to be that classic symptom much remarked upon by nineteenth-century observers: the opium addict's famed "indifference." But I knew that opium smokers were anything but indifferent. Like so much else about this drug, it was a misunderstanding on the part of nonsmokers. Roxanna's reaction wasn't indifference but a sense of detached observation that feels to the smoker like the wisdom of a sage who sits on a mountaintop and views life from on high. As Jean Cocteau explained it, life is an express train speeding toward a dark tunnel that is death: "To smoke opium is to get out of the train while it is still moving."

Roxanna lifted the little bottle of *chandu* from the tray and gave it a light shake. The blood-colored liquid mixing within was so toxic that if consumed orally, this small amount could have poisoned hundreds. She loosened the dropper from the bottle as she cradled the pipe against her breast. "Are you ready for more?" she asked.

"You know I am," I answered.

To be able to "cook" well is quite an art, and one of which an old smoker is very proud. A novice or a poor cook will bedaub himself and the pipe, and either overdo or underdo the opium, so that it is too sticky or too crisp to smoke well.

—H. H. Kane, *Opium-Smoking in America and China* (1882)

It wasn't long after my return to Bangkok that I heard from Roxanna again. She telephoned, sounding a bit lost, as though she had expected the number to be wrong. Roxanna wanted to visit me at my apartment, and I immediately assumed that I knew the reason.

I was excited, both at the prospect of meeting Roxanna again and because of some Pavlovian reaction to hearing her voice. Habitual opium use forms strong associations with sights and sounds. I learned just how strong on one occasion when Willi was passing through Bangkok and I met him for coffee at his hotel. Seeing his face and hearing his voice made my mind and body anticipate the thing that had always been instantaneously available each time we met. Whenever I had experienced this feeling in Vientiane there was a deliciousness to the angst because I knew that it would soon end. In Bangkok, however, there could be no joy. Willi and I both found our meeting excruciating, and without finishing our coffee we parted—but only after making hasty plans for me to go to Vientiane later that week.

With Roxanna, though, I was not sure where this would go. My mind raced. Was she expecting me to host, as Willi had? That was impossible, and I needed to warn her that I had no opium on hand—without uttering the word "opium" over the telephone. I could imagine what a trial it would be for someone with a prosthetic leg to navigate my Chinatown neighborhood with its narrow, vehicle-choked lanes. I could also picture her disappointment when she arrived to find that her efforts had been for nothing. Every horizontal surface in my apartment was crowded with antique opium-smoking paraphernalia, yet I had never even contemplated having opium there.

It was an old joke. Friends who visited my apartment took the sight of my collection on display as a cue to ask if they could try some opium. One friend bragged to another that he had patronized the secret opium den that I was running in my flat. I actively discouraged such talk. I saw myself as a collector and a scholar. My opium experimentation had always been tied to collecting and research, and I was able to rationalize it in the name of scholarship. Sharing opium with Willi was not the same as bringing opium into my home and smoking it. The drug was illegal in Thailand and its antidrug laws were strictly enforced. The country may have still had a reputation for narcotics, but that was simply a case of perception being slow to catch up with reality. In the 1990s, when I was doing freelance journalism for the wire service Agence France-Presse, an editor at the Bangkok bureau remarked to me—only partly tongue-in-cheek—that 90 percent of the Thailand-related stories that AFP put on the wire were either about sex, drugs, or elephants. "That sums up Thailand in a nutshell," he said. "It's what the West wants to read about Thailand."

During that time the entire country—and especially Bangkok—was being flooded with methamphetamine from Burma, and it made for some shocking scenes. In the Thai-language newspapers it was not uncommon to see lurid front-page photographs of some meth head's binge that had reached its tragic nadir—a last stand of extreme and deranged violence. When cornered by police, these meth addicts all seemed to react as if preprogrammed to do what onlookers would find most shocking: Their speed-warped minds commanded them to grab the nearest child and hold it hostage—usually with a knife to the throat and much bloodletting.

I doubt there are any reliable statistics on how many of these meth-fueled hostage incidents occurred in Thailand, but in 2003 something happened. Word on the street was that the prime minister's son had gotten hooked on meth. Suddenly things changed very rapidly. For two years extrajudicial killings were the order of the day. Thailand's officially sanctioned "war on drugs" is said by human rights experts to have claimed the lives of 2,500 people. At the time I was well aware that having opium in my possession would change the status of my entire collection from oddball antiques to dangerous drug paraphernalia.

There was a secondary, and to me no less important, reason for not letting opium become too familiar: My cherished trips to visit Willi and the Chamber—my escapes from the twenty-first century—would surely lose their magic if I allowed my mind to associate the sublime experience of opium with some-place as mundane as my living room. The mere idea seemed like gross sacrilege.

I groped for a way to discourage Roxanna by letting her know that I had no opium, but she quickly cut me off. "Just give me your address. My driver will find your apartment."

I told her, and she promised to see me within the hour. I

thought about lying and saying that I wasn't free, but I couldn't bring myself to do it. Instead I agreed, and as soon as I did the conversation was over. I put down the phone and stared at it. What might I say to get out of smoking at my apartment without offending Roxanna? I contemplated calling her back and saying that I had to go out unexpectedly, but I knew this would sound hastily fabricated and might put her off wanting to meet me again.

As I waited for Roxanna to arrive I began to reflect on how little I knew about her. We had spent a delightful evening in the Chamber and she had told some intriguing anecdotes, but regarding her present-day life she had said almost nothing. About all I knew was that she had relocated from Chiang Mai to Bangkok a few years back. Willi had been diplomatic when choosing his words to describe her. He referred to Roxanna's "habit," but had never uttered the "A" word. I wondered what I was getting myself into. Of course, I had met addicts in the past. Madame Tui was one, as were Mister Kay and his elderly patrons. What I had read in nineteenth-century missionaries' memoirs didn't worry me—all that drivel about moral decay and fiends who would stop at nothing to satisfy a yen. But there was something about Roxanna being a Westerner—it shouldn't have mattered to me, but it did. How on earth did she manage to get hooked? Was it intentional? Willi and I had often talked about how we were too careful to get addicted. We used the word "careful," but we were cocky and could just as easily have substituted the word "clever." Had Roxanna once thought the same of herself?

I began to wonder if perhaps Roxanna was bringing her own *chandu* and thought she might surprise me by showing up and offering to roll. I couldn't imagine that she would go to the trouble to carry a pipe and lamp with her—she was almost certainly expecting me to supply the accoutrements. I hit upon the idea of telling her that none of my pieces were anywhere near operable, that my pipes were fragile and would need repairs before they could be used; that all my functional bowls were with Willi; that my lamps were missing their chimneys and would leak oil.

I began removing pieces of my collection from their crowded display shelves, hunting for bowls that might still be usable and plucking them from the jumble. With each piece removed there appeared a footprint in the fine layer of Bangkok dust that blanketed every surface. I blew at the shelves to even out the dust and make the recent removals less obvious. I spirited away an opium lamp that was the centerpiece of my coffee table, one that I occasionally filled with oil and lit for decoration. There were so many pieces to hide and so little time that all I could think to do was line them up on my bed and throw a blanket over everything.

This is where I was when Roxanna arrived—in my bedroom, rushing to hide my collection from an opium addict. There were still many functional pieces on display, including a pipe on the living room shelf, but I had run out of time. I waited until she knocked a second time and then opened the door and illuminated the shadowy corridor outside with the dazzling afternoon sunlight that flooded my apartment. This never failed to impress guests and Roxanna was no exception. "Oh my, look at that view," she said, gazing past me and out the windows looking upriver.

She hobbled in, apologizing for not removing her shoes, and made her way to the sofa while I stood there, wondering if I should offer to take her arm as I'd seen Willi do. "I won't take up too much of your time. I can't stay long, my driver is waiting," she said while admiring the view. "I just had a little accident and I thought you might be able to help me."

"An accident?"

Roxanna was dressed more formally than when I had last seen her. She was wearing a maroon smock of Javanese batik over a pair of dark pants. On top of this she wore a collarless

cotton jacket dyed with indigo. Later I came to know that this
ensemble was of her own devising and something of a trademark. It was semiformal with a nod to Southeast Asian style, as
well as being cool and keeping her disability well hidden.

Roxanna seemed to be in a rush. Standing next to the sofa,
leaning on her cane, she looked around as though she were debating whether or not to sit. I urged her to and asked if she
wanted anything to drink. She refused both invitations, survey-
ing my living room but not remarking on anything, as though a
room full of opium paraphernalia was nothing out of the ordinary. Finally she spoke. "I had an accident this morning just before going to work. It's had me distracted all day."

"What can I do to help?" I asked.

"Well, I'll tell you. It's my pipe—my old pipe that I've had for
years. It split. There's a crack in the bamboo the length of the
pipe. I think it was that sudden change in humidity when it
rained last night."

"Do you want me to try and fix it?"

"I don't think it can be repaired. And besides, I was so flustered
when I found it broken that I dropped the bowl and its collar
broke off. Imagine the bad luck. And I don't have a backup pipe."

Roxanna's eyes found the pipe resting on a shelf. It was rustic,
a "workhorse" that had been imported from China to America
in the nineteenth century and rediscovered in New Mexico.
Unadorned, it was a no-nonsense pipe that had no doubt once
belonged to a serious smoker. But despite its simplicity, I did not
want to sell it. This particular pipe was special. A waxy red adhe-
sive that was used to attach the saddle to the pipe stem was
abundantly visible, and I had planned to have the substance
chemically tested and perhaps confirm anecdotal evidence that
old-fashioned sealing wax was used to seal opium pipes.

"I could help you find a pipe. It might take me a month or

two, depending on what you're looking for. Or there's a guy in Vientiane who makes them but that takes longer."

Roxanna had gone over to have a better look at my pipe on display. "What about this one?" she asked. "I really can't wait."

"I'm sorry, that's not for sale. Nothing's for sale. I just collect, I never sell anything."

She stood her ground. "I can't afford to pay you what it's worth, but I have other things you might be interested in."

"I do trades from time to time but only for other opium antiques."

Roxanna began fishing through her handbag, and I thought she might pull out a bottle of *chandu* and offer that, but it was a mobile phone that she finally produced. "I have to call my driver. I told him I would only be here a second to pick up something."

She tried to communicate with the unseen driver in heavily accented Thai and then repeated the message in English. "I need more time. Five more minutes, okay?"

As she put away the phone I had the feeling that I was greatly inconveniencing her. I wanted to help but the last thing I needed was for anybody to think that my apartment was some kind of one-stop shop for opium paraphernalia. I was very keen to know Roxanna and pump her for information about how opium was used in the days when it was still common in Southeast Asia, but my collection was more important to me than anything else. I tried to change the subject. "It must be nice to have a driver."

"The university provides a car and driver, but only for rides to and from the museum. I was able to talk him into coming here today but unless it's official business I really shouldn't be using the car."

"Which museum is that?" I asked.

"The Southeast Asian Ceramics Museum at Bangkok University. I'm the director. Didn't Willi tell you?"

In that instant I connected her name with an article that I had read somewhere about Chinese trade ceramics. I could feel my face flush with such intensity that I knew it must be visible. I smiled. I stammered. "Uh . . . no."

Roxanna smiled back. There is nothing to do in such situations but smile the awkwardness away. "Listen," she said, "I know you can help me and I'm prepared to help you. How come you've never learned to roll?"

"Willi says learning to be a world-class sushi chef would be cheaper."

Roxanna laughed. The bright sunlight on her face—highlighting sallow skin and mascara-ringed eyes—made her look like an actress in a silent film. "I'll teach you. For free. The first lesson starts today. Just get a stem and a bowl and come home with me. It's not far. We'll be there in half an hour, traffic permitting."

I didn't need to think about it long. She was the director of a respected institution, an expert on ceramics no less. One of my weak points was ceramic pipe bowls and their endless array of clays, glazes, and chop marks. I didn't see any need to learn how to prepare pipes, but there were questions that I could ask about her technique and how it differed from Willi's. I took a pipe from its storage place in an old suitcase. It was my "epiphany pipe," the one that I had since discovered was a reproduction. I wrapped it carefully before zipping it into a tennis racket case, and then led Roxanna down to her waiting car.

The vast majority of Westerners residing in Bangkok live on one of the hundreds of lanes branching off Sukhumvit Road. It is a relatively new part of the city—the streets were laid out in the 1960s—and it's also pretty characterless. Anonymous towers house luxury condominiums and overlook at least ten branches of Starbucks. There are spotless supermarkets selling imported brands of sandwich spread from Europe and America, as well as red-light entertainment complexes—two of three such areas in Bangkok that cater to Westerners. Sukhumvit Road is legendary for dense traffic and great expense. I knew a European Union diplomat whose high-rise apartment cost his employers $2,500 a month—a staggering sum in a city where the legal minimum wage at the time was the equivalent of $6.50 per day. Most Southeast Asian capitals have their version of this neighborhood, and this is where one invariably finds the expat community. If somebody had asked me which part of the city I would expect the director of Bangkok University's ceramics museum to reside, I would have guessed Sukhumvit Road.

Roxanna's house was only ten miles distant from the ex-patty glitz of Sukhumvit, but it was a world away in atmosphere. After turning off a main road we drove down a long lane lined with houses and family-run shops paralleled by a stretch of railway that terminated in Malaysia some six hundred miles away. Pedicabs ran from the wet market at the entrance of the lane nearly all the way to Roxanna's house, which could be accessed only via a narrow walkway overhung with banana leaves and barely wide enough for two people to walk abreast. As Roxanna and I walked the final few yards to her home, she pointed out that the walkway was actually a concrete causeway raised above the swampy ground. "It used to just be wooden planks on stilts above the mud. The city came and built the cement walkways in the nineties."

The area was densely populated, judging by the way the little wooden houses were nearly touching one another on all sides, yet everything was surprisingly quiet. In that respect Roxanna's neighborhood was Thai and very unlike Chinatown. I remarked upon this to Roxanna. She smiled and said, "Come visit some Sunday when all the men are home drinking and watching boxing on TV."

Roxanna's house was indistinguishable from those of her neighbors. The simple wooden structure rested on concrete stanchions and was two stories high. On a stick near the front door was a Thai flag slowly bleaching in the tropical sun. Inside, the lower floor was little more than a semi-enclosed hallway to a bathroom, two bedrooms, and a stairway leading to the upper floor. Crammed into this tiny downstairs space were a table and chairs for eating and a shelf of dusty books. The outer walls were simply rows of vertical wooden slats about two inches apart that allowed for cooling breezes to enter but did nothing to keep out insects or bar the gaze of passersby. Roxanna's bedroom was a plywood-walled room constructed within the larger room downstairs, and was clearly an afterthought designed to hold in conditioned air and afford some privacy. A second bedroom—as tiny as a closet—was occupied by Roxanna's son, Jamie.

As we entered, Jamie came out of his room with eyes that suggested a long nap, and stood silently to let his mother introduce us. I guessed him to be in his early twenties. He had shoulder-length hair and the good looks that have made children of mixed race a show business commodity in Thailand. My first impression of Jamie was that being introduced to me was the last thing he wanted to be doing. He was just a shade short of surly. I thought immediately that Roxanna must have raised him as an American—if Thais don't like you, they almost always make an effort to hide their feelings. I wondered what he knew of his mother's habit or if others had preceded me. Roxanna told him in English that we were "going upstairs to talk" and then she excused herself, saying she needed a minute to change out of her work clothes. Jamie went back into his bedroom without a word and I took the opportunity to use the bathroom. I was surprised to find that it was the traditional variety common in rural Southeast Asia: a squat toilet and a cement cistern filled with cold water. Plastic scoops were used for both bathing and to manually flush the toilet.

I was both puzzled and captivated. Why did the director of a museum at a private university live so humbly? Friends of mine sometimes teased me about "going native"—based on my fluency in Thai, the non-Westernized part of town that I lived in, and perhaps also my lackadaisical housekeeping. For me there were a few reasons: a natural ability to pick up languages, a constant shortage of money due to my compulsive collecting, and a healthy dash of laziness that I liked to blame on my being a third-generation Southern Californian. I also had a desire to see the exotic everywhere I turned. Why bother to live in Thailand if one was simply going to live in that bubble-like facsimile of the Western world on Sukhumvit Road? I looked around Roxanna's home and wondered what her excuse was. Was she consciously thumbing her nose at the expat community? If so, I could only admire her lifestyle.

When Roxanna emerged from her bedroom she was wearing the same sort of sleeveless smock she had worn at the Chamber. Although it was already six in the evening, the temperature was still in the nineties and the humidity high. As we made our way slowly up the narrow wooden stairs, the temperature seemed to rise a few degrees with each step. Once we were on the upper floor I saw why: There was no ceiling—I looked up and there were the rafters and pressed-asbestos sheets that made up the roof. The upstairs space was divided into two rooms with a door between them. Roxanna steered me into the inner room and locked the door. There were four windows in the room, all lacking glass or screens, but with solid wooden shutters. She asked me to shut them as tightly as they would close. Everything was made from an inferior type of wood and the warped shutters would not seat properly, but I did my best to pull them shut, knowing the reason behind the exercise was to prevent Roxanna's opium lamp from flickering.

The walls were bare and the only piece of furniture was an old desk on which sat a boxy television. Roxanna took a small key from a coin purse and opened a drawer in the desk. Inside were the components of her layout: a crude brass lamp; an opium needle evidently fashioned from a bicycle spoke; a cleaning rod made from a wire clothes hanger; and a jam jar that had been press-ganged into dross-storage duties. For a tray Roxanna spread out pieces of newspaper. After arranging her paraphernalia on the paper, she slowly lowered herself to recline on the bare floorboards. Her pillow was a small cushion filled with shredded coconut husks—the cheapest pillow on the market, I knew, because the stuffing made it hard as a block of wood.

The scene bordered on squalid and reminded me of the opium dens that Karl and I had visited in Laos for his story in *Time*. I couldn't help but feel a pang of pity for this woman, especially given her disability. Yet there was nothing in her demeanor that invited sympathy. This was the same Roxanna I had met at the Chamber—right down to that amused little smile. She joked about the contrast between her opium-smoking layout and the one that Willi and I had assembled. "If I could only afford something like that . . . wow. I could make myself believe I was the empress dowager," Roxanna said, referring to China's tyrannical ruler toward the end of the Qing dynasty. Putting on a stern face, she mock-growled, "Whoever makes me unhappy for a day, I will make suffer an entire lifetime."

"In that case I'd better get this pipe to work," I replied gamely. Sitting cross-legged on the floor, I cut long strips of cotton batik cloth from a piece that Roxanna kept folded in the drawer. These I dabbed with latex glue and wrapped around the collar of a pipe bowl that I had brought along. Then I began cutting half-dollar-sized patches for "gee-rags"—cloth gaskets that would create an airtight seal between the bowl and the pipe stem. The heat was oppressive, and I stopped frequently to wipe the sweat from my forehead. When I had finished, I brushed the bits of cloth off my trousers and went downstairs to splash my face with cool water. Jamie stuck his head out from his bedroom door as I was going back upstairs; he said nothing and closed the door as soon as he saw it was me. When I got back upstairs Roxanna was trimming the opium lamp's wick. I decided to broach a subject that had been on my mind since I'd arrived.

"Does your son know about this?"

"No, of course not," she answered, looking up from the lamp. "Nobody knows."

"Can't he smell it? And you're so close to your neighbors. I would think they could smell it, too."

"Well, maybe they get a whiff now and then but I doubt anybody knows what the smell is. They probably think I'm cooking American food!" Roxanna laughed. It was clear that she wasn't worried about it.

"Are you sure your son doesn't know? I just had this feeling when you introduced us that maybe he wasn't too thrilled to meet me."

"No, he's just like that. Jamie's quiet."

I didn't bring the subject up again. Instead I reassured myself that Roxanna would not have brought me home if there were any danger of her being found out. I wanted to ask how long she had been addicted, but without using that word. I tried to come up with an appropriate euphemism. "So have you been smoking daily since Vietnam?"

"Oh dear no," she answered, and then after a long pause added, "It's a long story."

The latex glue on the pipe bowl was tacky enough now for me to attach the bowl to the stem. In the old days the gummy opium itself served as a sealant, but that was when opium was as cheap and widely available as tobacco. I dampened one of the gee-rags and applied it to the bowl's collar before inserting the bowl into the saddle. The fit was perfectly airtight. Feeling proud of myself, I handed the pipe to Roxanna and then watched as she began cooking a few drops of *chandu* over the tawdry brass lamp. She talked without looking up from the bubbling *chandu*. "You haven't asked about my leg. Most people ask within minutes of meeting me."

"I figured that was probably the case. Which is why I didn't ask."

Roxanna finished rolling and lifted the pipe to her mouth. Before inhaling she smiled and said, "I'm sorry to disappoint, but it didn't happen in Vietnam."

"I really hadn't given it much thought, but you did say nobody you knew was hurt in the fall of Saigon and I assumed that included you, too. And if it had happened before that . . . well . . . anyway," I changed the subject. "So tell me about the opium dens in Phnom Penh. You mentioned at Willi's that there were two good ones there."

Roxanna was rolling a second pipe with her bicycle-spoke needle. Or perhaps it was the rib from an umbrella. If necessity is the mother of invention, drug use is surely its can-do father. Archaeological sites at nineteenth-century Chinese settlements in the American West—old mining and railroad camps—have turned up opium paraphernalia fashioned by enterprising tinkers from the most unlikely objects, such as pipe bowls made from glass ink bottles. I decided right then to make Roxanna a gift of a pair of my antique needles the next time I saw her.

"Yes, there were two opium dens in Phnom Penh that were open to Westerners. The original one was in a big old house, and it was run by a Chinese-Khmer woman named Choum. 'La Mère Choum' was what the French used to call her, 'Mother Choum.' Her place was very popular with the French. I used to go there with Bernard Groslier. He was the director of the École Française d'Extrême-Orient and an authority on Khmer art. Bernard didn't smoke, but Choum kept a bottle of cognac there just for him. It was the one place I ever saw him really relax. Toward the end, the Khmer Rouge had taken Angkor and occupied all the countryside, but none of that mattered at Choum's place. She had cotton sarongs to wear so you could get comfortable, and there were girls giving traditional massage, too. It was an oasis. An oasis of calm and civility."

"It sounds wonderful. What year was this?"

"The first time I went would have to have been around 1969. Then, not long after the coup in 1970, when Lon Nol deposed Prince Sihanouk, there was an influx of Americans into Phnom Penh. They liked Choum's place, too, but the French weren't too happy about that. They saw themselves losing influence in their old colonies, and Americans at Choum's was just another sign of that.

"I remember going with a group of friends to celebrate John Steinbeck's birthday in 1970. Not the writer, but his son. He was an army journalist in Vietnam, but after he finished his tour he stayed on in Southeast Asia as a freelance journalist. So that day we went to Choum's as a big group. The old house had two stories and the den was upstairs, taking up three private rooms and one big common room. We donned our sarongs and were looking for some space on the floor to accommodate us, and this made the French patrons complain, but we paid them no mind. It was John's birthday and we were not going to be turned away.

"Not long after that, Choum had one of her cousins open a new opium den and take some of the prettiest girls along with her. This new place we called 'Chantal's' after Choum's cousin. It was an instant hit with us Americans, but there were also quite a few French guests. There was a rumor that the French ambassador had an opium pipe at the embassy that he kept under lock and key but ready for use. Maybe this was true. I often used to see the French embassy staff smoking at Chantal's, but I never saw the ambassador himself there. I used to visit Chantal's so often that I became very good friends with her. She gave me this ring." Roxanna stopped rolling and held out her hand so I could admire a ruby set in solid gold.

When two friends smoke opium, the more experienced smoker is usually the one preparing the pipes, and it's customary for him or her to smoke a pipe or two before rolling for the other. Roxanna finished her third pipe, then rolled a fourth and offered it to me. I acted hesitant, knowing full well that I would turn it down. I thought that by seeming to be less than sure it might soften my refusal. "Hmmmmm. Nah, I just want to listen to your stories today."

"But what about your rolling lessons?"

"I want to stay sharp-minded. I'll forget your stories if I smoke."

"Well, okay. But if you change your mind . . ."

Roxanna vaporized the pill herself and then asked if I would mind going downstairs to bring her up a single cigarette. I suggested that while she smoked it, I might open the windows to let the heat flow out—the sun was just setting and the air outside was cooling. From the window I could see across the neighborhood. A line of betel palm trees stood sentry along a neighbor's fence—an increasingly rare sight in Thailand since

betel chewing began falling out of favor decades ago. The noticeable lack of any modern development made the surrounding
vicinity different from other parts of Bangkok, but the houses
themselves weren't very old, perhaps no more than twenty or
thirty years, and there was something odd about the way so
many of them incorporated pieces of scrap lumber and even old
election billboards in their construction. Roxanna explained
that much of the surrounding property belonged to the State
Railway of Thailand and that, technically, many living here were
squatters. She said her in-laws lived just a stone's throw away
along the edge of the tracks. By stringing together bits and
pieces of her story, I learned that she was supporting an extended family—that of her Thai ex-husband. They, in turn,
looked after Roxanna, bringing her meals and cleaning her
house daily. After Roxanna had finished her cigarette, I shut the
windows and she began rolling anew. I steered the conversation
back to opium dens. "What about Laos? Did you ever smoke in
Vientiane?"

"Of all the capitals of French Indochina, Vientiane's opium
dens were the poorest. Now that I think of it, Choum's and
Chantal's in Phnom Penh were the nicest, but even those were
just converted private homes and nothing fancy. Saigon was
strictly for takeout. There we almost always just had the pipe boy
come around to our apartment or hotel room to roll for us. But
Vientiane had some atmosphere back then and I always enjoyed
smoking there, even though the conditions were rustic. One
opium den was run by an old Vietnamese woman whose tongue
had been cut out by the Vietcong. There was nothing left of her
voice but a rough whisper."

Roxanna stopped smoking and sat upright. She used a small
screwdriver to scrape the dross from inside the pipe bowl. After
shaking the loose dross into the glass jar, she pushed the bowl

back into the saddle and started rolling another pill. She began to tell me about people she'd known in the old days; people whose names I might be familiar with. "I knew a lot of interesting people back then, but I'm sure none of them would remember me now. I met Paul Theroux in Singapore. I studied there for a time. Singapore was a popular destination for R & R, and I often had journalist friends passing through. They would stay for a few days and I would show them around town and take them to where we could smoke a few pipes. Can you imagine Singapore with opium dens?"

I could not. Hearing Singapore and any illicit drug mentioned in the same breath is a shock to anybody who has only known the city-state since it decided to become the Tropical City of Excellence. Singapore is now a sterile place known for its long list of laws and regulations (against the chewing of gum; requiring the flushing of toilets), and draconian punishment for minor infractions—including floggings with a waterlogged length of rattan. For serious offenses such as dealing in narcotics, including marijuana, the penalty is death.

Roxanna's Singapore predated all this. She was able to conjure up the decadent old city, home to opium dens and the wondrously sleazy Bugis Street red-light district. When I was in the navy in the 1980s, I heard sailors tell stories about a place in Singapore they called "Boogie Street"—about wild nights of liberty in smoky seaman's bars and being stalked by the region's most flamboyant transvestite prostitutes. When I visited Singapore for the first time in 1990, I was just in time to see the last of Bugis Street fall to the wrecking ball. On a subsequent trip a few years later, I found that a Bugis Street–themed shopping mall had been built on the site of the original. There is nothing like a sanitized present to make one yearn for the wicked past.

"My favorite place to smoke in Singapore was a den run by

a handsome young man from Sri Lanka named Eugene. It wasn't anything grand, but it was friendly and Eugene often let me smoke for free. Most of the smokers there were Indians and Eurasians, and he said having a 'European customer' was good for business. Then there was a no-name opium den on Malabar Street that catered to old Chinese smokers who used to squat around and stare at me and chatter at one another like I wasn't even there. I didn't mind it a bit. I couldn't understand a word of Hokkien, that Chinese dialect they speak in Singapore, but I could tell they were impressed to see me rolling my own pipes. The old Chinese proprietor must have heard that I was also a customer at Eugene's, because one time he asked me how I could smoke with all those Indians. That was typical Singapore. All the different ethnic groups were friendly to me but suspicious of one another. After the Singaporean government closed down the dens I heard Eugene couldn't kick the habit. He switched to heroin and died of an overdose."

As I had noted during our session in the Chamber, Roxanna lapsed into a slow, hypnotized monotone when telling stories. She rolled her pipes, now and then looking up at the blank wall as though a name or a face might be projected there. Outside, the chorus of birdcalls that accompanied the tropical dusk had waned into an intimate silence broken only occasionally by the low voices of neighbors conversing in the dark. A gecko chirruped in the rafters while the throaty whistle of a Malaysia-bound train floated in the distance. The atmosphere enchanted me. It was very different from Willi's place. This wasn't an idealized past that I had created for myself but a slice of the real past—and it produced in me a rising nostalgia that felt like butterflies in my stomach. I could feel myself falling under opium's trance despite not having smoked a single pipe. Was I becoming intoxicated from breathing secondhand vapors?

Again Roxanna offered me the pipe and again I refused, telling myself to fight the urge but knowing full well that I could not resist for long unless I left the room. I hadn't been there more than an hour but my willpower was nearly broken. I got up from the floor. "I'm sorry, I really have to be going."

"So soon? But what about your lessons?"

"Maybe next weekend," I said, knowing that if I came again this scene would repeat itself. "But please keep the pipe in the meantime. Keep it as long as you want."

I thanked Roxanna and apologized again when I realized that she would have to get up in order to lock the upstairs door once I had departed. On my way through the downstairs I passed Jamie eating tuna from a can. He didn't look up, so I said goodbye in Thai as I opened the front door. He answered "Goodbye" in English with a perfectly disinterested tone.

꧁

I took a taxi home, sitting in the front passenger seat so that I could aim the vent on the dashboard directly at my face. I asked the driver to put the air-conditioning on full blast. I felt relaxed, but my mind was sharp. I now knew for sure that by merely being in the same room with somebody smoking opium it was possible to feel a little tipsy. I was slightly tempted to have the driver turn around and take me back, and I probably would have had I known Roxanna better. Instead, I went home and immediately did an Internet search of her name.

There was no way to confirm Roxanna's wartime stories, but her expertise and position at the museum were there to see with just a few clicks. She had written a book about identifying and dating Southeast Asian ceramics and had been a speaker at universities and exhibitions, including at a recent symposium in Kuala Lumpur. This gave me something to think about. Like its neighbor Singapore, Malaysia also has harsh drug laws. The penalty for trafficking narcotics into the country—including importing the smallest amount of opium—is death. How could she travel to such a place if she was hooked? Willi was the only one who had said Roxanna was dependent on opium; Roxanna herself had never admitted it. Maybe he had exaggerated.

But then I remembered noticing the nicotine-like stain on the calloused index finger of her left hand. Others might have mistaken it for the sign of a chain-smoker, or perhaps a dab of iodine, but I knew differently. Emily Hahn, in her essay about her own addiction to opium in Shanghai during the 1930s, had developed a similar stain from smoking daily. "There was even an oily smudge on my left forefinger . . . that wouldn't easily wash off. It came from testing opium pellets as they cooled." Hahn's Chinese friends, also smokers, thought the stain was amusing and would call attention to it: "Have you ever before seen a white girl with that mark on her finger?"

Over the next two weeks I thought of Roxanna often. Every time she entered my mind the one image that accompanied my thoughts of her was that of her lamp. To me the opium lamp is symbolic of the romance of smoking. Most collectors are drawn to pipes, but they are cold, dead, useless things without the lamp—that twinkling beacon forever ready to warm the meticulously crafted pill and release its intoxicating vapors. Chinese artisans had enshrined this feeble, oil-fed flame upon an ornate pedestal. They well understood the lamp's importance and had given it attention that bordered on veneration.

Roxanna was a real discovery. I had the good fortune to have been befriended by and taken into the confidence of a person who had witnessed the last days of opium in Asia. If Willi was to be believed, she was the last of a storied breed: the Westerner lured to the Orient by adventure and then enraptured by the

A woman arrested for opium smoking is asked by the judge to give a demonstration of how the drug is smoked. A glass opium lamp sits on the bench above her. The photo was taken in 1936 in Chicago. (From the author's collection)

"soft beds of the East," now unwilling—perhaps unable—to leave it all behind. That lamp of hers, that sorry excuse for an opium lamp, bothered me. Something about its commonness, its complete lack of celebration, seemed to me to imply hardship and, ultimately, failure. I had no idea whether Roxanna herself saw it in that way, but I thought she deserved better.

I remembered that I was going to give her a pair of genuine opium needles to replace the one she had improvised. After locating my cache of needles, I began to browse through my lamps. I wanted something functional and easy to maintain. The chimney needed to detach easily so that trimming the wick, adding oil, and after-session cleaning were not a chore. Yet I also wanted a lamp that was elegant, one that would give Roxanna joy to look at—a lamp that would bring back memories of the days before such works of art were banned and destroyed.

After nearly an hour of pondering, I decided on a small, cylindrical lamp of brass. The openwork on the vent was a cloverlike pattern, and into four sides was delicately rendered the Chinese character denoting longevity. I had a feeling that Roxanna would have balked had the lamp I offered been too ostentatious or made from silver. This little brass offering would be perfect.

My initial trepidation about safety had begun to wane and now I had an excuse to call her. She answered as though she had been expecting me. "Oh, hi, Steven. I've been thinking about you all week. I'm hosting a group of curators from the national museum in Malaysia. Do you think you could give a talk at the ceramics museum?"

I said I might be interested and we set a date for me to stop by her house so we could discuss it. As it turned out, my next visit on the following Sunday morning was the beginning of a tradition. We agreed that I would arrive around eight, before the sun could begin baking the roof tiles, and before Jamie was awake. Roxanna left the front door unlocked and told me to creep upstairs, where she would be waiting for me with the layout already prepared. She was so happy with the lamp and needles I brought that I immediately promised to bring a proper tray on my next visit. There was no question about whether I would be smoking that day. I had barely slept the previous night in anticipation of this early morning session. Somehow her academic legitimacy also legitimized my visits—at least that's what I felt at the time. A visit to Roxanna's was really no different from a visit to Willi's—except now my lab was closer and I could conduct research without the expense of overnight train journeys.

My talk at the museum a week later was doomed from the start by Malaysian politics. The curators were young, ethnic-Malay Muslims—*bumiputra,* or "sons of the soil"—a label they used to distinguish themselves from Malaysia's ethnic Chinese and Indians whose ancestors immigrated more recently, when Malaysia was part of a British colony. The Malay curators had absolutely no interest in my talk about opium antiques. When I asked if they had opium artifacts in any of the branches of the national museum in Malaysia, one young woman told me (in a respectful tone) that Chinese items were not displayed at Malaysia's museums because the Chinese were not true Malaysians. The comment was no surprise to anyone familiar with Malaysia's fractured society, and anyway, I knew her claim about the country's museums was false. Having browsed the branch of the national museum in Penang on three occasions, I was aware that it was home to a very well-thought-out display of Chinese costumes and furniture. There was even a small exhibit of opium paraphernalia on the second floor. The pieces—one pipe, a needle, and part of a lamp—were unexceptional, but there was one particularly impressive hardwood opium bed that must have made its owner feel like a prince. On the ground floor of the museum, tucked away in a display cabinet situated under a stairway, I spied an opium smoker's travel kit made of lacquered boxwood and complete with its original lamp. The kit was not labeled, and its absence from the opium paraphernalia exhibit upstairs convinced me that the museum's staff had no idea what it was.

It made no sense for me to challenge Roxanna's guests with what I had seen in Penang, and of course there's never a good time to argue with Southeast Asians about local politics. Instead I saved my foundering show-and-tell by turning on a computer, getting online, and showing the young curators how to search for antique kris daggers on eBay.

I thought Roxanna might be disappointed with my presentation but she just laughed. After the curators had gone back to their hotel, she gave me a tour of the ceramics museum. It was small but the collection was fabulous, and the lighting and interactive displays—all designed by Roxanna herself—put everything I had seen at Thailand's government-run museums to shame. Roxanna suggested that we celebrate my "successful lecture" at her place with a pipe or two. I was glad for the invitation. In the back of my mind I had been hoping for one all along.

At Roxanna's later that evening, once the accoutrements were arranged and she had rolled three pipes for each of us, she began to describe the challenges she faced as the director of the Southeast Asian Ceramics Museum. There were the typical issues of being a foreigner: Some Southeast Asian academics resented outsiders who claimed to be experts in their art and culture—a resentment that no doubt had its roots in the region's experience with European colonialism. Thailand, having never been colonized, could not claim such a past, but Roxanna said there was a feeling in some quarters of Thai academia that non-Thais could not possibly understand the nuances of their art.

But sometimes Roxanna's being an outsider worked to her advantage. Southeast Asia has a long history of wars and conquests as well as a concept known to historians as "cultural augmentation." An example of this is "classical Thai" art and culture that, for the most part, was derived from Khmer art forms after the Siamese sacked Angkor in the fifteenth century and force-marched Cambodia's court dancers, artisans, and astrologers back to Siam. In turn, the Burmese invaded Siam 350 years later and made off with *its* cultural treasures. This partly explains why the arts of many of the civilizations in Southeast Asia look so similar—not that such similarities have fostered harmony between the neighboring countries. As has happened many times in the region, emotions quickly heat up when the fires of nationalism are stoked. In 2003, an angry Cambodian mob burned down the Thai embassy in Phnom Penh when it was reported (erroneously it turned out) that a Thai celebrity had suggested Cambodia's Angkor Wat belonged to Thailand. Roxanna's ceramics expertise covered the entire region and, according to her, she had been able to bridge gaps in the regional academic community simply because she was an outsider and seen as neutral.

But unfortunately that expertise was never taken on faith. Roxanna found it was something she had to prove over and over to each and every Thai she met. "How many times has some professor from the Thai government's Fine Arts Department come to visit the museum and then asked to meet the director, and when I introduce myself they just look right past me? Who is this little old *farang* lady? Where's Khun Rattana Ngerntongdee?" Roxanna laughed, using an honorific with her Thai name.

She explained that when she took Thai citizenship she was told by immigration officials that she was required to come up with a Thai name to go along with her new nationality. Her husband suggested "Rattana," which sounded fairly close to Roxanna. At home among her Thai family she was "Mem," a nickname based on the English word "ma'am" and commonly given to women of European or Eurasian ethnicity.

Then there was her leg, or the lack of one. Thailand is a country where much importance is placed on outward appearances, and Roxanna's disability was more of an obstacle than it might have been in other cultures. "It was a motorcycle accident. I was run over by a large truck. I survived, but you're familiar with the whole karma thing. Most Buddhist Thais, even the ed-

ucated ones, can't get past their belief that bad things only happen to bad people, that somehow I deserved it based on
something I did in a past life or earlier in this one. Of course,
they never say that directly to my face!" she said with a laugh,
showing she harbored no bitterness.

Roxanna went on to describe the world of collecting ceramic antiquities. "My biggest problem has been fighting the
tide of fakes that has flooded the market. You would not believe
the lengths dealers go to in order to convince collectors they're
getting the real thing. I've met collectors who have been to un-
authorized digs hundreds of miles from anywhere and watched
as fakes were 'unearthed' right before their eyes." Roxanna shook
her head in disbelief. "Imagine the collector who witnesses
something like this and who sincerely *wants* to believe he had
the luck to be there just in time to make the purchase!

"My museum was founded by the man who founded the
university. His Southeast Asian ceramics collection is extraordinary and it's the core of the museum's collection, but there are
fakes in his collection. One thing I've learned is that most collectors do not want to be told when they've been duped. They
just don't want to know about it. Okay, that's fine, but what do I
do when those fakes end up in the museum that I've hung my
reputation on, and the founder wants to know why I refuse to
display certain items? Do I open my mouth and risk upsetting
him? Most collectors would hate the messenger as much as they
hated the message being delivered."

It was clear how much passion Roxanna had for the subject,
but there was also a tinge of despair in her voice. While talking
about fakes she seemed so vexed that I tried to change the subject. It was the first time I had seen her agitated, and she obviously needed to vent. "The whole system is rotten. Perfect
replicas are aged and certified as antiquities while the few genu-

ine pieces that are being found are passed off as reproductions in order to export them. I seriously doubt anyone knows what's real and what's fake anymore. It's just gotten so jumbled that there's really no way to appraise anything. The value of something is simply what somebody is willing to pay for it. And if I'm the only one who can tell a piece is fake but nobody else believes me, is the piece really a fake? I don't know; you tell me."

"I'm sure glad that hasn't happened with opium antiques. There's not enough demand," I said.

"Oh, it'll happen eventually. Willi told me you're working on a book. Do you have a publisher?"

I told her about having finally found one, a small local publisher based in Chiang Mai called Silkworm Books. The writing was finished and the photographing of my collection had been completed, but the firm needed time to come up with the money to have my book printed. Despite the delays, I was grateful to have a publisher that understood my idea of presenting antique opium paraphernalia as art, and that was willing to take a chance on a book about it.

Roxanna said that I should use the waiting time to collect as much as possible before demand went up. She warned me that not only would values increase as demand rose, but that the number of fakes would increase as well. It is a cycle that feeds on itself, and it happens with every Asian collectible that becomes established with Western collectors.

"As soon as somebody publishes a book about something new, as soon as there is a reliable reference, not only does that get attention for a potential collectible, it will enable people who know nothing about it to start collecting. And once amateur collectors start throwing money around, nothing will stop the dealers from supplying them . . . with fakes if necessary."

I didn't think the warning applied to me and my odd little

niche. There were at that time probably no more than ten serious collectors of antique opium-smoking paraphernalia. Word
about the online auctions had already gotten out and competition had increased, but I was still able to buy stunning antique
pipes for only a few hundred dollars.

In 2003, I was one of a handful of people interviewed by a reporter from *The Wall Street Journal Europe* for a story—the premise of which was "Is there anything left to collect in Asia?"
Another collector of opium antiques was quoted in the article, a
Dutchman named Armand Hoorde who lived in Amsterdam.
He was also a collector of "Chinese erotica," painted and sculpted
images that were essentially very early pornography. He claimed
in the article to have been attracted to antique opium-smoking
paraphernalia because of the drug's historical associations with
prostitution in China. I remember reading that comment and
thinking about how journalists often latch onto some quote because of its color, not because it is relevant to the interview as a
whole. Over the next few years I heard bits and pieces about
Hoorde. He was said to be very wealthy, but he didn't make annual trips to Asia like Helmut P. Instead, he relied on Parisian
antiques dealers to bring pieces to him. Other collectors who
had glimpsed Hoorde's collection had pronounced it magnificent.

Not long after I began joining Roxanna for regular sessions,
I was contacted by Hoorde, who said he would be traveling to
Thailand with his family and wanted to meet me. I was glad for
the chance to get to know him. When he arrived I made my way
across town to meet him at his posh hotel. "Armie," as he insisted
I call him, was pushing sixty but a full head of hair made him
look much younger. He was warm and boyishly enthusiastic, and

we hit it off right away. Hoorde was traveling with his wife, who I later learned was descended from Javanese nobility, and their stunningly beautiful twentysomething daughter, Pearl.

Although I had for years been freely sharing photographic images of my collection via email to most anybody who was interested, I almost never invited anyone to come to my apartment to view my collection in person—a result of collector's paranoia combined with embarrassment at my having capitulated in the war against Bangkok's dust. Hoorde pleaded to see my collection, and because I had a good feeling about him, I brought him up to have a look. The visit went well. He asked good questions and professed abundant envy—the quickest way to a collector's heart. Later I took him to a nearby coffee shop, the old-fashioned kind of which there were once dozens in Chinatown: Occupying the ground floor of a shophouse, it had ceiling fans, marble-top tables, and highly sweetened coffee strained through a bag that looked like a sock.

Hoorde had some propositions for me. He asked if I would consider collecting for him, purchasing pieces in Bangkok and then reselling them to him. He promised top dollar. He also told me about an exhibition that he was working to arrange at a museum in Rotterdam. He said he needed help writing the exhibition catalog, intimating that if I agreed to this, an all-expenses-paid trip to Europe would be part of the deal, timed so that I could be on hand for the opening of his show. Hoorde said that he regularly smoked opium at his home in Amsterdam—where it was perfectly legal to do so—and that he was interested in observing my rolling technique. He asked if I knew how to roll. I lied and said yes.

I admitted to him that I didn't think I would be much of a source for opium antiques. As much as I liked buying, I never enjoyed selling no matter how much profit I could gain from it.

Old opium-smoking paraphernalia is so rare that it's not uncommon for an item to be completely unique—the sole surviving example of its kind. If I sold such a piece, there might not be any chance of discovering another, no matter how much I was willing to pay. I knew that anything I was interested enough to buy, I would have to keep for myself. There was no way my possessiveness would allow me to resell to Hoorde, despite his promise of lucrative transactions.

However, I was keen to contribute to the catalog. Work of this sort I didn't even consider work—the recognition that would come from being involved with the exhibition seemed payment enough—so I agreed to do it for free. The trip to Europe would be raisins in the pudding. Hoorde was very pleased, and he returned to Holland promising to be in touch. I had a year to prepare myself for Europe. I called Roxanna and told her the news, and we set a date for my first rolling lesson.

Roxanna was a patient teacher. She kept up a good-natured banter as I rolled her precious *chandu,* pretending not to notice when in my ineptness I wasted it by letting pills melt and drop into the lamp. It took several sessions before I gained some confidence, but just when I thought I was getting the hang of it there were days when nothing worked. Some pills inexplicably burst into flames as I toasted them over the lamp, flaring like match heads while I desperately tried to blow them out. Some pills stuck messily to the bowl as I was trying to shape them. Later, while seating the pill upon the bowl, some refused to adhere to its surface. Heating pills a second time for another attempt at sticking made them dry and delicate, and this caused some pills to shatter, the tiny pieces of opium skittering across the layout tray like bits of peanut brittle.

On days when I could do nothing right, Roxanna took over the rolling duties and amplified my frustrations by preparing one perfect pipe after another. "Don't feel bad. That happens to me, too. Opium is alive and has its moods. There are days when it's against you and there's not a thing you can do to get back in its favor."

To the uninitiated such claims will seem fanciful. I had read similar sentiments in old accounts—especially by French smokers—but before I started rolling I had assumed the authors were simply trying to romanticize their vice. Yet while learning to roll—toasting the fickle treacle over the flame—there were times when I could swear the opium was testing my devotion to it.

During those days of unsteady rolling I was treated to Roxanna's life story. She told me about growing up on a chicken farm in Illinois, the eldest child in a loveless family headed by a stern and belittling father. She talked about how she had left for New York as soon as she was old enough, finding a job at the World's Fair. Later, she flew to Australia and then Southeast Asia, where her brother was serving in Vietnam. She said she naively thought she could bring him home, but instead she found herself drawn to the excitement of the war. In Roxanna's bedroom I saw a souvenir of those days in Vietnam, a framed black-and-white photograph of a fresh-faced and beautiful Roxanna dressed in camouflage fatigues, and once she showed me an article in a back issue of the magazine *Soldier of Fortune*—titled "Between Roxanna and a Hard Place"—which portrayed her as a pistol-packing femme fatale. "That story is utter nonsense!" Roxanna said, laughing and obviously a bit flattered. "I contacted the author when I heard about it and he apologized, saying he thought I'd never see it."

After the war, Roxanna said, she gravitated to Hong Kong,

where she edited a magazine about Asian art. The Cultural Revolution had turned China on its ear, but British-run Hong Kong was a time capsule on the China coast, its illegal opium dens the last visible remnants of the infamous Opium Wars. Roxanna's recreational opium use, which had its beginnings in Vietnam, became heavier in Hong Kong—but unlike Southeast Asia, the British colony actually enforced its anti-opium laws. A colleague turned informer notified the police, and Roxanna was arrested and deported.

She next came to Thailand, where she married and put down roots. Jamie was born and she settled in with her new Thai family. Tacked up on a wall in her bedroom were snapshots of that happy time. Her motorcycle accident changed all that. Roxanna was not expected to survive and, to make her last hours as painless as possible, the doctors pumped her full of morphine. When she began to recover, after weeks of being rocked in morphine's gentle cradle, there was no easy way to discontinue the medication. Opiates would forever be a part of Roxanna's life. "I'm lucky. If I lived in the States or Europe I would've had to resort to methadone or, God forbid, heroin. At least here I can get quality opium. The main problem is worrying about whether or not I'll ever run out. I wish I could buy enough to always have a supply until I die, but it's so rare and expensive that it's just not possible."

After her accident Roxanna's husband left her, but her in-laws remained loyal. She confessed that she was in constant pain and each morning was greeted with the realization that she faced another day in agony. "Every morning I wake up feeling like a corpse that's been brought back to life. My whole body's in pain and too stiff to move. I have to set my alarm long before I go to work because it takes me a full hour to slowly stretch out every muscle and loosen up enough just to get out of bed. Then I have a few pipes to fortify myself before going to the museum."

Roxanna told me that the only thing that kept her going was her love for her son. Jamie had never been able to hold down a job, and Roxanna worried that he spent too much time shut up in his bedroom. She told me that he had gone to high school in America while living with her relatives there, but Jamie was shy and didn't fit in, so he had come home withdrawn and lacking confidence in himself.

A mild estrangement from her family in the States was something Roxanna often spoke of, but there was usually humor in her stories, and for me it was a relief to find somebody who understood the loneliness of self-exile in a foreign land. She, too, had felt the sensation, after many years abroad, of being trapped somewhere betwixt and between. Neither of us quite fit into our adopted country and yet we were no longer at home in the land of our birth, a place that had changed beyond recognition while we were away.

Sometimes there was real sadness in her tales of trying to assimilate into Thai society. Roxanna told me that Jamie seemed ashamed to bring his friends home. She assumed it was because of her, but when she tried to listen for clues as he spoke Thai to his friends on the telephone, she was unable to follow his slang-infused speech. It was that oft-told coming to America story turned upside down: Roxanna was the immigrant parent whose outlandish looks and kooky accent were causing her child endless embarrassment.

My lessons with Roxanna became more frequent. The original Sunday morning session was augmented by a midweek session, usually on Thursday evening after she had come home from work. Sometimes I wasn't able to smoke for a few weeks when updating guidebooks took me to Cambodia, Malaysia, or Laos. There were definite feelings of withdrawal during these dry periods but nothing too severe. Mostly it manifested itself as insomnia and what felt like a case of jittery nerves. I became convinced that the doomsday withdrawal symptoms that I'd read about in old accounts were as exaggerated as the stories about opium's hallucinogenic qualities.

The setting for our sessions in Roxanna's rustic house, besides being atmospheric, also debunked at least one opium-smoking myth. A dreamy passage in Cocteau's *Opium: Diary of a Cure* related how animals were naturally drawn to the pleasures of the drug:

> All animals are charmed by opium. Addicts in the colonies know the danger of this bait for wild beasts and reptiles. Flies gather around the tray and dream, the lizards with their little mittens swoon on the ceiling above the lamp and wait for the night, mice come close and nibble the dross.

In my laboratory open to the tropical atmosphere I found this to be completely untrue. Sparrows sometimes flew into the room through openings under the eaves of the roof, and they always flew right back out. Geckos avoided the rafters directly above the tray, and when on occasion Roxanna's cat scratched on the door to get into the room, it turned and fled as soon as I opened the door and it got a whiff of the proceedings.

Besides the rolling, I was also learning about ceramics from Roxanna. She taught me to recognize the difference between *zisha* and *zitao,* two types of pottery most commonly used for pipe bowls, and her knowledge of the settlements in China that had traditionally produced ceramics helped me map out what kind of bowls were produced where. Likewise, her groundbreaking use of salvaged shipwrecks to date Chinese trade ceramics inspired me to do the same for pipe bowls. I compared those

found on the wreck of the *Tek Sing,* which sank in the Riau
Archipelago near Singapore in 1822, with pipe bowls that had
been discovered in the American West. These latter bowls were
not likely to predate the California Gold Rush in 1849, and so
this enabled me to create a rough chronology for pipe bowls—
something that had never previously been done.

As the months passed, my visits to smoke with Roxanna increased to three or four a week. If some holiday created a three-
day weekend, we usually met on three consecutive days. My
rolling was becoming impeccable, and on the increasingly rare
occasions that I went to Vientiane to visit Willi, he was effusive
in his praise of my accomplishment.

Back at Roxanna's, I would spend entire Sundays curled up
next to the tray and peering through a pair of nineteenth-
century wire-rim spectacles in patient pursuit of the perfectly
rolled pill. On the way home, I would take the subway despite
its being out of the way and slower than a taxi—just so I could
luxuriate in the powerful air-conditioning and nod off between
stations. I was supremely impressed at my own uniqueness: I was
adept at using the world's finest *chandu* to prepare my own pipes,
and—I smiled to myself at the mere thought of it—I was surely
the only person in this city of ten million who rode the subway
while cooked on opium. I was an opium geek, even an opium
snob, but it never occurred to me that I was also becoming an
opium addict.

One of the marvels of opium is its ability to exalt sensitivity, it transforms the most boorish people into courteous creatures by establishing true equality between races and sexes.

—Max Olivier-Lacamp, *Le kief* (1974)

"Don't sell yourself short!" Roxanna said with insistence as I was vaporizing a pill. "And don't overestimate how much he knows. He wouldn't have flown all the way to Thailand if he knew enough to write his own book. If you give away your knowledge for free, Armand Hoorde will use it as his own and you'll have nothing to show for it."

"He said I'd be on a list of contributors on the title page."

"That's not enough. At least make him pay you for your work. . . . How many was that?" Roxanna interrupted herself as I handed the pipe back to her.

"I don't know. I forgot to keep count again. Sorry."

Awkwardly—because I was feeling too relaxed to bother sitting up—I reached toward the tray. Plucking three tamarind seeds from a small silver box adorned with a Chinese dragon, I dropped them into the box's cylindrical lid. During my trips to smoke opium with Willi, he had never once asked for monetary contributions—our sessions were infrequent and my gifts of paraphernalia and decorative objects for the Chamber were enough. But my visits to smoke with Roxanna had become so regular that she asked if I would mind paying for the *chandu* I smoked. She somehow figured the cost per pipe based on how many drops she used for each pill. It was up to me to keep count using the tamarind seeds, which were brown and smooth, about the size of coffee beans. The tamarind seeds' texture and stone-like hardness were appealing to my opium-sensitized fingertips. I chose them as counters for precisely that reason—no detail was too minute for opium's most fastidious fancier.

Roxanna and I were discussing whether I should be paid for my contribution to Hoorde's catalog. I had received a compact disc with the text and images that were to make up the publication, and I saw that it wasn't going to be some low-budget affair. The chapter I had agreed to contribute was already written— my job was to rewrite it. The original text had been penned by another Dutchman who had contacted me a couple years before, asking questions about opium pipe bowls and saying vaguely that he was working on "a paper." I didn't give him any information because at the time I was working on my own book. When I finally saw the makings of Hoorde's book, I was glad I had refused. Hoorde would not have needed my help had I been too free with my knowledge a couple years earlier.

I thought Roxanna was perhaps right about Hoorde's lack of knowledge. The images taken for his book, while beautifully photographed, included a number of fakes and pieces that had nothing to do with opium smoking. Seeing these pictures reminded me of when Hoorde was visiting Bangkok and I had taken him to the antiques shops at River City mall. Once or twice he surprised me by gushing over some piece that was clearly not a tool of the trade. In one case he became very enthusiastic about a small cloisonné tray that was being offered as a lamp tray. The pattern of the enamel indicated that it was

Japanese—and that alone is evidence enough that it was not crafted for smoking opium. The Japanese never produced opium paraphernalia for the simple reason that anti-opium laws in Japan were, from the earliest times, very severe and rigorously enforced. Still, I thought Hoorde might have just been testing me.

Roxanna was enjoying her cigarette break—she never smoked more than one or two per session. I took advantage of the pause in rolling to open the windows and turn on the electric fan. Then I went downstairs to get two glasses of ice and a bottle of Gatorade from the refrigerator. The sports drink wasn't exactly traditional, but Roxanna and I found it the best way to stay hydrated in the heat of that upstairs room. When I returned, Roxanna stubbed out her cigarette but continued on the subject of insisting on remuneration for consultation. She said she had once been hesitant to charge collectors when they approached her for ceramics appraisals—shyness and a low opinion of herself caused her to undervalue her own growing expertise. "Rewriting that chapter for Hoorde may seem easy to you, but think of how many years and how much money it's taken for you to get where you are today. All that collecting and studying. Your time and knowledge are just as valuable as any other professional's. Charge him accordingly."

At first I saw myself being compensated in other ways. Hoorde helped me acquire several pieces, including a porcelain stand for pipe bowls that he came across during a stopover in Hong Kong on his way back to Amsterdam. But as my smoking increased, so did my need for cash. By the time my trip to Europe was a month away, I was spending the equivalent of my monthly rent on smoking. So I renegotiated my arrangement with Hoorde, who agreed to pay me for my contribution to his book while generously keeping his promise to cover my journey to Europe.

Roxanna suggested that I could also make some cash by selling off duplicate pieces of my collection directly to other collectors. Despite what might have seemed like a major conflict of interest—now that I was paying her for each pipe smoked—I valued Roxanna's advice regarding my collection. For one thing, she was one of very few friends who understood and supported my decision to donate my collection to an institution—an idea I hit upon fairly early on.

A serious collector can't help but notice that the life span of a typical collection often only barely exceeds the life span of its owner. Once, at an antiques shop in Bangkok that specialized in antiquarian maps and books with Southeast Asian themes, I talked to the German proprietor of many years. He told of having European and American clients who visited Thailand annually, buying old books and maps to take back home to their collections. Often the collector had a wife and kids in tow. "He comes every year with his family and I watch as he gets older and his children grow into adults. I get to know them all very well. Then one or two years pass and he doesn't come to Bangkok and I wonder what happened to him. If he is already old I can guess what happened."

The antiquarian book dealer explained that sometimes his suspicions were confirmed when a deceased collector's family contacted him and wanted to sell the collection back. "I often get very good deals because the wife and especially the children have no interest in Father's hobby. Sometimes they are even a little hostile toward the collection because so much of Father's attention was given to his precious things. Families like this practically give back the books and maps to me for free."

I had observed something similar happening with the online auctions—where it was very common to see collections being scattered to the wind. The ones that I noticed being sold off piece by piece to the highest bidder had nothing to do with opium, but by using a collector's eye I saw things that others might not have taken note of. In one case I watched the dissolution of an extensive collection of vintage firecracker labels. I could see that they had been meticulously gathered, just as a serious collector of stamps would have done: Every little variation in design, no matter how small, was represented. When such attention to detail was obvious I could easily imagine the passion of the person who had spent years putting the collection together. To that collector, each and every piece would have a backstory about how and where it was acquired and, if the collector was inclined to do research, a detailed description of its history and provenance would also have been recorded. I watched this auction as the labels—stripped of all their history— brought in a few dollars here and a few dollars there, and the disparate lots went to buyers on different continents.

In 2004, a small but significant collection of opium antiques came up on eBay. The seller knew little about the items and would tell me only that the mother of a man who had died recently brought them in to be sold on consignment. The seller said that the mother didn't want her son's name disclosed, and so I could learn nothing about this collector except that he had lived in the Chicago area. I was able to buy some of his opium pipes, a few of which were very important pieces—including a pipe with a stem made from lacquered sugarcane that the seller didn't correctly describe (in the auction the pipe was listed as bamboo). At first I didn't recognize the pipe for what it was, either, but I bid on it and won the auction. It wasn't until much later—after I had used a photo of the pipe to illustrate my book and erroneously captioned it "an odd species of bamboo"—did I realize that I owned one of the few surviving examples of a sugarcane opium pipe. This is something the original owner himself might have known, but if he did, he took that information to the grave.

The notion that a similar fate might befall my own collection was enough to cause me sleepless nights. After dedicating a decade of my life to the one collection that had really caught my imagination, after the hours of meticulous research (all of it quite enjoyable, I had to admit), not to mention the money I had invested, the thought that the compilation I had put so much effort into assembling might someday end up on eBay—or worse, being haggled over by greedy shopkeepers and clueless tourists in Bangkok's antiques shops—was truly distressing.

I had long before decided that I would become *the* expert on opium paraphernalia. If I was going to be remembered for one thing, I wanted this to be it. Getting my book published was a start, but space constraints had meant that what was discussed and illustrated in my book was only a tiny fraction of what I knew and had collected. I needed a repository for both the goods and the information.

I toyed with the idea of opening a small museum in Bangkok's Chinatown. If my worst nightmare was having my collection shattered and scattered, my favorite daydream was to found and be the curator of my own museum—not some hall of institutional boredom with uninspired displays and labels that nobody bothered to read, but one of those weird little private museums that announces itself with a series of hokey roadside signs. I dreamed of something quirky enough to be hip yet academic enough to be taken seriously, a place where I could spend my days having conversations with visitors from all over the world. The more I thought about it, the more convinced I became that it could work. I even picked out a vacant century-old shophouse in a quiet lane near my apartment that I thought would be the perfect venue.

I discussed the project with an acquaintance—a Thai-Chinese businessman who was also a novice collector of opium antiques and who thought such a private museum might even turn a profit if it were done right. He had noticed the daily parade of tour buses hitting the Chinatown sights, such as the giant Golden Buddha at Wat Traimit monastery, and he felt a museum about opium would fit perfectly onto the tour companies' itinerary. He declared himself interested and set out to see if it could be done, but it didn't take long before he gave up on the idea. It seemed that the tour operators expected to be paid for each tourist they brought in; that each busload of visitors stopping by the museum would be accompanied by a tour guide with a smiling face and upturned palm. But before any of that could happen the tour companies would also have to be plied with substantial monetary enticement. When I heard all this, I was happy my collector acquaintance had lost interest. It was all too much like a business for my tastes.

Willi, too, thought my collection could be an opportunity to earn money. He suggested a friend of his in Hong Kong who might be able to get permission to start a museum there, but by that time I was wary of any moneymaking ventures. What if the museum went bankrupt? What if the authorities decided to just walk in and confiscate everything? Technically opium paraphernalia was still illegal in Hong Kong. Museums can get waivers because of their mission to educate, but who could trust a museum in China-controlled Hong Kong? China has been so intensely propagandizing its past, oversimplifying and emotionalizing its historic relationship with opium, that most Chinese— indeed most of the world—are convinced that the drug showed up on China's shores with the British, who then forced millions to become addicted at gunpoint. What would Chinese authorities make of Chinese-made paraphernalia whose opulence suggested Chinese complicity? I didn't think that China, or anyplace it controlled, would be right for a museum to house my collection.

Ideally I thought my collection would be best housed and displayed in America, perhaps in San Francisco's Chinatown, where opium smoking in the Chinese manner first got a foothold in the New World. Such a museum would be historically relevant to the entire country. Not only were a large percentage of the pieces I had acquired for my collection sourced in the United States, but late-nineteenth-century America had the largest population of opium smokers outside of Asia. But as I've mentioned earlier, the association of opium smoking with Chinese people has become politically charged in America, and so a museum presenting antique opium paraphernalia as an art form would probably be about as welcome in one of America's Chinatowns as it would be in China itself.

In San Francisco in 2004, I met Gaetano Maeda—an entrepreneur and filmmaker who was in town arranging the annual International Buddhist Film Festival. After graciously taking the time to listen to my ideas, he suggested that Las Vegas would be the only place in the United States that could host the type of museum I dreamed of opening. This was because the city's cultural diversions were aimed at visitors who were quickly jaded by the sheer depth of choices for entertainment. Investors were therefore always looking for something new and unusual to grab tourists' attention. If anyplace in America could host an opium museum *and* turn a profit, Maeda thought it would be Las Vegas. I thanked him for his advice, and then I promptly gave up on the museum idea. Nothing against Las Vegas, but my collection simply did not belong there.

I began looking for an institution that would take my collection as a donation in return for an agreement to keep it intact— and with my name on it—in perpetuity. Things did not look promising. According to Roxanna, most museums would never agree to such a binding contract. She said that unless I was lucky enough to find a museum or institution that just happened to have a director or curator who was very interested in opium antiques, it was unlikely I could even give my collection away. I was beginning to feel like some bearded old kook who, having amassed the world's largest ball of twine, demands that everyone take notice of his accomplishment.

Then I found a book edited by Dr. Priscilla Wegars of the University of Idaho's Asian American Comparative Collection called *Hidden Heritage: Historical Archaeology of the Overseas Chinese*. The book was a major discovery for me for two reasons. First, there was one whole chapter about opium paraphernalia that had been unearthed at old Chinese settlements in the United States. Many of these opium relics were found in what would have been trash heaps—alongside old bottles and such—and most were broken and had been discarded. Pieces of pipe bowls were a common find. What I thought most remarkable was not what the archaeologists had found, but what they had been able to glean from mere shards. By having minutely examined the broken pieces, the authors of the chapter were able to describe how the pipe bowls had been made—how some were thrown on a potter's wheel and others were molded by hand. I was so impressed by their findings that I contacted the editor. It turned out that Dr. Wegars was a former Peace Corps volunteer who had been posted in Thailand in the 1960s. She was due to visit for a Peace Corps reunion and would be stopping in Bangkok. We set up a date to meet and, after I showed her my collection, I offered it to the University of Idaho. Her enthusiasm gave me real hope that my collection had found a permanent home.

When I flew to Amsterdam from Bangkok in April 2007, my spirits were soaring as high as the plane. I had secured a permanent home for my collection, the University of Idaho having agreed in a written contract that the "Steven Martin Collection" would be incorporated into the university's Asian American Comparative Collection "for purposes of public display and enjoyment, education, conservation, and scholarship." On top of that, my book had finally been published just weeks before, and I was even able to bring along with me a few advance copies of *The Art of Opium Antiques.*

Armand Hoorde was at the airport to greet me, and because we had been communicating via email and telephone on such a regular basis, it felt like a reunion with an old friend. It was midmorning when I arrived, and he explained that the evening of the following day would be the opening night of his exhibition. The displays were not yet finished, and he expected to spend the whole day getting everything in order. Hoorde gave me the choice of going to his flat, where he said his wife would prepare breakfast for me and where I could get some rest, or going directly to the museum in Rotterdam to help with the displays. I didn't have to pause to think! We drove straight from the airport to the museum, less than an hour away.

The museum, known as the Kunsthal Rotterdam, was housed in a stark, modernist building that I might have mistaken for a car dealership sans the cars. The space reserved for the opium paraphernalia exhibit was in a room divided so as to keep visitors walking along passageways. One wall was covered with opium-related ephemera such as movie posters and illustrations from old magazines. A small area nearby was arranged with a screen and chairs like a tiny movie theater in which a film short, narrated in French and featuring Hoorde's daughter smoking opium, played over and over in a loop. Beyond this was a room within a room that could not be entered but could be viewed from an observation platform and through a window. This room on display was decorated with Chinese furniture and was supposed to portray an elaborate private smoking room complete with an opium bed.

Most of the exhibition was made up of antique paraphernalia in banks of display cases along the walls. These had not yet been sealed—the glass was not yet installed and the museum staff were hurrying to finish the displays. I noticed right away that the arrangement of the displays was based on the photos in Hoorde's exhibition catalog—whose layouts with sundry accoutrements had been arranged by Hoorde himself before the photographer captured the images. Apparently somebody had simply used the photos from the book as a guide for the displays. The problem was twofold: First, some of the paraphernalia on the layout trays were out-and-out fakes. But even worse in my eyes was the fact that Hoorde had managed to mix Chinese and Vietnamese components on the same layout trays. This may sound nitpicky to the layman, but imagine seeing a museum display of classical antiquities in which the curators carelessly mixed Greek and Roman relics. Vietnamese opium-smoking paraphernalia in most cases surpassed the Chinese model in its meticulous ornamentation. In my opinion, an exhibition such as Hoorde's should have been celebrating the Vietnamese contribution to the art form, yet nothing about the displays or on the labels differentiated the two.

Of course, there was no question of whether I would let the displays remain flawed. I pulled Hoorde aside and gently suggested that I rearrange the trays and remove the fakes. He didn't get upset or angry, but instead told the museum staff not to seal any of the display cases until I had had a chance to inspect and approve everything.

I quickly set about making the necessary changes. I wanted everything to be perfect—yet my motives were not without some selfishness. This museum exhibition had a sensuality that could not be properly explored or appreciated if its items were behind glass. So many of the pipes and tools on display had been crafted with textures that were meant to excite an opium-enthralled sense of touch. With the display cases open I was able to get my hands on some of the most sumptuous pieces of opium paraphernalia remaining in existence. The exhibition's show-stopper was a porcelain pipe, shorter than most at just over eighteen inches long. It was the only pipe on display in the whole exhibition that was without a pipe bowl—because it had been acquired without one and because no pipe bowl could be found that matched the pipe stem's magnificence. The porcelain stem was adorned with nine writhing five-toed dragons in low relief, whose bodies were sharply rendered with shimmering scales and surrounded by stylized flames. Glaze had been applied lightly so as not to clot the details. For a Chinese piece, the colors were subtle and harmonious, with a turquoise background and the dragons highlighted in pastel hues of yellow, lavender, and blue. The end piece and mouthpiece were thick cylinders of ivory with a mellow patina, and the silver rings that held them to the stem were hammered with two versions of the symbol for longevity.

Hoorde claimed the pipe once belonged to a member of the imperial household, but whether it was a genuine imperial piece or not, my hands trembled slightly as I lifted the pipe from its display case, feeling the scaly bodies of the dragons against the palms of my hands. I held the ivory mouthpiece to my lips and drew gently—had an emperor of the Middle Kingdom once done the same? Perhaps the pipe had belonged to Cixi, the empress dowager, who issued edicts against opium smoking and affixed her seal to them with one hand while rolling pills with the other. It was possible that this smooth, ivory bung had once caressed her thin, mean lips. While lightly inhaling on the pipe, the taste of caramelized opium resins that had long ago coated its bisque interior curled over my tongue like wisps of smoke. I then held the saddle's socket close to my nose and drew in deeply its heady bouquet. The experience of handling all those rare pieces of paraphernalia would have been nothing short of orgasmic had I been able to smoke a few pipes beforehand, but even in my stone-sober state it was excruciatingly good.

Later that night, after Hoorde and I had finished preparing the exhibits, we returned to Amsterdam. He lived in a flat on a leafy street lined with rows of brick apartment buildings dating from the 1920s. Hoorde said that the neighborhood had once been wealthy and stylish, home to much of Amsterdam's Jewish community before the Nazis marched in and seized the properties for themselves. His flat was reached via such a steep, narrow stairway that I expected the interior to be similarly cramped. Instead it was roomy and had an engaging view of the street below, which bustled with bicycles and the occasional tram. Hoorde's wife and daughter were there to greet me, and there was food ready at the table, but Hoorde suggested that we smoke a few pipes before eating in order to prime our appetites.

The living room of Hoorde's apartment was a wide rectangle, at the back of which was a low platform about knee level in height—a perfect "bed" for smoking opium. The smoking area was spread with Japanese tatami mats and beyond it was a picture window looking out into the back garden and toward the back side of an identical apartment building. I joined Hoorde reclining on the mat but couldn't keep myself from repeatedly peering out the picture window behind us. From where I lay I could see into the lighted windows of neighbors' homes, and they no doubt could see us if they bothered to look. It felt wrong to be smoking opium in such a wide-open place.

Hoorde laughed at my paranoia. "This is Amsterdam," he said. "Nobody cares what you do in your own home here, so long as you're not hurting anybody."

After speaking to him in Dutch, Hoorde's wife and daughter excused themselves and went upstairs to bed. Hoorde explained that they had already eaten and had only been waiting for us to arrive from the museum. I was happy—at that moment I couldn't think of anything I wanted more than a few pipes of opium.

Because all of Hoorde's collection was at the exhibition, his layout consisted of only the bare necessities: a pipe, a small brass tray, and a rather plain opium lamp known to collectors as a "coolie lamp." This latter piece was a Vietnamese model and more decorative than its Chinese counterparts, but such lamps with their heavy base and thick glass chimneys were once a staple in working-class opium dens all over the Orient. If Hoorde's lamp was a utilitarian Volkswagen Beetle, his opium pipe was a classic Cadillac, longer and wider than any pipe I'd ever used. Its bamboo stem was luxuriously sheathed in sleek tortoiseshell, dappled like the spots on a jaguar, and trimmed in ivory.

Unfortunately, Hoorde's opium was inferior in quality to what I was used to. He said it was from Iran and it looked exactly like tar—its having been mixed with too much opium ash gave it a shiny black color. It dawned on me that this was probably why Hoorde had titled his exhibition *The Black Perfume*. An odd choice of words, given that his opium had that characteristic odor of dross, which Peter Lee accurately described in his book as smelling like cat piss.

Hoorde rolled himself a pipe and then prepared several for me. The high morphine content of the dross-adulterated opium immediately made itself apparent. I felt a numbing buzz creep up the back of my neck and over my scalp while at the same time a ticklish itch danced across my face. Opium always made me itch—an intense, prickly sensation that affected not only my face, but also a spot between my shoulder blades, and, most embarrassingly, my crotch. The end of one's nose is especially susceptible to this itching, and the urge to scratch it produced what used to be known as "the opium smoker's gesture"—a constant pulling at the nose and nostrils with the tips of the fingers. To the uninformed this looked like some compulsive tic, but people blissing on opium could spot one another in a crowd by noticing this distinctive gesticulation.

Yet even in opium's peculiar side effects I found pleasure: I closed my eyes and lightly raked my fingernails over my face. Yes, the itch was incessant—but to scratch it was divine. There is a painting by French artist Henri Viollet executed a century ago called *Le vice d'Asie: fumerie d'opium*. The scene is an opium den, probably in Indochina, but perhaps in France. The proprietress, a dark-robed Chinese, is the painting's centerpiece. Below her are four French visitors to the den, a woman and three men dressed in summertime whites. Aside from the rather dramatic pose of the proprietress, this painting strikes me as a rare illustration that was created from a real-life experience. After taking in the proprietress, the eye of the viewer tends to rest on the French woman to the right, her chin resting in an upturned palm and her glazed eyes gazing dreamily at something beyond our view. But it is the Frenchman at the far left who adds real authenticity to this scene. He sits alone, facing away from the others, staring down at his own lap and, lost in the deliciousness of the itch, uses both hands to scratch his face and scalp. To a nonsmoker this pose is all but incomprehensible, but to those who know opium intimately, the mere sight of this smoker brings a tingle of delight to the tip of the nose.

Le vice d'Asie: fumerie d'opium, a 1909 painting by Henri Viollet, is rare in that the imagery was taken from real life. Note the man at left scratching his face— itching is a common side effect of opium smoking. (Courtesy of Barbara Hodgson, *Opium: A Portrait of the Heavenly Demon,* Greystone Books, 1999)

After Hoorde and I both had six or seven pipes we ate din-ner, and then I exhaustedly climbed into the bed in Pearl's child-hood bedroom, a tiny cubbyhole of a space upstairs above the living room. The next day, friends of his arrived from all over Europe to be in town for the exhibition's opening, and visitors to his apartment came and went throughout the day. Most inter-esting of those I met was Maurice, a half French, half Lao whose ability to speak fluent Thai made me feel very much at home. Once things quieted down, Hoorde brought out his layout and invited Maurice to prepare some pipes, explaining that he had spent many hours in the opium dens of Vientiane and was an accomplished roller. That Maurice was an extraordinary "chef" made itself apparent within minutes. He began by cooking the opium using a technique that I had only read about in old accounts, something that Emily Hahn also described seeing in Shanghai in the 1930s:

> Heh-ven never stopped conversing, but his hands were busy and his eyes were fixed on what he was doing— knitting, I thought at first, wondering why nobody had ever mentioned that this craft was practiced by Chinese men. Then I saw that what I had taken for yarn between the two needles he manipulated was actually a kind of gummy stuff, dark and thick. As he rotated the needle ends about each other, the stuff behaved like taffy in the act of setting; it changed color, too, slowly evolving from its earlier dark brown to tan.

This method of preparing opium is also memorialized in an early twentieth-century American invitation to indulge: "Let's twist up a few," the flappers used to say. When I asked Maurice if the technique was difficult to master, he immediately handed me the needles. "Try it," he said in Thai, and then when I balked, he gave me one more demonstration. This "knitting" turned out to be one of those uncommon exercises that looks much more difficult to do than it really is. By my third try I had found my rhythm and was feeling confident enough to prepare a pipe for one of the other guests when Maurice excused himself to look for some tea.

The gentleman I was rolling for was a Colombian multimillionaire who lived in Switzerland. He was a collector not just of antique opium paraphernalia but that of other drugs as well. Like a kid showing off a favorite toy, he insisted that I examine a Victorian-era morphine syringe cradled in a velvet-lined leather etui that he just happened to have with him. Although merely looking at the wicked harpoon of a needle made me woozy, I could appreciate and relate to the fervor for his hobby that drove him to carry such a relic around on his person.

That evening, opening night for *Opium: Het zwarte parfum* at the Kunsthal Rotterdam, was only the third time in history that opium-smoking paraphernalia had been gathered and put on display as an art form. The first exhibition was in 1979 at the Stanford University Museum of Art. More recently Taiwan's National Museum of History had attempted an exhibition, titled *Centuries of Smoke Stains: The Art of Opium Utensils.* Sadly, this 2004 exhibition was liberally peppered with fakes, and although I didn't go see the show, viewing the photographs in the exhibition catalog I could tell that nearly half of the pipes illustrated were modern reproductions.

Of course, there had been many informal exhibitions of opium pipes and paraphernalia through the years. Historically, whenever authorities were about to destroy a number of opium pipes, the condemned items were put on public display days before the bonfire was lit. I have collected photographs of such pipe burns in China and America, and Roxanna remembered seeing one of these displays in wartime Saigon. In 1909, during the days leading up to the Shanghai Opium Conference, hundreds of opium pipes were laid out on display and then stacked like cordwood and burned for attending journalists to witness. Opium-pipe bonfires were held every few years in San Francisco until the 1920s. The most remarkable of these events happened in that city in 1914 when Mayor James Rolph, who was presiding over a pre-burn ceremony, noticed the artistry of some of the pipes about to be incinerated. Under the headline "A Twenty-Thousand-Dollar Pipeful," a local newspaper reported that the paraphernalia to be destroyed included "several hundred pipes, centuries old, beautifully carved, and ornamented with gold and jewels." In a rare move that could only have happened in San Francisco, the mayor decided then and there to save the most magnificent examples and decreed that they be donated to the city's Golden Gate Museum. Where are those opium pipes today? I wish I knew.

The Kunsthal Rotterdam effort was a fine one. The opening night drew collectors, dealers, and aficionados from as far away as San Francisco and, of course, Bangkok. Among the crowd of attendees I was finally able to put faces on names, and in some cases, to put names on eBay handles.

As prone to cloak-and-daggery as collectors can be behind one another's backs, they can be quite charming in person. I was surprised and delighted by how many people at the exhibition seemed to know of me. I found myself being approached by visitors with questions about the displays and asked to pose for group photos with other collectors. Many knew that my book was out, and some asked how they might obtain a copy. Everyone I talked to was in perfect awe of the exhibition and happy they had made the trip to see the once-in-a-lifetime event. Only one person seemed not to enjoy himself—a French collector who was seen glaring at the treasures in disbelief and muttering curses under his breath.

But for Hoorde, the night was not without its complications. During the previous day he had told me that a third of the items on display belonged to an old friend of his, another Dutchman named Cees Hogendoorn, who was confined to some sort of institution. Hogendoorn had self-published an unusual book, whose cover claimed it was a "supplement" to Hoorde's catalog and, much to Hoorde's chagrin, Hogendoorn managed to get his book on the shelves of the Kunsthal Rotterdam bookshop. The book was oddly named *Opium: The Art of Lost Collections,* and between photos of the author's opium antiques was the story of how he had come to be institutionalized. Hoorde told

Confiscated opium paraphernalia, including hundreds of pipes, are publicly burned in San Francisco in 1914. Though this was common practice during official campaigns to combat opium use, this particular pipe burn is notable because San Francisco's mayor saved the most opulent pipes from incineration and had them donated to the city's Golden Gate Museum. (From the author's collection)

me about how his old friend had agreed to lend his collection for the exhibition but then later became convinced that Hoorde would keep the best pieces for himself. Was Hogendoorn really justified in thinking that his collection was "lost," or was this an example of the collecting impulse taken to its furthest extreme— a descent into madness?

After having dinner at a restaurant with Hoorde, his family, friends, and the museum staff to celebrate opening night, I accompanied Hoorde and his family back to their apartment where all of us—except Hoorde's wife—had a smoke. Later Hoorde explained to me that his wife did not approve of his opium smoking, but that he and his daughter often smoked together. "I'm afraid Pearl likes it a little too much," he said.

I had taken an immediate liking to Pearl. She was one of those young people—in her mid-twenties at the time—whose maturity allows them to mix naturally with adults twice their age. I sat next to her during the opening night dinner, and my conversations with her didn't make me feel old—as encounters with young people sometimes can—but instead her infectious enthusiasm made me feel half my age. Pearl had tried to talk me into accompanying her to one of Holland's famous "coffee shops" to sample the marijuana, hashish, and mushrooms. It would have been fun with Pearl as a guide, but I begged off. Experiencing the sights and sounds of Europe for the first time was exciting enough. There was no need for hallucinations when I wasn't yet bored with reality. Besides, I was convinced that nothing was better than opium.

I was also beginning to acquire a taste for Hoorde's drossy concoction. The high-morphine content gave me a buzz that I remembered from smoking at the opium dens in Laos. It was a feeling I thought I would never go back to after experiencing the sophisticated bliss produced by Willi's fabulous *chandu,* but by day three in Holland I found myself craving that numbing buzz. Dross has a bad reputation that stretches way back. There are nineteenth-century paintings on rice paper done by forgotten Chinese artists that depict wretched dross smokers begging for handfuls of the potent opium ash to sustain their habits. In old China, smoking dross was the end of the line—a smoker's declaration of abject poverty and failure.

In old American and Canadian accounts, dross was known as "yen shee," a loanword from Cantonese. When opium was cheap and plentiful, yen shee was used in North America as it was in China—as a way of cutting pure opium to make it last longer and give it a kick. Later, when opium in America became scarce as a result of the enforcement of anti-opium laws, the much cheaper dross was smuggled in from China as an alternative. Opium ash by itself was difficult to smoke—rolling it into a pill shape was not always possible—but dross could also be mixed with coconut oil and made into pellets that were taken orally. If mixed with sherry or port wine, yen shee became "yen shee suey"—a colorful example of an American-coined pidgin Cantonese term. However, like the drinking of laudanum, the oral consumption of any dross concoction was considered by opium smokers to be a barbaric, last-resort substitute for smoking. Dross was said to be extremely hard on the liver as well as to cause a number of uncomfortable physical side effects, such as chronic constipation. This leads us to yet another piece of vintage slang: the dreaded "yen shee baby." This was when weeks of constipation brought on by the smoking or eating of dross culminated in a large and painful bowel movement that one imagines was accompanied by teary eyes and much cursing.

Despite knowing the history of dross, I wasn't too worried about smoking Armand Hoorde's dross-heavy opium. I saw my all-expenses-paid trip to Europe as a grand holiday—something I might never in my life be able to do again. Why spoil the fun by putting limits on my opium intake? I could always cut back when I got home to Bangkok.

The day after the exhibition opening, Hoorde declared that he was ready to take a road trip to Paris. Hoorde, Pearl, and I climbed into a black SUV and drove south through Belgium, bringing along Hoorde's basic layout, including the ivory and tortoiseshell pipe, and a quantity of opium. He explained that France was in no way as lax toward drugs as the Netherlands, and that it was not unusual for vehicles coming from Holland to be searched at the French border. Was he joking? That was enough to sour me on the idea of a cross-border trip. Hoorde claimed that he'd done such a journey before and that we didn't have to worry because we didn't fit the drug-smuggler profile. If this observation was meant to be a calmative, he quickly reversed it by launching into a story about how he had narrowly avoided being searched at a police roadblock in Paris by acting like a lost tourist.

Because I naturally tend to fall asleep when I'm worried, this information had the effect of knocking me out. When I woke up we were at a rest stop in northern France. Relieved, I asked Hoorde how the border crossing went. He laughed: "Both you and Pearl were sleeping like angels when we passed through the border. The police were there stopping cars today but they were busy searching a carload of Muslims when we came along and they let us drive right through."

I wasn't sure if Hoorde was pulling my leg or not, but if it had really been a close call, I didn't want to know. Suddenly I had a strong urge for a pipe, and I laughingly admitted this to Hoorde. "Oh, don't worry. We will have a session as soon as we check in to the hotel. It won't be long now!"

On the expressway into central Paris, Pearl spotted the Eiffel Tower in the distance and pointed it out to me. "Seen it," I quipped. I had meant to sound cheekily dismissive, but the tone was lost on them. Then, remembering how Hoorde had felt obligated to drag me to a handful of less-than-fascinating tourist sites in Holland, I thought I'd better make clear my complete lack of desire to see the famous cultural landmarks of Paris. No Champs-Élysées or Arc de Triomphe for me; no cathedrals or monuments or museums. A view of the Eiffel Tower from the expressway was more than enough. What I wanted to see were the antiques shops. I wanted to see opium accoutrements that had been carried to France on steamships; pipes that had been slowly seasoned in the sleepy ports of French Indochina; lamps that had last been lit when Brassaï was posing prostitutes around them.

Hoorde agreed. He said that he needed to make some calls after we arrived but promised we would visit all the relevant antiques merchants. "All you have to do is help me out. I have a small favor to ask of you. Just let me confirm things first and then I will fill you in. If everything works out we will be spending many hours at the biggest Asian antiques store in all of France."

By late afternoon we had checked into Delhy's Hotel, a small inn hidden down a flight of stairs in an alley off La Place Saint-Michel. Hoorde said he always stayed at this one-star place because it was quiet, cheap, and comfortable. We all shared a room on an upper floor overlooking the alleyway. Before I had even removed my coat, Hoorde and I were scouting the room for a convenient place to recline. The small room was crowded with two beds, so there wasn't enough space on the floor to smoke. We next tried the beds themselves, but these were too soft. Because we had only a small lamp tray and lacked a wide layout tray, any movement might cause the top-heavy opium lamp with its tall glass chimney to tip over and possibly spill oil on the bedclothes. Finally, we hit upon the idea of using a large coffee-table book as a foundation for the lamp tray.

It worked. As the light outside began to wane, we pulled the curtains across the windows to ensure that nobody from the building opposite could observe our smoking session. To record the moment, Pearl stood on the bed and took photographs from above, one of which I am looking at as I write this. While Hoorde takes a draw on the tortoiseshell pipe, I stare into the glowing lamp, hypnotized.

Later that night we took a walk along the Seine, crossing a bridge to the Île de la Cité. While descending a urine-reeking staircase we were approached by a spike-haired Arab youth who offered to sell us heroin. Instantly, Hoorde and I burst into loud guffaws, causing the drug dealer to step back and look about suspiciously before hurrying away. If only he could have seen that our eyes shone with a sharp twinkle, that rare, pupil-less glimmer that only a century ago would have been instantly recognized in Paris as the mark of an opium smoker.

We strolled along the edge of the island, past young people strumming guitars and drinking in cross-legged circles. There was nothing menacing about the scene, and had I been tipsy with drink I might have been tempted to linger and enjoy their high spirits, but the easy bond that ties opium smokers to one another does not extend to nonsmokers, no matter how sympathetic. We walked by them as we might have strolled under a tree full of songbirds—charmed by the serenade but aware that attempting to interact with such a distant species would likely disappoint. Back at the inn we lit the lamp and smoked until the wee hours. I imagined that the grateful ghost of Jean Cocteau discovered us by following tendrils of fragrance that slipped out the window and wafted over rooftops. Hovering above our session in that little hotel room, he thanked us for bringing the pleasures of opium back to the city once known for its decadent dens in Montmartre.

In a 1910 book about drug use called *La drogue: fumeurs et mangeurs d'opium,* by Dr. Richard Millant, is a photograph of an opium smoker in a Montmartre den. This wonderful photo is perhaps the best surviving image of a lavish opium-smoking establishment in France. Captioned "Un coin de fumerie Mont-martroise," it depicts a young man, looking slightly effeminate in a full-length robe and with his hair parted down the middle in the style of the 1910s, reclining on a plush couch. A Japanese screen lends privacy as he tends his ample layout, which sits on a coffee table before him. Like the Manhattan opium den described by *The New York Times,* the room is a mélange of Asia, an Orientalist's fantasy of the East; not an accurate depiction but an idealized version—which is exactly how opium smokers prefer to view life anyway. The face of this mystery smoker is like a mask—ageless, unlined, serene. It is clear that he is savoring every moment of his vice.

I had seen photographs of Jean Cocteau and knew that he did not look like this smoker in the old book, but when I imagined Cocteau smoking, this was how I saw him: pre-cure and contentedly preparing pipes, reclining on a couch in some Parisian den so willfully outlandish that it could be mistaken for the lobby of Grauman's Chinese Theatre. On that night at Delhy's Hotel, I was certain Cocteau's ghost was hanging like an imp somewhere above and watching—perhaps gazing down at us from the same vantage point that Pearl had captured in the photograph.

There is another photo of me taken by Pearl during that session, and in that one I am smiling. Anyone who happened across this photo without knowing the circumstances would assume the subject was a grinning drunk lying on a rumpled bed. But it was at this exact instant that I realized why Cocteau's cure hadn't taken. As Pearl snapped the shutter I was celebrating Cocteau's weakness. Of course he had gone back to the pipe. Was there something so wrong about being hooked? Wouldn't it simply mean feeling like this all the time?

I toasted Jean Cocteau with a last pipe and then, stunned by the dross, I drifted into a dreamless sleep.

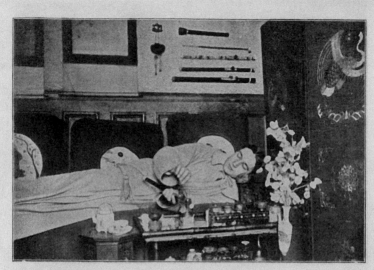

UN COIN DE FUMERIE MONTMARTROISE

A photograph of an opium smoker in a den in Paris from the book *La drogue: fumeurs et mangeurs d'opium* by Dr. Richard Millant, published by René Roger, Paris, 1910. (From the collection of Aymon de Lestrange)

Adam Kahn was the godfather of opium antiques in Paris. We found him at his shop, after a long walk along the Left Bank that would have seemed much longer had it been anyplace else. Kahn was dressed in a suit and tie, and I later heard that he was a Holocaust survivor and wore a fresh boutonniere each day as a way of giving thanks for having survived the Nazi death camps. To me he looked presidential, less a merchant than a patient head of state who just happened to be sitting in a room full of opium pipes. Hoorde had brought along a copy of his exhibition catalog, and he and Kahn leafed through it while I browsed the shop. Kahn had generously allowed me to take photographs, and I was trying to contain my excitement and control my shaking

hands so I wouldn't have to use a flash in a shop that surely toler-
ated very few cameras.

Spotting a rosewood and silver travel kit on a shelf, I spent
much time trying to get a sharp shot of the intricate repoussé
and chased work that some nameless Vietnamese artisan had
hammered into the kit's silver components. This was the sort of
thing I had wanted to see up close, the opium relics brought
from Indochina by expatriate French returning home. I am convinced there are more opium antiques in the basements and attics of France than anywhere else in Europe. But the French
value their antiques, so when these items appear in shops, prices
are always very high. I was lucky Monsieur Kahn allowed me to
take photos—there would be no souvenirs for me from his shop.

After visiting more shops in the same neighborhood, Hoorde
and I went back to the hotel to prepare for that evening's activities. Earlier he had given me the details of the favor he wanted
to ask me. The "biggest Asian antiques store in all of France" that
Hoorde had mentioned the day before was owned by a couple
who were dear friends of his and who had supplied him with
many opium artifacts over the years. They were also renowned
for procuring antiques for some of the most discerning patrons
of Asian art in Paris. The dealer couple had asked Hoorde if it
would be possible to arrange a demonstration of old-time opium
smoking for some of their most favored clients. Hoorde had
agreed—this was why the bare-bones layout had been brought
along to Paris. But the dealer couple wanted to ensure that their
special guests were greatly impressed. The demonstration had to
be the event of the year—and something that would be whispered about for years to come.

Hoorde asked me if I would be comfortable preparing pipes
before a live audience. I couldn't think of any reason why not—
as long as I was allowed to smoke some of the pipes I was pre-

paring. Hoorde thought we might need one more alternate roller, and asked Maurice, the half-Lao gentleman I had met in Amsterdam, if he, too, could participate. Then Hoorde set about borrowing from a local collector the pieces of paraphernalia that were needed to make two complete layouts.

That afternoon, Hoorde and I drove to the outskirts of Paris for the demonstration. The antiques store was a big, concrete-block box located in a strip mall—not the kind of place one pictures finding in Paris. In fact, the surrounding area could have been mistaken for suburban San Diego. Fortunately, things got better once we entered the building. Inside the cavernous store was a wooden "tea house"—a one-room structure that Hoorde claimed had been shipped from China piece by piece and then reassembled within the store. Here the dealer couple served tea to their clients while discussing the merits of items that were brought in from the larger store "outside." From inside the tea house it was possible to forget what lay beyond it, especially after the sun went down and the dwindling ambient light through the larger glass-fronted building allowed the store to darken. Before this could happen, however, I had a chance to look over the offerings in the store's jam-packed display cases.

I had already told myself not to expect any bargains in Paris, but within minutes of browsing the displays I spotted a small, conch-shaped pipe bowl. The conch shell is a Buddhist symbol, and although opium paraphernalia is rife with Buddhist symbolism, I could recall seeing no more than three or four such pipe bowls in several years of collecting. I stood there and debated whether to ask the price. The cups of oolong tea they were serving cost more than what I usually spent on a week's worth of meals in Bangkok.

I finally got up the nerve to ask and was pleasantly surprised to learn that the bowl was fairly priced at only 190 euros. I paid for the bowl and then showed it to Hoorde, who had been pre-occupied and hadn't seen the transaction. I did this with some dread because, despite Hoorde's usual joviality, I had gathered that he could be ruthless and unstoppable when there was some-thing he wanted—not to mention the fact that I was traveling on his dime. But I had to show him; it seemed wrong to hide it from him. Upon seeing the bowl his eyes bulged, his nostrils flared, and his face flushed in that way collectors' faces do when they've lost out on something. I quickly offered him the bowl as a gift—and was relieved when his face relaxed into a smile. In the end, he let me keep it.

It was nearing 10 P.M. by the time all the guests had arrived. The dealer couple locked the doors and all the lights were put out, except for two or three dim ones within the tea room. The spectators were mostly older couples, dressed to the nines, which I thought was appropriate: Opium smoking is such a rare ritual that it should be a black-tie affair. The guests occupied three sets of tables and chairs carved from rosewood. Tea was served, and then Hoorde said a few words to them in French before he, Maurice, and I took our places upon bamboo mats that had been spread out on the floor. The layout trays were perfectly ar-ranged, the opium lamps were lit, and soon the unforgettable smell of opium permeated the room as pills were carefully toasted.

As soon as we began smoking, the room became hushed as if some delicate piece of surgery was being performed in an oper-ating theater. It was so quiet that I was sure the spectators could hear the soothing burble of the pipes as vapors were inhaled through ceramic bowls. Hoorde rolled three pipes for himself and then six for me before rolling for himself again. Now and then a whispered comment came from the direction of the ta-bles, but if not for that and the occasional knock of porcelain

against rosewood, I might have forgotten that our every movement was being keenly ogled. The opium had its effect on me
and I grinned at the curiousness of the circumstances. The reaction of the spectators was similar to what I had seen at sex shows
in Bangkok, when set demonstrations of sexual positions (some
of them quite acrobatic) invariably caused observers to go silent
with astonishment.

After my tenth pipe or so, I decided to try to break the ice by
approaching one of the tables. Hoorde urged me on. "Go see if
you can interest any of them in trying a pipe."

I got up slowly and stood still for a moment to keep from
getting dizzy. Hoorde's opium was strong, and it would cause
Vientiane-style moonwalking if I wasn't deliberate in my actions. As I stood there, I saw that everyone was watching me. I
walked to one of the tables and, pulling out a vacant chair, slowly
lowered myself into it. To my right sat a thin, elderly man, perhaps in his seventies, who was nattily dressed in a billowy white
shirt. He stared straight into my eyes, and in his face I saw intense curiosity mixed with apprehension. It was the sort of look
you might see in the eyes of someone who had come across a
dazed space alien near the site of a recently crashed flying saucer.
Partly out of amusement and partly because I'd lived in Thailand
so long that it came naturally, I smiled back. His eyes widened
with alarm and he immediately looked away from me.

A small porcelain teapot and cup were placed in front of me
by one-half of the dealer couple, and she began translating for
her guests as she put questions to me about how I felt. At first
they looked at me as though I were a talking head in a crystal
ball. I found myself suppressing laughter and the temptation to
play games with them.

Instead, I answered their queries about dreams and hallucinations and even one question about heightened sex drive. They

listened intently and, after I felt they had relaxed a bit, I invited the most inquisitive one, a woman in early middle age who had asked about opium's reputation as an aphrodisiac, to try a pipe. She smiled at the old gentleman next to me as though challenging him to forbid her and then answered me in English, "Yes, I try."

Her efforts were watched with great interest by the spectators, who were now away from their tables and standing at the edge of the mat. Only the old gentleman remained seated. Maurice rolled for the woman and coached her on inhalation technique, and on her second try she got the pill to vaporize. After her third pipe another of the guests took her place, and then another. Finally, even the old gentleman lowered himself onto the mat and held the mouthpiece daintily between slender fingers. After he had successfully exhaled the vapors of his first pipe, the others politely applauded. The atmosphere of the tea house became casually genial, like a reunion of old friends, and we all smoked together until nearly three in the morning.

Gone were the old romantic notions of wild drug orgies and heavily flavored dreams, but I didn't regret them, because the truth was much better.

—Emily Hahn, "The Big Smoke," *The New Yorker,* February 15, 1969

I arrived back in Bangkok flush with excitement, having made valuable contacts with collectors and antiques dealers and even managing to bring home a piece for my collection. My arrival was on a Monday in May, and I knew the Southeast Asian Ceramics Museum was closed on Mondays, but it was the middle of Bangkok's torrid hot season and Roxanna usually went to the museum even on her day off just to escape the heat. I called her as soon as I walked out the airport doors and toward the taxi queue.

Roxanna's cheery hello was just what I was hoping to hear—it emboldened me to invite myself over under the pretext that I could tell her about my trip. In truth I was craving a pipe after the long flight from Amsterdam. The feeling was not unpleasant. It was excitement for something I was looking forward to, like the giddy anticipation one feels at the prospect of a hearty meal after a day of going without food. Roxanna said she would call her driver and arrange to leave the university and go home immediately. I was traveling with a single bag but would have gladly lugged two or three suitcases over that narrow causeway to Roxanna's house if there was going to be a pipe waiting for me. I got into a cab and told the taxi driver where I needed to go.

Back on the old floorboards, my pores open and oozing sweat for the first time in ten days, the whole whirlwind of a trip felt like a dream from the night before. Roxanna listened to my stories and was wowed. "You took an opium tour of Europe!" she laughed. "I'm jealous!"

But there was a problem. Over the course of half an hour, Roxanna rolled ten pipes for me and I eagerly smoked them, but they had no effect on me. I explained to her that Hoorde's opium had been very drossy and that, having smoked the morphine-laden stuff constantly while in Europe, I probably needed more of her subtle *chandu* than usual to feel anything. I also told her that I hoped she wouldn't get tired of my company, because I would need a daily session for a week or so in order to taper off my usage. Then my heart sank when Roxanna told me that she had to leave town and would be gone for a week.

"A whole week?!" I exclaimed. "What am I going to do?"

The idea of not smoking opium for a week seemed tragic. It wasn't that I feared withdrawal. In Europe I had noticed hay fever–like symptoms and mild headaches a couple of times when Hoorde was slow to offer me a pipe. Not that I couldn't manage it, of course—it was just that going a week without opium would be like enduring a week with a head cold. As my mind skittered about for a solution, I remembered that I could roll proficiently and there was no reason why I couldn't smoke alone. "What if I were to buy a week's worth of *chandu* from you?" I asked Roxanna.

"Sure. Why not? How much will you need?"

Taking a break from smoking, I counted out drops into a spare medicine bottle that Roxanna had on hand. The amount was supposed to be enough for twenty pipes a day, which would be much more than I needed since my plan was to smoke just enough *chandu* to comfortably wean myself off Hoorde's dross. I twisted the dropper cap tightly onto the little brown bottle and then zipped it in my overnight bag with my razor, toothbrush, and deodorant. Even in the totally unlikely chance that I was stopped and searched, no policeman would ever guess what that little bottle contained. If questioned, I could always say the iodine-colored liquid was some traditional herbal remedy— perfectly plausible since they were very popular in Thailand and often came in unmarked packaging. I had no doubt that I would be believed if somehow I had to resort to this story.

I didn't have the money with me to pay Roxanna for the *chandu,* but she waved this information away as though she were trying to dispel a bad smell. "Oh, come on. Just pay me when you can."

Back at my apartment, I took the bottle out of my bag and put it in the refrigerator. I left the rest of the bag unpacked and, after having a hot shower, climbed into bed. Among other things, opium is the perfect cure for jet lag. I spent a wonderful night reliving my journey to Holland and France and, while I didn't get much real sleep, I got up the next morning feeling refreshed.

I had a week's worth of email to catch up on as well as some light work—a synopsis for a guidebook to Cambodia that I had been asked to update—which took me most of the day to finish. By late afternoon there was a nagging angst in my stomach. I thought of the bottle of *chandu* that I'd left in the fridge after coming home from Roxanna's the night before. Hours in the chilled air would have made the liquid thick and rich. In my mind's eye I could see the *chandu* slowly dripping from the drop- per into the little wok . . . and then it struck me that my wok for evaporating *chandu* was packed away in a box somewhere. I was also lacking a working pipe—all were with Willi or Roxanna. The antique paraphernalia at my apartment hadn't been used for many decades at the very least; pieces would need hours of modification before I could smoke.

This realization set me to thinking. Until now I had never even contemplated smoking in my apartment. By keeping opium at a safe distance I had been able to rationalize my smoking in the name of research—and the infrequency of my smoking was an important part of that rationalization. How could I justify smoking in the name of research if my behavior was no different from that of a common addict? I sat and stared at my computer screen until it went black. The screen saver suddenly launched a parade of images that glided to and fro. They were photos of some of my most prized pipes and lamps. A splendid little idea came into my head, causing me to smile and nod.

I set about gathering paraphernalia to form a layout—one that would be very different from the previous two working layouts I had put together. The one at Willi's had taken years to assemble and was a work in progress, like the Chamber itself. It was meant to electrify emotions and evoke feelings of time travel back to a more elegant era. There was no way to outdo the Chamber layout in terms of opulence or the harmonious nature of its matching paraphernalia. Conversely, the one I had put together for Roxanna was durable and had a reliable functionality that was necessary for somebody who was going to smoke daily for years. Of course, when building both layouts I had kept the rarest pieces to myself. I would not, for example, have thought to use my pipe with the sugarcane stem because there were very few such pipes in existence.

But if only *I* would be smoking from the pipe—and for only one week—there was little worry about anything getting damaged. I knew how fragile my accoutrements were and how best to handle them. With this in mind, I decided that my personal layout should be a platform for experimentation that allowed me to do things I'd never done before. I had a full week to try out pieces that were too fragile to travel, and because my collection was all there in my apartment, I could dig out whatever I needed to put any theory to the test. When questions or ideas had come up at Willi's or Roxanna's, I sometimes didn't bother to jot them down and then forgot them altogether, my train of thought severed by conversation. Alone in my apartment I would have a notebook and pen at my side at all times. I would turn the exercise of reducing my opium intake into a windfall of knowledge.

By 10 P.M. I was on the mat. It was a Cambodian woven-cane affair, about ten by twelve feet, that I had long ago carried back from a trip to southern Laos. The mat had been rolled up and propped in a corner for years and would not lie perfectly flat on my living room's wooden parquet floor, but that was not a worry. I placed a large rectangular rosewood tray inlaid with mother-of-pearl in the center of the mat. This would be my layout tray. I then spent nearly an hour selecting and symmetrically arranging various boxes, tools, a lamp, and two smaller metal trays upon the larger tray. The mother-of-pearl patterns on the layout tray were mostly floral but punctuated with birds and butterflies. There were also depictions of four vases filled with bouquets of four types of flowers, which in Chinese culture represented the four seasons (winter—plum blossom; spring—peony; summer—lotus; fall—chrysanthemum).

Besides the depictions of flowers and insects, bits of opalescent nacre had been painstakingly cut into straight pieces as thin as kite string and buried into the rosewood. These lines divided the layout tray into sections—and were meant to be used as a diagram for whoever was setting up the tray. Using these patterns to guide me, I looked for accoutrements sized to perfectly fit within the mother-of-pearl delineations. The most obvious of these was a rectangle in the very center of the layout tray that marked a space for the lamp tray. Once I had finished arranging, the paraphernalia neatly conformed to the pearly schematic, allowing the flowery symbolism to show through.

Taking an idea from the Chamber, I brought from my bedroom a vintage gooseneck desk lamp and placed it on the mat at one end of the layout tray so the light would shine straight down on the accoutrements. On top of the mat where I would lie, I spread out a Burmese sarong of metallic green silk. I then folded a smaller length of silk into a square to use as a cushion atop the block-like porcelain pillow. As I am right-handed, I would lie on my left side facing the tray. Behind me were a bottle of mineral water, my notebook and pen, and, of course, the opium smoker's scepter: a back scratcher. When everything was in place I lit the lamp.

Smoking opium alone was something I'd never done before. Sure, there were times when Roxanna catnapped while I was learning to roll, but other than that, smoking had always been a social event for me. Being alone with my thoughts was something I did after the session had concluded.

In his 1882 book, *Opium-Smoking in America and China,* H. H. Kane, who spent years interviewing opium smokers in New York City, stated, "I have never seen a smoker who found pleasure in using the drug at home and alone, no matter how complete his outfit, or how excellent his opium." But Kane never met Jean Cocteau, who was born seven years after Kane's book was published, and who said, "Smoking *à deux* is already crowded. Smoking *à trois* is difficult. Smoking *à quatre* is impossible."

On that first night I found I was somewhere between these two opinions. Smoking fine *chandu* made me animated and chatty—as it did everyone I had ever smoked with. But smoking alone turned out not to be such a solitary activity after all. In the same way that I'd noticed I could vividly recall entire conversations immediately after sessions—while lying alone in bed—I was delighted to learn that I could also effortlessly imagine conversations while I was rolling. I first noticed this while concentrating on preparing a pipe. I imagined Roxanna making one of her usual remarks about the way I was letting the *chandu* evaporate without stirring: "Stir it or it's going to burn."

This should not be mistaken for "hearing voices." There was no sensation of an audible noise—Roxanna's remark was clearly in my mind. It was just that opium seemed to sharpen my imagination, for music as well as voices. I'm one of those people who often have songs playing in their heads—sometimes the same song for days on end. I don't hear the song constantly; it comes and goes until some other tune takes its place. While smoking in a silent room I soon noticed that opium amplified these songs, making them crystal clear and impossible to ignore—now and then to the point that I had to turn on my stereo or get online and listen to some other piece of music, just to "change" the song playing in my head.

Of course, I'm no expert on the subject. Perhaps this is all nonsense and these non-aural songs and conversations were caused by some wrinkle on my brain. I don't know. But my solo opium-smoking sessions were enjoyable from the start and, if some lonely people drink alcohol for the company it gives them, I can say that smoking opium alone also afforded me an imagined companionship that in time I would find preferable to the company of real people.

I was adamant that my plan to smoke just enough opium to taper off from the dross habit I'd formed in Europe go as scheduled. I was strict with myself, keeping a record in my notebook of how many pipes I smoked. That first night I smoked fourteen pipes and then promised myself that each subsequent night I would reduce the dosage by two. Every pill that I rolled would be made with no more than seven drops of *chandu,* ensuring that they would be about equal in size. I did not rush to finish the session but instead drew it out over nearly three hours. Between preparing pipes and smoking I passed the time examining a group of tools and accoutrements that I had lined up on the mat around the layout tray.

The largest of these items was a porcelain stand for pipe bowls, about eight inches high and shaped like a miniature chest of drawers. Two levels of horizontal surfaces were pierced with a total of five holes, each about the size of a quarter. Upon these holes rested clean pipe bowls sitting at the ready in case I needed to replace a dirty, dross-filled bowl with an empty one. The mystery of this whimsical little piece of opium furniture was a sixth hole, twice the size of the other five and positioned on a vertical surface, front and center on the piece. If this were really a miniature chest of drawers, this mystery hole was situated where a round mirror should have gone, but there was no mirror, just a hole and an empty, boxlike space in the porcelain behind it. A small, rectangular porcelain lid capped the space behind the round hole. The bowl stand was not unique. I had seen several others in various collections—although most bowl stands of this type were missing the aforementioned lid. What was this vertically positioned hole for? What purpose did it serve? The question had long bedeviled me.

Other collectors were convinced that the round hole had once framed the face of a clock, and that the space behind it would house the clock's workings. It was an interesting idea, but on close examination of the bowl stand it just didn't make sense.

The space was too small even for an old-fashioned pocket watch
to fit into it. Some collectors had pointed out that clocks were
status symbols in old China, reflecting the modernity of their
owners, and this was true. It was also true that a clock was handy
to have while smoking, especially since opium could make time
seem to slow down or speed up, depending on how much experience one had with the drug. Yet I was still unconvinced by the
clock theory.

I owned four examples of this type of bowl stand, and so I
placed one of the little porcelain mysteries at the foot of my
layout tray. I then put pipe bowls on four of its five horizontal
holes. The bowls I chose for this were some of my most colorful,
and that first night I spent an hour gazing admiringly at this
wonderfully incongruous piece of drug paraphernalia—an almost kitschy creation that could have been mistaken for Grand-
ma's vintage toothbrush holder—but which in fact was crafted
to make an opium smoker's messy vice more convenient and
orderly.

The following night I began my session at the same time as
the first. The tray was still arranged; I had simply slid it under my
coffee table, put the bottle of *chandu* back in the fridge, and
rolled up the cane mat. Once the session was well under way and
I had smoked six pipes, I began once again to contemplate the
porcelain bowl stand. Its odd configuration seemed as mysterious as ever.

Then, after my twelfth and last pipe of the night, I pushed the
porcelain pillow aside and rested my head on the folded bolt of
silk. Instead of going to bed, I decided to simply turn off the
electric lamp and allow the oil-fed flame of the opium lamp to
burn itself out, my slumber bathed in its diminishing glow. Lying
supine, my whole body was relaxed and drifting like a raft on a
placid sea, when suddenly an idea hit me with such force that it

seemed to light up the room. It was nothing short of a revelation, and I knew instantly that I had solved the mystery. I sat up
and turned the electric lamp back on and went into my bedroom to look for a white cotton T-shirt. When I found one that
I didn't care about, I used the lamp-wick scissors to cut the shirt
into gee-rags—the small, doughnut-shaped cloth gaskets that
when moistened form an airtight seal between the pipe bowl
and the metal fitting on the pipe stem known as the saddle.

My mind was sharp and clear, and I sat on the mat working
at my task until I had cut a handful of gee-rags, making a small
pile of the curling cloth gaskets. Then I lifted the little lid from
the porcelain bowl stand and stuffed the gee-rags into the space
behind the vertical hole. The natural clinginess of the cotton
kept the gee-rags bunched together and not a single one fell
from the hole. Then, using two fingers, I reached into the vertical hole and pinched a gee-rag. When I pulled, it came out as
easily and neatly as a tissue being plucked from a box of Kleenex.
This made perfect sense! What would a smoker most likely need
when changing from a dirty bowl to a clean one? Not a damned
clock—but a fresh gee-rag, of course! I was so elated by my discovery that I hopped up from the mat and strutted around the
room with my arms raised high.

To the layman my little discovery may sound like the height
of useless arcana, but opium paraphernalia is full of these diminutive mysteries, bits of knowledge buried and forgotten like
so many pieces of driftwood beneath the surface of a sandy
beach—and each small mystery solved brought me that much
closer to being *the* expert on my favorite subject.

My experience that second night was repeated twice more
during my week of smoking alone. It felt as though the opium
itself was giving me insight, guiding me and illuminating my
path as I diligently worked to unlock its secrets.

A nineteenth-century porcelain stand for the storage and display of opium pipe bowls. The compartment behind the circular opening is for clean gee-rags, cloth gaskets that were used to make an airtight seal when a pipe bowl was attached to the opium pipe's stem. (Photograph by Yves Domzalski)

It wasn't until later that I remembered reading about the so-called hop-head hunch—uncanny powers of the mind attributed to opium smokers in American underworld lore. The phenomenon was recorded by Jack Boyle in an anonymously written essay in *The American Magazine* in June 1914. While relating his story of being an opium-addicted criminal in turn-of-the-century San Francisco, Boyle told of his own experiences with opium-induced revelations: "In the underworld there is a species of foresight termed 'hop-head hunches.' They are regarded with superstitious awe the country over."

In Jack Black's memoir of crime and opium smoking in western America and Canada of the same period, he, too, experienced a similar revelation when the solution for cracking a problematic safe came to him while smoking opium.

So, you ask: Was the hop-head hunch a bunch of hopped-up hooey?

"The Eureka Hunt," an article in the July 28, 2008, issue of *The New Yorker*, asked a question with its subtitle: "Why do good ideas come when they do?" The story explained how relaxation, not concentration, is what allows the brain to have sudden bursts of creative insight—the same reason that solutions to problems seem to come to us while we are taking hot showers or during the minutes just before drifting off to sleep. Opium seemed to bring on these "eureka moments" with an amazing frequency.

Although my opium-induced revelations were the highlight of my week of weaning, I was also glad to learn how easy it was to get off the dross. After just over a week of smoking an ever-decreasing dosage of Roxanna's opium, I "fasted" for five days to see if I could handle the withdrawal. Days three and four were uncomfortable—it felt as if I had a nasty cold—but by day five I was on the mend. I called Roxanna and made arrangements for a visit the following weekend, and for the next two months my smoking was limited to weekends.

Since turning forty, birthdays were something I did my best to ignore, but in mid-July 2007 I used the occasion of my forty-fifth birthday as a reason to bring home another quantity of *chandu*. Roxanna protested mildly when I told her my plan to spend my birthday smoking alone, but she, too, had been impressed by the little discoveries I'd made during my week of solitary research. She consented to sell me some, and so I measured out half a bottle drop by drop in front of her, counting in advance the hours and days that I would spend riding my magic carpet high above Chinatown.

Money was no longer a problem. By this time I had found a
novice collector in Las Vegas whose hunger for antique paraphernalia was matched by his wealth. The collector was looking
for tools to make two complete layouts and was willing to pay
hundreds of dollars for each piece. Roxanna allowed me to use
her PayPal account to receive the payments, so the cash went
directly to her. In the past I had been adamantly against selling
anything from my collection, but I came to realize that I owned
plenty of duplicate tools because I was in the habit of buying
items even if I didn't need them—as long as the price was right.
Now this strategy was paying off. I was able to sell for $200–
$500 pieces that had originally cost me $20–$50. I now had
more than enough money to pay Roxanna for her opium. I put
the half-full dropper bottle in a small paper bag with the logo of
a local hospital and took the subway home, buzzing with the
feeling that I was about to take a long-awaited vacation to some
wonderful and exotic locale.

My move to Bangkok's Chinatown predated my interest in collecting antique opium-smoking paraphernalia by a couple of
years. Once I started collecting, I began asking antiques merchants if they knew where Bangkok's old opium quarter had
been located. None that I talked to seemed to know. "Chinatown," they said vaguely, forcing a smile to indicate that was all
they knew.

One day I stumbled across an old-style antiques shop—more
of a junk shop compared to the gallery-like spaces of the River
City mall—in an exhaust-blackened shophouse on Bangkok's
oldest road, a long, narrow thoroughfare lined with low buildings, known to most expats as "New Road." The junky antiques
shop was located opposite Bangkok's imposing main post office,

and after mailing off a parcel one day, I spied its cluttered display window from across the street. I almost put off having a look—the road is difficult to cross on that block because a lack of traffic lights lets vehicles get up to speed—but a gap in the flow suddenly opened up, allowing me to sprint across.

Seen through the glass door, the inside of the shop looked deserted, but I tried the knob and it opened to the sound of jangly brass bells. The proprietor—a smiling Chinese gentleman whom I later learned was in his eighties—came in from a back room. He welcomed me with rather good English, but I switched into Thai as I began a spiel that would lead to a description of what I was after. This narrative was well rehearsed and allowed me to keep the conversation going toward my goal in a way that sounded natural and unhurried. It also kept the antiques merchant from wasting both my time and his by giving him too much freedom to offer me items that I had no interest in buying.

I began by asking if he had an example of the most ubiquitous piece of opium paraphernalia in existence: the porcelain pillow. Unlike a pillow for sleeping, the porcelain opium pillow was a raised platform for the head, enabling a smoker to comfortably lie on one side and allowing for an unobstructed view of the pipe bowl as it was held above the opium lamp. Every antiques shop in Bangkok seemed to have one or two of these on hand. The old gentleman indeed had one, but its green-hued glaze was badly chipped. After pretending to give the pillow an appraising look, I asked about other opium antiques. He went into the back room and returned with an old soup dish containing a selection of pipe bowls in one hand and a porcelain Chinese teapot in the other. The antiques merchant invited me to drink a cup of tea, letting me sit and examine the pipe bowls at my leisure.

During our conversation it came out that he was originally

from Talat Noi, the neighborhood in Chinatown where I was living. Without any prompting he then told me about how he had visited the Chinatown opium dens as a child while accompanying his uncle, who was an enthusiastic smoker. The old merchant mimed smoking a pipe, and his gestures—he cocked his head to one side as though reclining—left little doubt he had witnessed the ritual firsthand.

I asked him where the dens used to be located and he smiled and said he didn't know the present-day names for the warren of alleys that once made up the old opium quarter. Speaking in Thai, he attempted to give me directions: "The opium dens were located off Prosperous City Road, this road in front of my shop, the one you Westerners call New Road. Follow it across the bridge over the canal and then turn left down Lane 22. Then walk about a hundred meters and turn left into the first alley. Back then, Lane 22 was known as 'Dog Shit Lane' and the principal alley with many opium dens was called 'Raw Ghost Alley.' Go in there and ask the old folks; they'll point to where the dens used to be."

I bought a bowl from the proprietor, although it was rather common and plain, as a way to thank him for what I felt was a fascinating bit of local color. I wondered why I'd never before heard those vulgar old street names, but it was typically Thai to withhold such history on the assumption that a shady past would reflect badly on the present. On the walk back to my apartment I stopped at a hole-in-the-wall eatery that specialized in stewed duck and ordered my usual lunch of duck over rice.

As I was waiting for my order, I started a conversation with "Old Uncle," the patriarch of the family-run restaurant, who was always puttering around collecting empty glasses and wiping food scraps from the stainless tabletops. I showed him the pipe bowl that I'd just bought and asked him to guess what it was. He knew. I then asked the old man if he had ever heard of "Raw Ghost Alley." He laughed upon hearing the name. "One way into that alley is right there," he said, pointing to a narrow walkway that passed right through a motorcycle repair shop next to the eatery.

"Do you mean there were once opium dens around here?" I asked.

"You're sitting in an old opium den!" he said and laughed again, waving his arms around to indicate the very restaurant where I had lunch practically every day.

The news that I was living in Bangkok's old opium quarter didn't surprise me. At that point I was ready to believe that fate had drawn me to the neighborhood in the first place. Days later, I again brought up the subject with Old Uncle at lunchtime, and this time he elaborated on Raw Ghost Alley, pointing to another entrance some twenty yards away from the eatery and next to one of the neighborhood's best preserved traditional Chinese homes. Despite having lived in the area for years, I had never explored these narrow alleys. I was curious but something always held me back. Just a peek down the alleys—there were toddlers playing among slumbering dogs and oldsters lounging in the shade—had been enough to convince me that I would be intruding had I strolled on in. I decided instead to let the sleeping dogs of Raw Ghost Alley lie, leaving it all unexplored for the time being.

Many months later, during the two-week opium smokefest that my forty-fifth birthday developed into, Raw Ghost Alley came back into my thoughts. The name was intriguing. Anyone who has lived in Southeast Asia for a longish spell will have noticed that ghosts are widely believed in throughout the region. While living in the Philippines, I often heard about people who had been visited by spirits—although I never met anybody who admitted to having actually seen one themselves. Later, when I began doing guidebook work, I frequently came across ghost stories—most often associated with hotels that were supposedly haunted—in Laos, Burma, Cambodia, and Thailand. In fact, some Thais seemed to be so terrified of the supernatural that it was difficult to get them to talk openly about ghosts; my inquiries about hauntings often produced bulging eyes and silence.

However, the ghosts referred to in the alley's informal name weren't the disembodied spirits of deceased opium smokers. In Thai, *phi dip* directly translates into English as "raw ghost," but the meaning is actually more akin to the term "the living dead." In other words, opium smokers in old Bangkok were thought of as zombies—people dead to the world yet still walking around among the living. Interestingly, "ghost" was also an American underworld term for opium smoker. But I didn't think the imagery these words evoked was meant to paint opium habitués as slack-jawed ghouls. Instead, I felt the meaning probably conveyed the idea that opium smokers were withdrawn and no longer took an interest in society.

Rudyard Kipling's short story "The Gate of the Hundred Sorrows" opens with what the author claimed was an old opium-smoker's proverb: "If I can attain heaven for a pice, why should you be envious?" ("Pice" is the old Anglo-Indian spelling for "paisa," a near valueless copper coin, one hundred of which made up a rupee.)

As I spent my birthday blissfully preparing one pipe after another, I could very much relate to the sentiment raised by Kipling's proverb. Good quality *chandu* was no longer available for pennies, but why *should* anyone object if opium made the lives of those who chose to partake of it so delicious?

Why was opium illegal? From my vantage point next to the layout tray, the historic anti-opium crusades *did* look like petty envy—resentment soured by large doses of ignorance. Surely the banishment of opium was just another example of Victorian efforts to truss up society in a rigid corset of morality; the same kind of righteous zealotry that begat the temperance movements that led to the Volstead Act and a decade of Prohibition; the same hysteria that caused most countries in Europe to ban absinthe after a mass murder was wrongly attributed to the drink in 1905.

Starting in the last week of July 2007, I again forced myself to fast, this time abstaining from opium for an entire month— longer than I had gone without the drug since I began smoking with Roxanna. My birthday celebration, with its round-the-clock rolling, was exquisite, but during that two weeks of indulgence I'd done no work. It was time to catch up on some assignments. I found the weeklong detox period uncomfortable but manageable—reinforcing my belief that the torment of opium withdrawal had been grossly overstated. While working at my laptop, I noted that my mind often wandered to the mat, but I had no problem keeping to my fast, despite seeing the bottle of *chandu* rolling around on the egg shelf of my refrigerator every time I opened it.

In mid-August I was visited by an old friend whom I'd first met years before when she was posted at the U.S. embassy in Bangkok. Lisa Bailey was a Southerner who managed to shatter all the Southern stereotypes. She was also the first of what would become many American embassy friends whose transcendent coolness debunked my preconceived notions about whom the State Department sends abroad. I best remembered Lisa for an informal Bangkok nightclub she introduced me to. In a city known for its nightlife, this place was unique. Lisa and her friends had dubbed it "the Japanese speakeasy" because it apparently had no liquor license and was run as a hobby by a Japanese fashion designer who rented the building—a century-old mansion on a quiet back lane. There was a tiny, handwritten sign on the gate out front, but other than that, there was no indication the house was anything but a private residence. Here was a nightclub minus the loud music, flashing lights, and gyrating pole dancers. Instead there was a genteel atmosphere behind high hedges where one could throw house parties—imagine a scene from *The Great Gatsby* if West Egg had been in tropical Asia. There my embassy friends drank vodka tonics and bemoaned having to work in offices overseen by the sneering visage of Dick Cheney.

Lisa's August 2007 visit to Bangkok immediately followed her having been posted in Afghanistan. We met at the tiny riverside café up against the Sheraton Hotel, which had become my usual place to meet people—this was where Helmut P. had begged me to stop collecting a few years before. Lisa was very excited about my recently published book and had bought a copy. We talked about what I had been doing to promote it, and I told her about the website that I had paid to have constructed, OpiumMuseum.com, on which images of my collection were displayed together with historical photographs of opium smokers in China, Southeast Asia, and America.

"Have you had a book launch party yet?" she asked.

"Who would pay for it?" I asked. "My publisher?"

"Why not?"

"I have absolutely no complaints about my publisher, but Silkworm Books is a small operation. I don't think anybody gets a book launch party."

"Well, why don't you let me arrange one for you?" Lisa asked with an eager look in her eyes that told me she was serious.

It sounded like fun, but my first reaction was to decline. Lisa pushed the idea in a playful tone, but then let it drop after making me promise to let her know if I changed my mind. She had only a few more days left in Bangkok and said she was going to have a small get-together with friends to see her off. "We could make it into a goodbye party for me and a book launch party for you."

I said I would give it some thought and we parted with a hug. On the walk back to my apartment I remembered how much I'd enjoyed the opening night of the exhibition in Rotterdam— which was unusual for me because getting a lot of attention was always something that made me uncomfortable. And then I remembered exactly why I had enjoyed both opening night and the demonstration at the tea house in Paris a few days later: Beforehand I had been smoking Armand Hoorde's opium. I pictured the sweet little bottle of *chandu* in my refrigerator and felt a wave of excitement just like a kid feels during the last days of school before summer vacation. I decided then and there that I would break my fast for a worthy cause: my book launch party.

A few days later I was in a taxi arriving at a modern high-rise— the residence of the American embassy's cultural attaché, who through Lisa had offered to host my party. Alone in the elevator, I straightened my collar before a wide mirror that covered the back of the compartment. My pupils were pinpoints, but I could detect no other clue that might give away the fact that I had broken my monthlong fast by smoking fifteen pipes prior to leaving my apartment. I had purposely arrived at the party early to get accustomed to the surroundings and help with setting up, but the host had already seen to all the arrangements: There was a table in the dining room, every inch of which was covered with platters of Thai food. Two stacks of copies of my book were arranged on a coffee table in the living room.

Lisa was already there. She was booked on a flight back to the States later that night so we took advantage of the quiet and talked over things before the guests began arriving. She said that quite a few people from the embassy would be there, although except for the host, I knew none of them because all of my embassy friends had rotated to new postings outside of Thailand. It didn't matter. Atypically for me, I was looking forward to being in a room full of new faces.

I've known U.S. embassy people to be punctual, and these were no exception. By 7:30 P.M. the apartment was crowded with guests and I was kept busy being introduced and signing copies of my book. At one point there were sharp, ringing taps on a wineglass and I was asked to say a few words. Speaking in front of crowds has always been one of my least favorite tasks, but I was aided by the confidence-bolstering properties of opium—which seemed to turn my leaden tongue to silver.

The rest of the evening was spent chatting and answering questions. People approached me one at a time or in groups of twos and threes. Many of them had been in Southeast Asia for some time—not exactly old hands but savvy enough to know the score. After complimenting me on my book, they all seemed to ask the same question: Was it possible to smoke opium in Thailand?

Recreational drug users are well known for wanting to "turn on" others to an activity they find highly enjoyable. But recreational drug use, by its very definition, is something outside the realm of work or study—and for that reason I didn't see myself as engaging in it. I was using opium for research, and, enjoyable as my experiences might have been, I knew there was nothing to be gained by introducing others to the bliss that I had found within the glow of the opium lamp. In fact, there was much to lose by doing so.

I smiled patiently as one person after another worked through some introductory small talk before popping the question. Was it my imagination or did I detect a glimmer of hope in their eyes? I became convinced that many of them wanted me to answer with a wink and a whisper. Instead, with the pupils of my eyes as tiny as poppy seeds, I shook my head with feigned regret as I shut the door on their hopes. "I'm afraid nothing remains of that old world," I said.

Doctors would have us believe that opium dulls us and takes away our sense of values. But if opium pulls the old scale of values from under our feet, it sets up another for us, superior and more delicate.

—Jean Cocteau, *Opium: Journal d'une désintoxication* (1930)

The fast now broken, my appetite for opium became voracious. Opium's slow, decade-long seduction suddenly flared into a passion of an almost sexual nature. As I watched my hands performing the rituals: trimming the wick, cooking the *chandu,* and then rolling pill after perfect pill, I was mesmerized by them. Instead of taking a break between each pipe as I had before, I allowed myself to roll and smoke as many as seven pills in succession before putting the pipe down and closing my eyes to savor the effects. Before I realized it, I was smoking daily. I kept up my standards just as before—showering and dressing in a silk sarong and crisp linen shirt before reclining; always reminding myself that what I was doing was rare and special and never to be taken for granted. I slept at dawn and awoke in the late afternoon still feeling pleasantly fuzzy from the night before. By nine or ten that evening I was on the mat again.

I began listening to music during the long, languid breaks that I took between vaporizing pills. My taste in music had always been varied; the cabinet below the shelf that supported my stereo was full of cassette tapes and CDs featuring everything from traditional bluegrass to 1970s funk to Burmese heavy metal bands. But now I had absolutely no desire to listen to anything even remotely modern. It was as though the opium was pulling me back to a time when composers might have used opium themselves, creating songs while under the influence of the drug and perhaps even making music with the enjoyment of opium smokers in mind.

It is not far-fetched to surmise that ragtime great Scott Joplin had experienced opium. At least one of his collaborators, the now largely forgotten Louis Chauvin, became addicted to the drug in the opium dens of St. Louis. There is something about Joplin's piano rags that, when played at the correct tempo (modern pianists tend to play them too fast), perfectly complement opium's subtle buzz. I found compositions like "The Easy Winners" most soothing and especially fitting for the bittersweet hours just before dawn.

Early in the evening I usually desired something bouncier, such as Dixieland jazz: Red Nichols's snappy 1929 version of "Chinatown, My Chinatown" kicked off many a session. I was also charmed by the buoyant optimism of Depression-era crooners, their cheerful messages going hand in hand with opium's uplifting effects. Even the blues couldn't bring me down. I discovered Billie Holiday and ordered a three-disc set online so I could listen to her for hours on end. I'd close my eyes and let her lilting voice wash over me while I searched the lyrics for evidence of her alleged opium addiction.

Not every minute of my nightly revelry was spent reclining. Ideas popped into my head and sent me to the shelf of books that I called my library, or more often, to my laptop for an Internet search. These mind rambles were not limited to opium-related subjects. I tended to avoid news and current events but instead spent hours on Wikipedia, clicking links until I'd forgotten what subject had brought me to the website in the first place. I also frequented Flickr and dedicated much time to exploring the accounts of members who collected and uploaded old portrait photographs. I knew that if the photos depicted Americans and dated from the 1880s to the 1910s, there was a slight chance they were also opium smokers. With this in mind I spent hours staring into the eyes of these sepia-toned faces, searching for a telltale glint. I felt I had more in common with the dead people in these images—these aloof souls guarding their secrets as old airs played endlessly in their heads—than I did with the millions of live people to be found just beyond my apartment door.

To entertain myself during the wee hours, I began scanning old photos of my travels in Asia and uploading them to Flickr. I followed a blog aimed at middle-aged Americans who were feeling nostalgic for the Disneyland of their childhood, and the reddening snapshots of Adventureland circa 1970 brought back some good old memories. Yet despite my almost complete apathy for the present, I had no problem keeping up correspondence with friends outside Thailand via email, even finding the time to leave posts among strangers on online forums. Nobody had any idea of what I was going through. The only clue to my state of mind was that I seemed to be awake at all hours. That friends many time zones away noticed this was evident when I once received an email message—addressed to myself and several others—whose subject line asked the question "Does Steve ever sleep?"

I almost never left my apartment during the day other than to take short walks down the lane to buy food—except when I was on some odd quest inspired by my nocturnal musings. One such opium-inspired project sent me on a search for an old-school Chinese tailor who could fashion me a linen suit like those once worn by the colonials of French Indochina. A friend visiting from Cambodia showed me where I could buy quality linen at a shop in Sampeng, a tunnel-like alley that runs through Bangkok's Chinatown. For the equivalent of seventy dollars, I bought four meters of buff-colored linen for the suit and three of beige rayon for the lining (the shopkeeper claimed that silk would counteract the cooling properties of the linen).

The tailor I found was only about a mile from my apartment and near the Oriental Hotel. Had I not been pointed in that direction by one of my American embassy friends, I would never have thought to look there. Many tailors' shops line the lanes surrounding Bangkok's oldest and most famous hotel, but most are what you'd expect in an area that is flush with rich foreign tourists: blatant attempts to separate the visitors from their money. These tailors are mostly from India and are almost as transient as the tourists they target—none of their shops seem to last more than a season or two before changing hands. Such operations are easily pegged because the tailors themselves often stand outside their own shops and tout their wares: "A fine silk suit for you, sir?"

By contrast, the tailor that my friend directed me to was Thai-Chinese and had been in the same shop for decades. Thinking there was a good chance that he could make the suit I wanted, I brought with me a still from the French film *The Lover* that I had found online. It was a photo of Tony Leung Ka-fai as he was dressed when he met Jane March on the ferry to Saigon. This movie, by the way, has the best opium smoking scenes of any I've ever watched. The paraphernalia are authentic antiques, and the smoking is realistic. The film is also rare in that it really looks and feels like Southeast Asia: The light is right; the colors are correct; the background noises ring true. A friend of Roxanna's, a former Vietcong who had become the curator of the Da Nang Museum of Cham Sculpture, once told me that he was astounded by how this film seemed to bring colonial Vietnam back to life.

So, with an image of Tony Leung Ka-fai wearing a tropical linen suit in hand, I presented myself to the tailor, and in my most polite Thai tried to talk him into cutting a suit that was in none of his catalogs or magazines. The tailor was probably about sixty, born too late to have actually seen anyone wearing what I was asking him to make—but he was amiable and game to try. He didn't seem too interested in the photo of Tony Leung Ka-fai, handing it back to me after I explained what I wanted. I took this to mean that he already had an idea in mind and didn't need the photographic cue. I stood for measurements and told the tailor that I was in no hurry—I didn't want the typical three-day suit. As long as I got the vintage style I was looking for, I didn't care how long it took to finish.

When I came in for my first fitting a week later, the suit jacket was still little more than a chalk-marked vest. The tailor had misplaced the trousers, and after fifteen minutes of looking he gave up and suggested that I try them on during my next visit. A second week passed and I came in again for another fitting—the last before the suit was to be completed. But something was wrong: The jacket was alarmingly tight. I pointed this out to the tailor, but he seemed unworried. He asked if I wanted authentic vintage style, and I affirmed my original request and left it at that. I have a knack for opening my mouth and complaining too soon, and, especially in Thailand where being quick to question is considered poor form, there had been many times when I wished I had simply held my tongue. I thought this might be another such instance, so I let the matter drop. Instead,

I made an appointment to come in and pick up the finished suit the following week, and then headed back to my apartment for a mind-soothing smoke.

On the way home I ran into a friend from River City mall, the Thai manager of an antiques shop that I visited weekly when I first started collecting. My trips to the mall had slowed once I began buying most of my opium antiques online, but over the years I still made an effort to stop by and chat with her now and then. After I fell into smoking heavily, it became too much of a bother for me to get to her shop before the 6 P.M. closing time, so I stopped visiting. On this day it struck me as soon as I saw my friend that it had been many months since we'd last met.

"You've gotten thin," she said in Thai.

Her remark might have been taken for a typical Thai greeting: People who haven't been face-to-face for long periods of time often comment immediately on any perceived change in weight. This wasn't the usual greeting, however—my friend sounded concerned. "Have you been sick?" she asked.

"I've been in Cambodia," I replied.

This was the lie I had been telling everybody. It wasn't the first time I'd heard the remark about getting thin, and I was hearing it more frequently. The more opium I smoked, the less food my body seemed to need. Traveling in Cambodia was the best way to explain away weight loss. All Thais think of Cambodia as a barbaric place where the food is unspeakably filthy, so they expect you to get sick and lose weight during visits there. My friend smiled sympathetically and advised me to get plenty of sleep. Then it was my turn to smile as I thought about just how blurred the line between my sleeping and waking hours had become.

A week later I was back at the tailor's shop trying on the finished product. I stood there dumbstruck by my image in the mirror. Nothing fit. The jacket was too tight, the sleeves sliding halfway up my arms when I held them out in front of me. The trousers, on the other hand, looked like the bottom half of a zoot suit: They were balloon-like and with an excess of cloth bunched at my shoes. This wasn't some strange redistribution of weight caused by the opium—the tailor had ruined the suit.

Losing one's temper in Thailand is always a mistake. There was nothing to be gained by blowing up, but I had to know why my suit had gone so wrong. After some questions, the tailor led me back to the innermost area of his shop, and there I learned where he formed his idea about how my suit should look: On the wall was a poster of Stan Laurel and Oliver Hardy. The jackets on both men were a couple of sizes too small. The tailor helpfully pointed out that Charlie Chaplin also had his suits cut in the same manner. A small jacket and baggy trousers were authentic vintage style.

But those guys were clowns! I thought to myself, yet no such protestation left my lips. Breaking the tailor's face would have been counterproductive. Instead I told him that I'd changed my mind. I wanted a suit that fit in the modern way. The tailor assured me there was enough material left to make another jacket and so I again stood for measurements. When I returned two weeks later, a stunning piece of work awaited me. The suit fit perfectly.

I brought my suit home, added a white cotton shirt to the ensemble, and immediately had a few pipes while wearing it. The linen was stiff and had a smell that brought a fabric store to mind, but I hoped the opium vapors would permeate the waxy fibers with each bowl that I smoked, giving them that unique *chandu* scent and a patina as soft as the honey-hued ivory mouthpiece of my favorite pipe. How many decades had it been since somebody rolled pills to ragtime while wearing a suit? I decided to wear it every Saturday night, making the opium-smoking ritual a bit more formal than my usual sarong-and-guayabera-clad sessions.

Regardless of what I was wearing, I spent every night like a pasha on a divan, holding court before the friends, relatives, and acquaintances who crowded my imagination. They pushed in for a look, asking questions that allowed me to ramble on about my favorite subject for hours. My imaginary guests were not limited to people I actually knew. During the course of one late evening I tutored Johnny Depp in the fine art of rolling. I had seen his botched performance in the opening scenes of the film *From Hell,* and I sympathized with his predicament. "Of course you had no idea how to roll," I assured him. "There was no way for you to research the scene. Here, let me show you. . . ."

On another occasion I prepared pipes for Francis Ford Coppola and Sergio Leone while playfully chastising both men for their attempts at opium-smoking scenes in *Apocalypse Now Redux* and *Once Upon a Time in America* respectively. "Your opium lamp didn't even have a chimney!" I railed at Coppola in tones of mock outrage. "The opium would have burned to a crisp the moment Aurore Clément held the bowl to that naked flame! How on earth did Martin Sheen manage to get high?"

"Oh, believe me, Martin was high on other things," Coppola replied after exhaling a column of vapors.

I decided to cut the director some slack; the opium had put me in a forgiving mood. "Really, though, your omission can be excused. The Shanghai Lil sequence in *Footlight Parade* made the same mistake. James Cagney stumbles through an opium den and sees two beautiful women having pipes prepared for them"—I paused for effect while leveling my own pipe above the lamp—"over a flame without a chimney! And that movie came out in 1933! There's no excuse for it; there were still opium dens back then!"

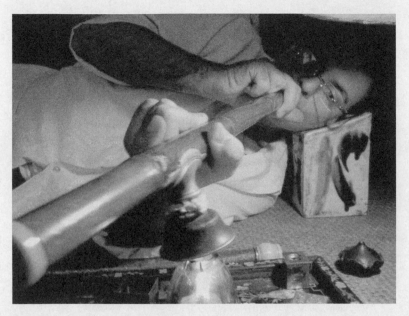

The author smoking opium at his Bangkok apartment in 2007. During this time he was nursing a twenty-pipe-per-day opium habit. (Photograph by Jack Barton)

Burning the midnight oil night after night, I arrived at some new phase of opium geekdom. My interests had become so narrow and the depth of my knowledge so great, that like a lonely soul trapped at the bottom of a mineshaft, only by resorting to my imagination could I enjoy some like-minded conversation.

My old books claimed that opium smokers needed ever larger doses in order to maintain the desired effects, but I found this to be untrue. As long as I was smoking high-quality, dross-free *chandu,* the same number of pills—five to seven—was enough to bring on the bliss. That said, I actually did steadily increase my dosage, because I wanted to keep rolling throughout the night.

So even when I didn't really need more opium, I kept smoking just for love of the ritual. I noticed, too, that the feelings brought on by intoxication were not quite the same as when I used to spend nights in Willi's Chamber of Fragrant Mists. If anything, my sense of well-being was more all-encompassing than before. I felt safe and warm and looked after, a feeling that I dimly remembered from way back: I was a child, sick with some mild childhood malady, being lovingly doted on by my mother. These were feelings of safety and comfort that only a child knows, when all the world is under a warm blanket in a cozy bed— feelings that are lost as one grows older and learns of the risks and uncertainties of life on the big outside. As long as I smoked opium I was continuously enveloped in this protective blanket of contentment.

Weeks passed. I was unable to focus on work but had already received an advance from Rough Guides to update their guidebook to Cambodia. The on-the-ground research would take at least three weeks, and I intended to do it—as soon as I tapered back on my smoking. There was no way I could up and leave town unless I was willing to take the opium with me, and that was something I was not prepared to do. Instead, I scheduled a week's worth of decreased smoking as I had done after coming back from Europe. I wasn't too worried about it—I was sure this time would be even easier since my opium was pure and not the dross-laden stuff I had smoked with Armand Hoorde. I set a date a week before my new regime was to begin, but my sense of time was warped by the opium—time flew by. Before I knew it, the date had passed without my having started reducing. I set another date, but as the time to start weaning myself off the opium approached, I found a reason to push it back another week. It was procrastination of the most blatant sort, but how could I say no to just one more week of heaven? The damned guidebook could wait.

At some point I remembered that my visa for Thailand was soon to expire. I had less than a week to get out of the country, but luckily my multiple-entry visa would allow me to simply exit Thailand and then reenter for another three months. Still, I felt a rising panic. The thought of leaving my apartment even briefly brought on anxiety, but there was no way around it. I got online and started looking at options. I wanted to leave the country and return without spending the night away from home. A single night absent from the lamp would bring on the initial symptoms of withdrawal, and with regional immigration officials still jittery about the so-called Bird Flu, I didn't want to take the chance of being sick for the pipe while traveling.

Singapore was the one place I could fly into without a visa in the morning and be assured of a flight back to Bangkok later the same day. Other destinations such as Vientiane and Phnom Penh were risky, since there was not as much traffic between these cities and Bangkok, and I would have to gamble that Thai Airways wouldn't cancel the return flight. Going to Singapore was an ironic choice since its antidrug laws are the strictest in the region, but I had no intention of leaving the airport, and of course I would take nothing incriminating with me. I booked a morning departure and an afternoon return and then went back to the pipe and rolled until I regained my confidence.

The night before my flight I smoked lightly and tried to sleep, setting my alarm clock to wake me early so I had time to have a few pipes before leaving for the airport. In the morning I didn't overindulge, stopping at eleven pipes and dropping a large dose of Visine into my blinking eyes. I also wore a pair of non-prescription glasses to help obscure my eyes and, hopefully, to give myself a square, bookish appearance—the sort of person who would never be involved with drugs.

The flight landed in Singapore just past noon, and after completing immigration and customs formalities, I ran through the airport to the check-in counter of the departures area, arriving just in time to board the very same plane to Bangkok that had brought me to Singapore. Walking on board, I noticed the bemused smiles of a couple of the stewardesses who recognized me from the morning flight. "You don't stay in Singapore?" asked one.

"I miss Thailand," was my reply. By late afternoon I was back at my apartment, lighting the lamp and having a self-congratulatory smoke.

❧

"Opiates are a slippery slope," warned my friend Jake Burton. He was a freelance television journalist and through me had become an amateur collector of opium antiques. He also claimed to have a friend confined to a nursing home in Australia whose downfall was heroin. I listened politely to his sorry story and then replied: "Apples and oranges."

Jake was the one Bangkok friend whom I had let in on my big secret. Years before, Jake had discovered a little stall in Bangkok's Weekend Market that specialized in Chinese antiques. Along with the usual blue-and-white porcelain vases and carved wooden deities, the vendor had a few choice pieces of antique opium paraphernalia on offer. Seeing how excited I was about his discovery and knowing how seriously I took my collecting, Jake graciously shared his find with me and then stood aside and let me have the pick of the booty. The source lasted nearly a year before the shopkeeper began trying to pass off fakes, but for a time her stall was a fairly rich vein.

To pay Jake back, I invited him to my apartment to take part in a session after a back injury began causing him difficulty in shouldering his video camera. "I'm bloody laid up with a bad back. It's completely oucho-imobilizo," he had said.

I badgered him out of bed, saying that I could guarantee relief, but only if he would catch a taxi to Chinatown. He arrived at my flat within an hour. Watching the opium work its pain-banishing magic reminded me what a miracle it could be, and I asked Jake to return once his back had healed so he could experience opium in a purely recreational sense.

From the time of my monthly visits to Willi I had been keeping a record of my smoking sessions with still photographs— self-portraits that I shot at arm's length or with a timer. My digital camera had a screen that rotated free from the camera's body, allowing me to see what was in the frame while the lens was pointed at me, and I used it to take scores of photos of myself lying next to the tray. I also wanted to document my rolling technique in a way that would catch the subtleties of my method. Video was the only way. Jake was a video whiz, having shot and edited many hours of television news stories for the English-language services of Agence France-Presse and Al Jazeera.

The two of us set a date and time, and when he arrived at my apartment late one evening, I was pacing the living room in anticipation. Outside, the strains of a Chinese opera were booming from a joss house situated between my apartment building and the river. Normally, I enjoyed the exoticness of these sounds— the catlike vocals shrilly punctuating sawing fiddles, whistling flutes, and crashing cymbals—but that night I was too distracted to think about anything but a smoke. Upon awakening around noon I had decided that the video might be more interesting if I abstained from smoking until Jake could record my first pipe of the day. As Jake set up his camera and began testing angles, I fiddled with the accoutrements on my layout tray and gritted my teeth in an effort to enforce patience. Time crawled. Once Jake was finally ready and the camera was rolling, I began making preparations for my first pipe. Jake asked me to lift the bottle of *chandu* and hold it to the light, and I did that much, but his other requests were ignored as I rushed to inhale that first lungful of divine vapors.

Three pipes into the session and my haste was forgotten. I rolled a couple pills for Jake, and after smoking them he continued to film me for the better part of an hour. Then he put the camera aside and we smoked until just before midnight when he suggested that we wander down to the joss house and watch Chinese opera for an act or two. Out in the street, the night air was perfumed with the fragrance of jasmine mixed with the swampy smell of the Chao Phraya River, which flowed unseen behind a row of century-old shophouses that bordered the western edge of my apartment building. Jake and I admired the old teak and stucco façades as we walked with a light step toward the direction of the music. A makeshift stage had been set up opposite the entrance to the joss house, positioned so the performance would be visible from the ornately carved stone altar just inside the temple's open doors. In actuality the show was for the Taoist deities within, but in front of the stage two dozen metal folding chairs had been arranged in uneven rows just in case any mortals might want to watch as well. Only a handful of these chairs were occupied, primarily by elderly Chinese women looking strangely uniform with their permed gray hair and flower-print pajamas.

Jake and I took a seat front and center so as to get an even blast of music from the stacks of speakers on either side of the stage. Once we were seated, Jake craned his neck around slowly to take in the whole scene before turning his glazed eyes and contented grin on me. I knew exactly what he was thinking. There would be no more talk of Australian nursing homes. Jake lived across town in the Westerners' glitzy ghetto off Sukhumvit Road—far from any joss houses reeking of incense and idolatry. If for him a trip to Chinatown was a taste of the exotic, watching Chinese opera while high on opium was nothing less than a feast.

I smiled in reply, but all I could think about was getting back to my pipe and lamp. Here I was surrounded by what should have been the height of exoticism; a setting that went hand in hand with my cherished vice. Many times I had read John Blofeld's tale of the opium-addicted singing master, star of both a troupe of opera performers in 1930s Peking and the smoking scenes that were my favorite passages in *City of Lingering Splendour*. Attending a midnight performance of Chinese opera in the courtyard of a Taoist temple should have produced exhilaration, yet something akin to a restless boredom kept me from enjoying my surroundings.

I was reminded of an opium-wise character in Claude Farrère's collection of stories *Black Opium*. As a novice smoker, the character had decorated his private smoking room in the most exotic manner he could think of—by covering the floor and walls with the skins of tigers whose taxidermied heads were permanently frozen in fang-bearing snarls. Later in his smoking life, the character realized that no sights, sounds, or other external stimuli—not even snarling tigers—could compete with opium's internal sorcery. It was as though the narcotic had the ability to make one evolve into a being whose interests lay entirely within oneself.

When I had first read Farrère's story during my early days of experimentation, it sounded like so many other passages of French opium literature that had been translated into English:

pompous and ridiculous in equal parts. How could opium make the outside world uninteresting when recapturing a childlike sense of wonder was what it did best? Time and opium answered that question for me. The intervening years had changed my tastes until I found myself anxious to trade the dizzying sights and sounds of Chinese opera for sensory deprivation in the form of a quiet, dark room that allowed me to be alone with my thoughts and imagination.

At the time it seemed like a simple preference and a logical one—a preference for silence over noise. But then something happened. I went from preferring these things to absolutely needing them. The change was subtle and gradual. I could not pinpoint when it happened exactly, but I did know what seemed to be driving the change: a strange skittishness that I could not control. Loud noises—especially sharp reports like the sound of a firecracker—began to terrify me. I might be walking down the lane in front of my apartment building, on my daily trip outdoors for sustenance in the form of stir-fry, when a backfiring motorbike would cause me to react like a shell-shocked war veteran. Even loud sneezes—the Thai often amplify their sneezes with an accompanied shriek—would completely unnerve me. I would jump visibly, clenching my fists and scrunching up my shoulders as my eyes involuntarily slammed shut—a reaction that was impossible for others not to notice. Even when I knew the loud noise was coming there was simply no way for me to remain calm and collected. It was as though the opium had tapped into some deep well of animal instinct, reanimating primal fears that a lifetime had taught me were of no real danger.

There were other things. During my monthly trips to visit Roxanna and refill my bottle of *chandu,* I discovered that riding in a taxi on the expressway made me short of breath. Had historic opium smokers ever traveled at such high speeds? I asked

Roxanna if she had ever experienced the same fear. "Not that I can recall," she said with a smile and just the slightest hint of sarcasm. Did she think I was making it up?

In mid-October 2007, for the first time in almost a year, I traveled to Vientiane to visit Willi and the Chamber of Fragrant Mists. Normally I would have taken the night train, using the trip as an excuse to treat myself to a cabin in the first-class sleeping car. Each stateroom had a wide, sofa-like seat and a mirror on the opposite wall, into which I could look up and smile at myself whenever I made some opium-related discovery in one of the old books I always brought along to read. There was a small table for writing and even a miniature sink and drinking glasses with the logo of the State Railway of Thailand. And for about twenty dollars more than the standard first-class fare, I could have the two-passenger cabin all to myself. As soon as the train pulled out of the station and my ticket had been inspected, I would lock the cabin door and change into a T-shirt and a sarong. The only decision confronting me then was whether to eat dinner in my cabin or take a sightseeing stroll down the rolling aisles of the second-class cars that led to the diner.

Yet I had not taken a long train ride since I began smoking heavily. I knew that going the whole night without opium would make the trip horribly tedious, and the overnight trains were sometimes delayed for hours. Just worrying about such a delay would take much of the enjoyment out of train travel. Tempted as I might have been to bring along an abbreviated layout and have a few pipes while reclining on the rocking train, I knew that such an idea was pure idiocy: The smell of something burning would immediately bring the conductor knocking.

I decided instead to fly, and during the hour-long flight from Bangkok to Vientiane, I made another discovery: I could no longer fly comfortably. If high speeds on the expressway were frightening, flying—especially takeoff and landing—felt like imminent doom. I gripped the armrests and sat bolt upright, my feet firmly planted on the vibrating floor as though coiled and ready to spring through a hole in the fuselage, jumping to safety, should the plane just happen to break up in midair. Willi noticed the fear in my eyes when he picked me up at the airport. "Was there turbulence?" he asked.

But this particular visit was most notable for a different realization. During the ride to his house outside Vientiane, Willi explained that he and his wife had the previous week hosted a houseguest—a rather obnoxious Briton—who, as Willi described it, had driven his wife to threaten to abandon him if she didn't get some peace and quiet. Willi apologized profusely before telling me that he had booked a room for me at Vientiane's finest hotel. "I'm sorry; it really can't be helped. I'm paying for the room, of course. And I'm preparing a big dinner tonight for all of us."

Upon arrival at Willi's, we adhered to custom just as we always had, bringing the Chamber back to life step by ritualistic step: lighting candles and incense; starting the pendulum clock. It was nearly 5 P.M. by the time we finally reclined for our first shared pipes in nearly a year. Yet something was off. Willi counted four drops of *chandu* into the miniature copper wok and meticulously rolled two pipes for each of us. The pills were tiny. Barely the size of a half grain of rice, they were much smaller than the pea-sized pills I rolled for myself. I asked if he was getting low on opium. "No, not at all, but these days I rarely smoke more than once a week and I'm limiting myself to two or three pipes per session."

"Is two or three pipes enough for you?" I asked.

"Yeah, sure. When I smoke more than my usual dose, it makes me irritable the following week."

"I see."

Willi had not blown out the lamp, but I felt he was signaling an end to the session. I asked, "So are we finished smoking for the evening?"

"Of course not! But let's take a break and have some tea while I check on how dinner is coming along."

I sat in the pavilion above the lotus pond, sipping oolong tea while feeling frustrated at my lack of a buzz. As I drained the tea from its tubelike cup, I heard the rolling crunch of a car approaching slowly up the gravel drive, followed by loud greetings with an English accent. Dinner "for all of us" turned out to be a more crowded affair than I had anticipated. Besides the Englishman and his Lao wife, there was another couple—a Canadian and his Thai wife. The food and presentation were flawless, brought out to the pavilion by Willi's servant one dish at a time and perfectly on cue as Willi described the ordeal he had gone through to procure the extraordinary ingredients. As always, there was also plenty of wine on hand, although I wasn't drinking.

I tried to follow the conversation but soon gave up. It started with that sort of inane chatter in which almost nothing of any real meaning is said. The men, all of whom were expat entrepreneurs, then started talking shop while the women switched into Thai and began discussing the plot of a soap opera. As the alcohol flowed and the time passed, I tried not to look at the clock on my mobile phone. Then the word "opium" caught my ear and I was astonished to hear the Englishman ask Willi if he would be smoking opium later that night. Willi replied in a vague way, saying that he had to be up early the following morning.

I stared at my half-empty glass of mineral water and thought about what Willi hadn't said. This was the former houseguest who had overstayed his welcome—and who in the process had managed to spoil my welcome. He had no doubt been staying in the Chamber, using the paraphernalia I had so painstakingly assembled. If he had been smoking Willi's opium, that was none of my business, but I couldn't help but feel insulted. What I had come to think of as my own private getaway had been usurped by this loutish philistine.

What was worse, it was already late and Willi looked half drunk. I could picture him asking his dinner guests to drop me off at my hotel to save himself the trouble of driving into town. Was this payback for my having neglected to visit for so long? Since I had begun smoking with Roxanna, I'd been more attentive in supplying her with the accoutrements necessary for maintaining her habit. Had she told Willi about this, and had he taken it the wrong way? I had no idea, but there was one thing I did know: If I didn't get more opium into my system, my night at the hotel was going to be less than restful. I got up from the table. "Willi, I'm sorry, I just need to lie down for a bit. Do you mind?"

"No! No, go right ahead!"

I excused myself to the other guests, left the pavilion, and walked the few paces to the Chamber door, shutting and quietly locking it behind me. Then I lit the opium lamp and started to prepare a pipe, propelled by an emotion that I'd never before experienced while on the mat—anger.

Whatever his reason for sharing our secret, whatever his reason for relegating me to the backseat, I didn't care. At that moment, all I cared about was smoking as much opium as possible before Willi realized what I was doing and perhaps put a stop to it. After about fifteen minutes, Willi called to me from outside, saying that they were about to have dessert. Two can play at that game, I thought to myself. "Please go ahead without me. I'll join you as soon as I'm feeling a little better."

I did not rejoin the dinner party. An hour after dessert was served the guests were getting up to leave, politely saying their goodbyes to me through the locked Chamber door. I replied in kind. It was easy—my anger had subsided as soon as the opium brought a ticklish itch to the tip of my nose.

When the guests were gone Willi knocked on the Chamber door and let himself in—I had quietly unlocked the door as the guests were driving off—and then he stretched out on the other side of the tray. I offered to prepare Willi a pipe and he accepted. Nothing was said by either of us about how the evening had transpired and the drive to my hotel was mostly quiet.

As I lay on my back on the hotel bed, I decided that there was no longer any reason to visit Willi and the Chamber of Fragrant Mists. I felt no resentment or hard feelings. The five years that we had collaborated had been an exceptionally good run. But things had changed. I now greatly preferred to smoke alone.

Opium, an equivocal luxury in the beginning daintily approached,
becomes ere long under the clamorous demands of a perverted appetite
a dire alternative, a magisterially controlling power.

—Alonzo Calkins, *Opium and the Opium-Appetite* (1871)

Forbidden fruit is always the most pleasing to the palate. Not only is opium illegal, there is also the added gamble of potential addiction. Back in the days of the Chamber of Fragrant Mists, I had doubted the possibility of opium addiction, but by October 2007, I was forced to rethink everything.

Willi once related a story to me about an old German expatriate living in Bangkok whom he knew in the 1980s. The German told Willi that he smoked opium only once a year—to celebrate Christmas. Yet the old man claimed that even though he smoked only that single time every year, during the week leading up to his annual session he would become very agitated. Moreover, after smoking his Christmas pipes the old German was annually hit with the classic opium withdrawal symptoms: It was as though he had caught the flu. I laughed at Willi's story and remarked that the case sounded psychosomatic to me.

Later, when I, too, experienced physical symptoms that I believed were all in my mind, I had to wonder about yet another of opium's mysteries—the nature of addiction. Did opium have the ability to hijack the mind and body in order to force its continued usage? Was the drug some demon seed planted in my brain—an alien life-form that was using me as a vehicle to perpetuate itself?

Plant species have developed remarkable knacks to assist in propagation. Take the jackfruit tree: Its fruit can grow as large as a small child and is covered with a thick, spiky skin. Growing on the tree's trunk, the heavy fruit hangs low and free from the tangle of branches. The seeds are numerous and as big as walnuts, but rounded and smooth—perfect lozenges for passing easily through the digestive tract, but only that of a really large animal. Humans have taken a liking to the jackfruit, but evolution targeted the elephant—or perhaps I should say, the elephant has been the jackfruit's facilitator in the process of natural selection. Elephants can deftly pull the low-hanging fruit down from its tree, breaking through the thick skin that repels other animals in order to eat the fruit's sweet yellow flesh. The seeds that pass unharmed through the elephant's digestive system are deposited in a pile of fertilizing dung. A jackfruit sapling sprouts and the species is furthered.

Then there is opium, whose unparalleled ability to relieve pain and control diarrhea was discovered in ancient times and led to the cultivation of the poppy. Opium was the first wonder drug. Its value as a painkiller is well known even today, but opium's effectiveness at suppressing diarrhea was once of equal importance. For the ancients (as in undeveloped countries of today), diarrhea was a frequent and dreaded killer—especially of young children. Opium saved lives. But there was a catch. If too often resorted to, opium had to be used again and again. If not, the pain that opium initially drove away would come back tenfold;

the diarrhea that opium once kept in check would return with a vengeance, leaving the body as drained and lifeless as an empty chrysalis.

"Opium, the Judas of drugs, that kisses and betrays," was how career criminal Jack Black described the narcotic, calling the six months that it took him to wean himself off opium "the toughest battle of my life." My problem was that opium made life so sweet that I longed to do it every day. I had gone from looking forward to the time when I was wrapped in its blissful blanket to loathing the time when I wasn't. With opium, a porcelain pillow on a hardwood floor seemed as soft as a feather bed; without it, every surface felt like a bed of nails. Once a taste for the drug is acquired, it takes an extremely self-disciplined personality to keep from surrendering to its delights on a more and more frequent basis. Unfortunately, self-discipline was never my strong suit. Opium preys on compulsive behavior. The same traits that made me a passionate and successful collector also rendered me unable to resist its siren song.

I thought of Jack Black's self-detox ordeal—six months of cutting back on his daily dosage—and I wondered if I had the discipline to do the same. I remembered seeing a young Frenchman at Mister Kay's Vientiane opium den. His name was Xavier and he was an entrepreneur who had come to Laos some years before. I had exchanged words with Xavier on a couple of occasions, but he wasn't the talkative sort, and the few times that I saw him at Mister Kay's he was in and out within fifteen minutes. One day, just after Xavier had left the den, I remarked on his brief visits to the other habitués. They told me what they knew about him. Xavier came to Mister Kay's on a daily basis, usually in the early evening. He smoked two pipes a day—no more, no less—and then he left. Xavier never missed a day, but he never lingered after his second pipe was finished. His socializing was limited to brief greetings for the proprietor and the regulars.

At the time I didn't give much thought to Xavier's odd routine, but now I had to ask myself: What else but trying to cut back on one's opium use could explain such behavior? And if a mere two pipes could keep him coming back day after day, how tightly would the grasp of twenty or thirty pipes a day hold me?

Not since the beginning of August had I made a serious attempt to stop smoking. Sure, I had gone full days without a session, but agitation always drove me to the pipe before the clock struck midnight. I needed answers. There was nothing to do but visit Roxanna and be frank. The previous week I had sold some antique paraphernalia—several rare tools—to the collector in Las Vegas, and I was due to pay Roxanna a visit to get more *chandu*. I resolved to tell her everything.

On a drizzly Sunday morning I took the subway to its terminus and then a taxi the remaining couple of miles to Roxanna's house. Walking the deserted narrow lanes, melancholy with puddles and dripping eaves, I thought about what might be the real reason behind her austere, "authentic" lifestyle. There was tragedy in Roxanna. It wasn't just her leg—there was something else that I could feel but couldn't quite put my finger on.

Roxanna had left the front door bolted but unlocked, instructing me over the phone to reach through a hole in the door's wooden slats and let myself in. I found her upstairs dressed in one of her trademark sleeveless smocks, a Javanese batik with a black spiderwebby pattern that contrasted with the bare wooden floorboards. She was holding the mouthpiece of her bamboo pipe to her lips as the ceramic bowl softly gurgled. The house was silent—Roxanna's son was still asleep—and I whispered a greeting as I positioned a porcelain pillow on the floor next to the tray and lay my head upon it. After letting Roxanna prepare three pipes for me, I asked about buying more *chandu*. She looked up from the pill she was rolling. "At the rate you're going you'll need another refill in three weeks. How many pipes a day are you smoking?"

I tried not to sound concerned. "I haven't really been counting. Maybe between twenty and thirty?"

Roxanna didn't even try to conceal her shock. "What? Oh dear, you've gotten in way too deep. Even if you have the money to keep this up, I won't have enough to supply you much longer."

I had never asked Roxanna how many pipes she smoked each day. I had just assumed it was around twenty. She surprised me by claiming to smoke only six or eight pipes per day: a few in the morning upon waking and a few more in the evening after work. "On Sundays I sometimes splurge," she said. "To tell the truth, I haven't been doing that so much since you stopped coming over."

"What should I do?" I asked. It was no use for me to try to explain or make excuses. Roxanna picked up the little glass bottle of *chandu* and removed its dropper cap. She counted seven drops into the miniature copper wok. "You would use a lot less opium if you took it orally. Just take micro-doses. One drop under the tongue is equal to five pipes and six drops is equal to thirty. And six drops is less than I use for a single pill."

As she said this the seven drops of *chandu* began to boil in the wok, the water evaporating in a frantic sizzle. I watched but said nothing. The word "micro-doses" had set alarm bells ringing in my head. Opium eating sounded like an admission of addiction. It sounded like failure. It was also totally bereft of romance. The words "Confessions of an American Opium-Eater" flashed in my head and made me wince. I hadn't gotten into this to become a modern-day Thomas De Quincey. Allowing myself to go the route of opium eating might also lead to other opiates that I viewed as barbaric. I had an absolute horror of needles. What could be worse? I thought of the corpulent, waxy-faced Hermann Goering, rolling up an impeccably tailored uniform sleeve to inject a daily dose of morphine. But what if I used opium eating as a way to scale back on my smoking?

Back at my apartment I tried taking a single drop orally. It tasted so indescribably bitter that I made a face into the bathroom mirror as I held the burning liquid under my tongue. Roxanna had said to keep it there as long as possible—where it could be absorbed into the nest of blood vessels below the tongue. Swallowing the *chandu* would slow the drug's effects.

Within an hour I felt a light tingling sensation at the back of my head and neck, and I knew the opium had passed into my bloodstream and was massaging my nervous system. Roxanna was right—the physical effects that I felt were similar to what I typically experienced after about five pipes. The high was less complex than smoked opium, because there was no vaporization process to shuffle opium's alkaloids to the advantage of the smoker, but the feeling was near enough to what I had become accustomed. I tried to do some work and found that I could focus as well as if I had smoked a few pipes. Yet a niggling feeling told me that something was missing; that something wasn't quite right.

By late that evening I knew very well what was missing: the ritual. Like a cigarette smoker who quits and suddenly has nothing to do with his hands, I missed the feel of the needle rolling between my fingertips. I longed for the kiss of ivory against my lips. I pined for the warm glow of the lamp. I didn't have a favorite TV show I never missed, or even a television on which to watch it. Instead, my entertainment was watching myself conduct a nightly black mass.

There were also some side effects to eating opium that I didn't notice until the following day. My digestive system all but shut down, seemingly frozen into hibernation by the drug. The result was constipation and a bloated, unwell feeling in my guts that lasted all day. That night, the physical discomfort subsided, but there was something else that kept luring my mind back to the mat—what Victorian-era Americans knew as "nostalgia for the pipe."

I was able to keep from reclining until just after midnight, but once I did, my reduction strategy was quickly abandoned. I began rolling and inhaling, losing count of how many pipes I had smoked and ruining any chance of making use of the drop of opium I had eaten earlier to lessen the night's dosage. I told myself it wasn't a problem. Roxanna had showed me a way to reduce and I was sure it would work—as soon as I seriously put the method to use. But that could wait. Another night passed by the glowing lamp wouldn't make any difference.

I had all but stopped collecting. Indeed, I'd been selling off some of my minor pieces in order to afford more and more opium. However, there was one piece of paraphernalia that as a smoker I could not do without: the pipe bowl. In my collection there were literally hundreds of bowls, but almost none were of any use to me. This was because the seating of one pill after another upon the needle holes long ago had caused a barely visible enlarging of these tiny apertures. The needle hole is crucial to the vaporization process: If the hole is the right size, the opium will vaporize efficiently and uniformly. However, if the hole is too large because of having become worn from use, opium gets sucked into the bowl without being vaporized, wasting significant amounts of the costly drug with each inhalation.

The two pristine antique bowls that I had bought on eBay years back—the ones discovered behind the false wall in Vancouver's Chinatown—were both in use. Willi had one and Roxanna had the other. The chances of finding more of the same were very slim, but I put the word out to a handful of antiques merchants and waited.

In October I received an email from Alex, my longtime dealer in Beijing, with photo attachments of some opium antiques he had on offer. I didn't expect to find unused pipe bowls in China. I cannot speak for other types of Chinese antiques, but opium antiques that are sourced anywhere else are more likely to be in good condition. Antiques that had the misfortune of being in China during the twentieth century did not have an easy time of it. Wars and political upheaval are never good to old things—when refugees pack their belongings, antiques rarely make the list. Then there was that unique Chinese event, the Cultural Revolution, or as the Chinese now call it, the "Ten Years of Chaos." During this turbulent period, keeping an innocuous heirloom such as a Qing vase might cause the owner to be targeted by the fanatical Red Guards, who under Mao had absolute power to stamp out the bourgeois trappings of Old China. Opium-related relics were even more likely to get their owners in trouble, and as a result, countless thousands of opium pipes, lamps, and other accoutrements were destroyed.

In the past I had purchased pipe bowls from Alex that I suspected had been thrown down wells or buried in gardens, and these were sometimes well preserved, having been covered with a protective layer of soil until later discovery. However, such bowls had been used prior to being discarded, and the needle holes always had wear that made them unsuitable for smoking.

The photos that Alex had attached to his email message were only large enough to get a cursory look at what he was offering.

The items were laid out on a yellow towel alongside a U.S. dollar bill for scale. There were some brass tools and a pair of scissors for trimming an opium lamp's wick. There were also three pipe bowls, all about the same size and shape, and all with the same odd, splotchy patina. Something about the bowls caught my eye, and so I zoomed in on them until the image blurred with pixilation. I wasn't absolutely sure, but the needle holes seemed to be identically small on all three bowls. I emailed Alex asking for larger photos of the bowls, and within a couple of hours the images arrived in my in-box. The needle holes were tiny and perfectly formed as if the bowls had never once had a needle thrust into them. This was luck.

I quickly emailed back and asked the price of the bowls. As always, Alex's price was fair. He would sell me all three bowls for a hundred dollars. I agreed immediately. The transaction was the best kind—one of those in which both the buyer and seller are sure they've gotten the better deal. At a glance I knew the three bowls would have generated little interest in anyone other than myself. Their ceramic surface was covered with blackish and whitish stains from mineral deposits that had leached out of the soil in which they were once enveloped. Neither ornamented nor fitted with brass collars, the bowls lacked the two features that collectors usually look for. However, when they arrived in the mail, I saw that my observations had been correct: The bowls had pristine needle holes that had never been used.

My guess was that the pipe bowls had been new when their original owner decided to ditch them, perhaps throwing them down a well or digging a hole and burying them. I cleaned the bowls under a running tap, using a soft-bristle toothbrush to scrub away the lichen-like incrustations from the terracotta surface. After an hour of gentle scrubbing, the bowls were clean and looked like new. Next, I picked through a drawstring bag full of spare brass collars, looking for three that would fit snugly onto the necks. Once this was accomplished, there was only one thing left to do: Take the bowls for a test drive.

All three worked perfectly, burbling sonorously as I drew opium vapors into my lungs. I marveled at my good fortune in finding them, and vowed not to share them with anybody. With luck, a well-made pipe bowl might last a year or more, and so I figured that I had at least three years of not needing to worry about this essential piece of paraphernalia. Then, extraordinarily, Alex emailed me again with two more bowls that he wanted to sell. Immediately I noticed that these two new bowls had the same exact patina as the first three. Had somebody in China found a cache of "dead stock" pipe bowls stashed away in a cave? The thought intrigued me.

I had already decided to buy these latest offerings, but I feigned hesitation in order to extract more information from Alex. As we conversed via Skype enhanced with cams, I saw that he was bundled up against the chill of a Beijing autumn and laughing nervously. Alex at first pretended he knew nothing about the pipe bowls' provenance. Then, after some goading, he finally admitted that he thought all five bowls had been robbed from the same century-old grave. "Tomb bowls" was how he began referring to them.

"The smokers in old times were buried with opium and tools to smoke," Alex explained, "so they will not suffer in the afterlife."

I asked, "Would the family of the dead smoker buy new paraphernalia—new tools—or use old pieces?"

"I'm not sure. Maybe one or the other. Maybe a favorite pipe and lamp but also maybe some new bowls for use when the favorite bowl no longer works."

This made perfect sense. I surprised Alex by jumping at the

newly offered pipe bowls. He again laughed uneasily and asked if I wasn't afraid of ghosts. I was not. On the contrary, it wasn't just that the bowls were in perfect condition and would improve my sessions by preserving precious *chandu*. I was also morbidly fascinated by the idea of using paraphernalia that had for a century been cradled by a corpse. I imagined a link between myself and this long-dead smoker whose spirit was soothed by the presence of opium and paraphernalia with which to smoke it. It was true that some rude spade had shattered his time capsule and grasping hands had desecrated its sanctity; but a smoker is a smoker and I was sure that the original keeper of these bowls, if he had some way of knowing, would break into an admiring smile upon seeing me put them to work.

That night, in the darkened living room of my apartment above Bangkok's Chinatown, I drew vapors through one of the pipe bowls and marveled at its perfection. The taste was superb— not a hint of brimstone. What would the ghosts of Raw Ghost Alley think? There was no mistake—I could hear them cheering me on. Their roar of approval could not be confused with the noise of inane carousing that at that moment was emanating from the booze cruises on the nearby river. In my increasingly withdrawn state, the sounds of human revelry had begun taking on a sinister quality, while in my head the imagined shouts of encouragement from the neighborhood's old opium spirits rang with the familiarity of family.

The world outside the confines of my apartment now seemed a hideous and brutal place. Every night I became Charlton Heston in the 1971 film *Omega Man,* living in an elegantly appointed mansion that also served as a fortress. Inside the mansion's thick walls were sanctuary and civilization: Heston's character, dressed in a smoking jacket, plays chess with a bronze bust and sips scotch, while outside chalky faced mutants clad in soiled cowls shriek and howl for him to come out and face them. Once in a while Heston might step out onto the balcony—the mere sight of him causing the mutants' keening to crescendo—and pump a few rounds from a high-powered rifle into the orgy of flapping robes. Yet for the most part Heston simply ignores the rabble.

Okay, the shooting part was taking it too far. Of course I didn't hate people, but my feelings of uniqueness at being able to smoke opium had somehow morphed into a cold sense of superiority. I felt no kinship with people. Their concerns were not my concerns; their worldly joys and desires struck me as absurd. People were lining up for blockbuster movies or to eat in trendy restaurants or to buy the latest version of some video game—and I saw no point in any of it. To the contrary, my one great joy was knowing that I didn't *need* any of it. There was euphoria in what felt like the ultimate act of rebellion against modern society. Opium was setting me free.

Even the eventual demise of my libido felt liberating. The ability to see beauty in the human form was still there, but all consequent sexual desire had vanished. It felt no different from admiring marble nudes in a museum. Yet to me this didn't seem like loss—quite the opposite—it was as though I had conquered a base instinct and risen above it. Like some Buddhist ideal, this extinction of desire brought about an end to suffering. Except that a single desire remained: I needed a fix every few hours or my mind and body would go to pieces.

❧

"Okay, but this is the last bottle. There's really no way I can sell you another refill unless you chip in to help with buying a shipment through Willi."

I had been dreading this day for what seemed like a lifetime.

I knew it was coming but had purposely avoided asking Roxanna how low her stash was. As for the who, what, when, and where of procuring the *chandu,* I always felt that the less I knew, the better. I wanted to keep a buffer between myself and the ones handing money to the procurers, whoever they were. Even now, the only thing I wanted to know was how much money I would need to raise in order to invest in opium futures.

"Well, I'm never sure exactly how much it will cost until I get the *chandu,* but if you gave me five thousand dollars, that should take care of it."

It was a good thing I had saved this conversation for the end of my visit or it would have ruined our session. I had less than a week to come up with the money—longer if I began eating the *chandu* instead of smoking it. I was broke. I had already spent much of my advance for the guidebook to Cambodia—the one that I had not yet begun researching. There was only one way to come up with such a large amount of money in such a short amount of time: I had to sell something from my collection.

On the subway ride home I started taking inventory in my head, going through boxes and examining pieces in my mind's eye. When I arrived back at my apartment I immediately began taking stock of what I might part with, opening boxes that contained hundreds of pieces of paraphernalia, each individually wrapped but not labeled. I relied on my memory and the feel of an object through the plastic Bubble Wrap to help me decide what to unwrap and examine.

During the preceding year I had been selling bits and pieces to a wealthy amateur collector in Las Vegas. The tools I let go were mostly ones for which I had acquired duplicates. This, of course, allowed me to sell without worrying that I might never find replacements for what I had sold. Opium antiques are so rare that finding exact duplicates is the exception, not the rule.

Many of the pieces that I had collected were unique; during all my years of collecting and research I had never seen another. But in order to raise such a large amount of money I would need to sell off some of these unique pieces, and this made it very difficult to choose. I might instead sell one major item—such as an ornate pipe—and with its sale get the bulk of the cash I needed. I gave both options some thought and came to the conclusion that it would be less painful for me to sell off a lot of minor pieces than one or two major ones.

I picked through the boxes that contained the bulk of my collection, but after hours of queasy indecision I had made no progress. The experience was exactly like going through my belongings as a kid after having been told by my parents that it was time to throw things out. Back then, I always ended up daydreaming; playing with toys that I had neglected for years; leafing through old magazines; minutely examining the contents of cigar boxes filled with coins or streetcar tokens. Hours passed and no decisions were made. Part of my problem was that as a kid I was convinced that inanimate objects had feelings, and so throwing out old toys or bits of collections felt like individual acts of betrayal. I vividly recall sitting cross-legged on the carpeted floor of my bedroom, taking everything out of bureau drawers (most of which were "junk drawers"), and scattering their contents on the floor around me—making my bedroom an even bigger mess than when I had started. And there I would sit frozen, unable to discard anything.

Of course, as an adult I wasn't troubled by thoughts that pieces of my collection might grieve being sold to a new owner. Still, in an odd way my collection provided companionship of sorts. Collecting opium antiques was the principal activity in my life. For years it had been my main source of entertainment—until I discovered how entertaining opium smoking could be.

Now my opium-smoking habit was threatening to change everything. What it was coming down to was this: Opium paraphernalia collecting or opium smoking—I had to choose. If I continued smoking opium, I knew that my collection would literally pay the price. My plan to donate my entire collection to the University of Idaho would be shelved, and as a result, what I had hoped would be my legacy—what I would be remembered for long after I had left this world—was going to be undone as well.

It was with this dilemma in mind that I finally made a decision: I would quit cold turkey. Previous attempts to gradually scale back on my daily dosage had all failed. Every effort had ended the same way: As soon as I started smoking, the inevitable tendency to procrastinate took over. Somewhere along the way my opium optimism had become opium fatalism.

I had already tried stopping abruptly, fighting the urge to smoke as soon as I awoke in the afternoons and then spending sleepless nights sneezing and wiping my nose until it was raw. On three occasions I made it all the way until dawn before breaking down—frantically preparing pipes to calm my jagged-edged nerves and allow me to sleep. But this time quitting would not be some spur-of-the-moment decision. I would make a plan and stick to it. Halloween was a few days away and that seemed a fitting date to quit. I had a week to prepare and do research.

During the many years that I had been collecting opium antiques I spent countless hours reading about every aspect of the drug. While looking for clues as to how opium's mysterious paraphernalia was used, I had gone through every book and magazine article written in the English language that I could find. In some of those publications—the older ones dating back to the late nineteenth or early twentieth centuries—I had run across dire descriptions of opium withdrawal. In the past I had skimmed over these passages without much notice—back then I was interested in learning to smoke, not learning to quit. Now I went back to my library and nervously reread those same passages to get an idea of what I might be up against.

My first move was to seek out the advice of the good doctor from New York City, H. H. Kane. Despite the great age of his words (Kane did his research in the 1870s), I felt that he was solid and reliable. I had found the majority of Kane's observations matched my own, and while no doubt a product of his time, he was atypical in that he did not assume a high moralizing tone when discussing opium use. Kane also seemed to feel, as did I, that opium addiction was less harmful than alcoholism. This attitude, also rare for his time, made me trust his words. I opened the book to a passage that I was already familiar with:

> Between opium-smoking and chronic alcoholism there can be no comparison. The latter is by far the greater evil, both as regards its effects on the individual and on the community. The opium-smoker does not break furniture, beat his wife, kill his fellow-men, reel through the streets disgracing himself or friends, or wind up a long debauch comatose in the gutter.

I nodded at this forgotten truth as I continued leafing through the book. On page 44, Dr. Kane had this to say: "A man who smokes large amounts of opium daily is, in this country, called a 'fiend.'"

Even in my desperate state I couldn't help but chuckle at these words. I didn't feel particularly fiendish. Then, on page 84, I found this: "The shackles that he has lazily and indolently riveted upon himself now refuse to be unloosed, and he finds himself bound to an idol that he despises." And finally, on page 100, there was this description of opium withdrawal:

> A peculiar, dry, drawing, burning pain in the throat, and tearing pains, most marked in the calves of the legs, in the loins, and between the shoulders, are felt. These pains are usually very distressing in the worst cases. If no opiate is used and the vomiting and diarrhoea continue, the restlessness and flushed face give place to quiet, with paleness, sunken eyes, collapse, and death.

For good measure, Kane quoted one Samuel Wells Williams, an American diplomat and Christian missionary who lived and traveled widely in China in the nineteenth century and wrote a book about the country's social life and customs. Williams's description of opium withdrawal symptoms were much the same:

> At this stage of the habit his case is almost hopeless; if the pipe be delayed too long, vertigo, complete prostration, and discharge of water from the eyes ensue; if entirely withheld, coldness and aching pains are felt over the body, an obstinate diarrhoea supervenes, and death closes the scene.

I also discovered the contemporaneous *Opium and the Opium-Appetite* by Alonzo Calkins from 1871. Calkins, a doctor like Kane but one whose research among Americans focused more on laudanum and opium eating, paraphrased one addict's own words when saying this about opium withdrawal: "With the 'horrors' upon him, the sensations were what no imagination could conceive, much more what no pen could describe."

I also searched online, but, as with the paraphernalia, knowledge about withdrawal seemed to have vanished along with opium smoking. My Internet searches for "opium addiction" brought up websites for a number of American detox clinics, but every one of these lumped it together with addiction to heroin and other opiates, seeming to mention it only as an afterthought. I didn't think the websites had reliable information. For one thing, from what I had gathered by reading other sources, the symptoms of withdrawal from heroin were milder than those of opium. I wondered if the clinics had actually treated any opium addicts.

Back with the leather-bound books, I learned that both doctors Kane and Calkins warned against trying to cure an opium habit without a qualified doctor's supervision. The cases that both doctors saw probably involved people who had been using the drug regularly for years, so I wasn't sure if their warnings applied to me. It was true that I had been experimenting with opium for about a decade, but I hadn't become a regular smoker until a couple of years before, and had been smoking heavily and daily without a break for only a couple of months, since the end of August 2007. From reading Emily Hahn's memoir I deduced that her length of serious experimentation with opium was about the same as my own. She claimed to have overcome it with the help of hypnosis.

As Halloween approached I became more and more determined to quit. All I needed, I told myself, was to believe that I still had the self-discipline. I reminded myself that when I really put my mind to doing something, I always did well. It was a simple case of mind over matter. I kept a stream of such thoughts running through my head during those last days, steeling myself for the business of quitting even while I was smoking.

On the afternoon of the thirtieth of October I began my session as soon as I woke up. I was going to have my last pipe before midnight rang in the thirty-first, and I wanted time to have a full session in order to say goodbye in style. After a few pipes to limber up my sleep-sore muscles, I showered and donned my linen suit. For company, I propped a framed photograph of Miss Alicia de Santos on the opposite side of the layout tray. Miss de Santos would have been the first runner-up beauty queen of the Manila Carnival in 1931, but she cried foul and declined the title. There was something about the wronged look in her eyes that made her an agreeable opium-smoking companion.

My usual layout mascot, a century-old brass Billiken figurine grinning like some species of cheeky Buddha, would keep the conversation lively even when Miss de Santos became petulant. I rolled a few pills and told them both how much I would miss their company. In the last couple of months I had come to understand the fondness of old-time opium smokers for whimsical pipe bowls shaped like jolly Buddhas and laughing children. How much easier it was to anthropomorphize your pipe if its bowl smiled back at all your witty pronouncements.

What was to be my last session flew by with the rush of a roller-coaster, leaving me breathless and euphoric. Just before midnight I blew out the lamp and pushed my layout under the coffee table. I thought that perhaps by breaking opium's routine I could lessen the impact of withdrawal, so instead of passing the rest of the night blissfully drifting on the mat, I broke with custom and went to bed. I was determined to wake in the morning as normal people do—not on the living room floor, but in bed.

Three days later I was back on the mat chuckling at my own folly. Nothing had changed except that my apartment looked as though a tornado had ripped through it. There were fresh bruises on my arms and legs as well as aching in my guts and bowels from days of oral and anal purging. I spent two days smoking and

recovering from the Halloween Massacre. There were no more
thoughts of quitting. Billiken smiled; Miss Alicia de Santos stared
beseechingly. As soon as I had rested, I selected some items to
sell, photographed them, and emailed the files and a price list to
the collector in Las Vegas. Within a couple of weeks I would
have enough of a payment to show Roxanna that I was serious.
For the time being I could stop worrying about the ever-
decreasing level of *chandu* in the little brown bottle.

I had been smoking a thousand years. The calendar didn't
concur—it had been just over a week since my failure to quit on
Halloween. Yet it was obvious that I had passed some sort of
milestone—descended into some previously unvisited level of
opium surrender. I no longer needed a clock or a calendar.
Opium became my timekeeper. It alone would let me know
when it was time to smoke and when it was time to sleep. Hunger no longer had much sway over my body clock. Food became
increasingly unnecessary, and sweets were all I desired. Did the
husband and wife from Canton who ran the minimart on the
ground floor of the condo notice that I was living almost exclu-
sively on ice cream? If so they said nothing. The only remark I
ever heard from anybody about my appearance was that I looked
"tired."

Near dreamless sleep had been the norm since I started
smoking with Roxanna, but that changed, too. Every afternoon
I awoke with memories of lonely images, such as abandoned
stone temples in airless jungles or rusting hulks of automobiles
upon bleak stretches of desert. These dreamscapes all had one
thing in common: They were totally devoid of people. While
sleeping I perspired profusely and upon waking my sheets and
pillow were soaked with a tea-colored sweat that smelled of

opium. I showered twice a day, washing off an oily opium sheen that coated my skin. I thrived on hot water, tolerating the highest of temperatures even on the hottest of days. Conversely, lukewarm showers felt as though they were freezing cold.

In mid-November I called Roxanna and arranged for a visit. I had received money via Western Union, nearly four thousand dollars, and I wanted to hand it to her in person instead of merely having the money transferred to her PayPal account. I wanted to make a point, to show that I was ready to carry my weight. Selling pieces of my collection was traumatic—I almost backed out of the deal at the last minute, going into something of a panic at the post office. But with the money now in hand I felt it was all some strange sort of fate, as if my collection was predestined to bankroll my habit, allowing me to experience this rare lifestyle.

I arrived at Roxanna's on a Saturday afternoon during the preliminary stirrings of Bangkok's "winter," a period of relatively cool and dry weather with pleasant daytime temperatures in the low seventies and nippy nighttime temperatures in the high fifties. This respite from the heat and humidity might last a couple of months or barely a week. Some years the temperatures never dropped at all, but the prediction for late 2007 and early 2008 was an extended and chilly cool season.

During weather like this, smoking in Roxanna's upstairs room seemed cozy and inviting. There was no need to open the shutters and turn on the electric fan between pipes, and we punctuated our session with hot tea instead of the usual Gatorade. Time sailed by and we smoked until long after dark, the whistle and clatter of a passing night train reminding me to look at the clock. It was almost nine. The pedicab drivers would already have gone home, and soon even the knot of teenage boys who hung out on the corner and made extra cash by using their motorbikes to ferry the occasional pedestrian to the main road would take their earnings and head for the nearest all-night snooker hall. I needed to think about hitting the road soon or I would have to walk that lonely half mile, stray dogs barking abruptly from the shadows and scaring the bejeezus out of me. I brought out my wallet and counted out the flesh-toned thousand-baht banknotes onto the layout tray.

"That's enough for now. I'll cover the rest," Roxanna said while folding the bills and snapping them into her coin purse.

"Great," I replied, "I'm almost out again. Do you think it will take longer than a week?"

"A week?" Roxanna gave a half smile as though unsure of whether I was trying to be funny. "It will take two months at least. Luckily for us this is harvest season. Sometimes it can take half a year before anything is available."

I forced a yawn—a tactic to disguise my rising panic. "And how about if I take an advance on my share?" My voice cracked slightly on the word "advance."

"I'm sorry, I just don't have it," Roxanna said with a finality that silenced me. She began rolling a pill and I let her finish and smoke it—a long five minutes—before making one last plea.

"Could I at least get one more refill?" I was desperate. If she agreed, I might be able to stretch out the amount over two months. This would mean opium eating but I saw no way out. If only I could hang on until the new shipment came in, then I could relax for a while.

"Oh, all right."

Her tone was mock annoyance but I knew Roxanna was okay with it. My having come up with the money to chip in surely mattered for something. She let me count the drops of opium into my bottle as she took a cigarette break. I pushed the tip of the dropper as deep into her bottle as I could, believing the *chandu* was thicker at the bottom. When Roxanna was preoccupied with stubbing out her cigarette, I pinched a couple of uncounted squirts into my own bottle.

A week went by. A third of the bottle vanished but I had yet to start taking the opium orally. I dreaded it. The taste was absolutely hideous—a grimace-inducing bitterness unlike anything I had ever experienced. Then there was the fact that eating opium affected my digestive system like liquid cement. Worst of all, eating this rare *chandu* was a ridiculous act of desperation. It was like eating Havana cigars just for the nicotine. I couldn't bring myself to do it. It was low. It was base. The next thing I'd be doing was smoking dross like Armand Hoorde.

I thought about the pieces of my collection that I had sold, a layout tray and matching components that I would never in a million years find again. It was a huge waste, and all it got me was a couple ounces of the narcotic and perhaps more in the distant future. When in need of a pipe, I may have been too muddled with yearnings to see things clearly, but smoking a few pills made my mind lucid, and I was under no illusions. I could now admit to myself that opium was firmly in control, but I still believed there must be a way out.

Again, I went back to my books. Curatives for the opium habit have a long history. In China, the first asylums for treating opium addicts date to the late nineteenth century. Physicians of the day reasoned that if there was a cure for opium addiction, the abundant Chinese pharmacopoeia—thousands of years in the making—would contain it. Yet after trying myriad substitutes, including deadly belladonna, arsenic, and strychnine, Chinese doctors concluded that the only "effective" remedies were the ones that contained opiates. Dross was mixed with herbs and the resulting pellets were sold as an antidote for the opium craving.

Opium smokers got hooked on the pellets but often went back to the pipe, taking their opium orally only when there was a need for secrecy. In times when opium use was actively suppressed, Chinese authorities opened treatment centers that were nothing more than prisons—and so rife with corruption that those who could afford to pay bribes were able to smoke their way through treatment.

Christian missionaries in China also got in on the act, establishing hospitals specifically to cure the opium habit. Compared to Chinese institutions, these were usually better staffed and equipped. The missionary doctors had read up on the latest Western methods of rehabilitation—yet these were fundamentally no different than the dross pellets of the Chinese. Morphine was for a time used as a substitute for opium, and daily injections by the missionaries created among the Chinese untold thousands of "morphine Christians" who crowded churches, clenching Bibles and howling out hymns as their withdrawal-wracked bodies shuddered in anticipation of the post-sermon fix.

Some missionary doctors forbade the use of opiates to cushion the agony of withdrawal, believing the addicts' passage through detoxification should be as painful as possible so that the miracle of the Christian cure would be indelibly impressed upon their memories. When it came to cruelty, however, the Chinese authorities were not to be outdone. An opium addict with a history of relapse might be "rehabilitated" through mutilation: a notch of flesh was cut out of the upper lip, making it impossible to get an airtight seal on an opium pipe's mouthpiece.

In America, there was no end to the quackery on offer for the desperate. Denouncing them all, H. H. Kane wrote:

There are quacks in the West who put up medicine which will, they claim, enable a smoker to abandon the pipe without suffering. It is a cunning bait, but a delusive one, it having led many to ruin; for containing some preparation of opium or morphine, they often fix the victim in the double habit of smoking and taking the drug by the mouth. These rascals deserve a punishment that no law now in existence can give them.

I have in my collection an advertisement for one such American cure, "Dr. S. B. Collins' Painless Opium Antidote." An illustration on the ad shows an opium pipe, lamp, needle, and container, as well as a "Chinese opium smoker" putting the paraphernalia to use. For anyone in the know, however, the drawings instantly put Dr. Collins's cure to question—whoever drew the illustrations for the ad had certainly never witnessed opium being smoked, or its paraphernalia, firsthand.

A read through Dr. Kane's description of his own opium cure might make one wonder if he had more in common with Dr. Collins's ilk than he cared to admit. Kane listed some of the remedies used at the De Quincey Home, his opium addiction treatment center in New York. These included chili peppers, iced champagne, and a tincture made from cannabis. The patient was treated to "electro-massage, hot baths with cold spray" and "a course of reading . . . to elevate the mental and moral tone of the individual."

For me, seeking professional medical help in Thailand was absolutely out of the question, and not just because I was short on cash. Entering a hospital and being completely frank about my opium addiction was a great risk because I wouldn't know until it was too late if the staff was obliged under the law to alert the authorities.

Thailand may still have a reputation for tolerating illicit narcotics, but that is the Thailand of the past. A devastating meth-

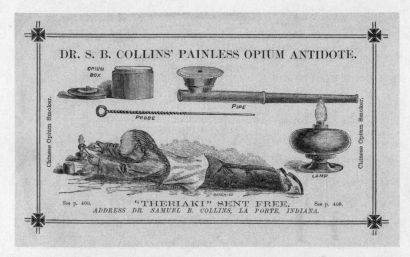

An advertisement for a nineteenth-century quack remedy for opium addiction. The woeful inaccuracy of the ad's depiction of opium smoking and paraphernalia cast grave doubts on the remedy's effectiveness. (From the author's collection)

amphetamine epidemic that began in the 1990s was answered by the government with firepower. The ensuing "war on drugs" killed thousands. Not that people no longer get addicted to illegal drugs in Thailand—they do. It is well known that wealthy Thais go mainly to the United States for drug rehabilitation, checking into the same posh institutions that look after American celebrities. They do this not only to avoid scandal in Thailand, but to keep the authorities from becoming involved. As for the average Thai, I had no idea where they turned when saddled with an addiction.

I continued to search the Internet for ideas. Then I remembered reading about something years before—a certain Buddhist monastery located in a province near Bangkok. Known as Wat Tham Krabok, the monastery had a long-established drug detox program that was unusual enough to have been the subject of the occasional news story. This place might be just what I needed:

an effective, discreet, and inexpensive way to get unhooked. The monastery had a website and I read through it all, the photos and testimonials giving me real hope. The more I read the more I was certain I'd found the right solution. After emailing the *wat* (Thai for "Buddhist monastery") to make sure there was a vacancy, I asked if they could send a car to pick me up near my apartment. It would have been just as easy—and probably cheaper—to take a taxi, but I didn't want the agitation of having to evade a taxi driver's nosy questions about why I was visiting a drug detox center.

On November 18, 2007, I set a date and time: the 21st at one in the afternoon. It had been roughly seven months since my trip to Europe had primed me for daily smoking; four months since I used my birthday as an excuse for a solo binge at my apartment; three weeks since my attempt to quit on Halloween. I spent the remaining three days physically and mentally preparing myself for detoxification. Some of the few things that I needed to bring were toiletries and a sarong. Most everything else would be provided.

On the morning of the 21st, I woke up at ten. For breakfast I ate a triple-decker peanut butter and jelly sandwich on raisin bread and washed it down with goat's milk. After eating and showering, I reclined to seven bowls. My concentration was poor: Pills burned and collapsed, and pipe number five was wasted. I just wanted enough opium to keep my system tight— to be free from sneezing or yawning or any of the other initial symptoms of withdrawal. I had broken down most of my layout the previous night and begun washing *chandu*-stained accoutrements and putting them away. My layout that morning was down to the bare essentials: pipe, lamp, needle, and tray.

I rolled my last pill without any ceremony—it seemed counterproductive to make a big deal of it. Then I quickly began taking apart the pipe, flushing dross and gee-rags down the toilet, wiping down everything, and placing the pieces back onto dusty shelves. Upon rolling up the woven-cane mat, I saw that my constant reclining over months had worn the lacquer from the wooden parquet floor underneath. There was a ghostly mark on the hardwood: an outline of my body in repose. If I was successful at quitting—and I was determined to be—this scar on my living room floor would be the only remaining physical evidence of my opium habit.

Better [for the smoker] to die breaking off opium than to live with the
sin upon him. . . . If he thus died God would be pleased with him.

—A. P. Quirmbach, *From Opium Fiend to Preacher* (1907)

When Thailand closed its government-licensed opium dens in 1959, the move created an exodus of opium addicts from Bangkok. Opium detoxification centers were so few and so inadequately staffed that for the vast majority of smokers the chance for rehabilitation was nonexistent. In the neighborhood of Talat Noi, known for its warren of licensed opium dens, regulars were turned away and went home to smoke the last of their supply, knowing full well that to buy more would be an expensive and dangerous proposition. Some turned to heroin. Others, knowing they were doomed but unwilling to be a burden on their families, plotted a final escape. One by one they toasted their last pills and then, before the pain of withdrawal could cause them to lose their courage, the addicts slipped away into the night, hitting the road for sparsely populated rural provinces where they could die alone and unknown.

One such hopeless addict happened upon a Buddhist monastery in Saraburi Province, some eighty miles north of Bangkok. All monasteries serve as very basic places of accommodation for traveling Buddhists, and the addict stopped there to ask for a place to sleep before journeying on. The abbot granted permission and at that point the addict confessed his predicament and begged the abbot to help him, explaining that if he didn't get some kind of relief from the pain of withdrawal, he was sure to die during the night. The abbot demurred. He had no experience with opium addiction and knew of no way he might help. The man was desperate. He implored the abbot to aid him in any way he could. Finally, simply to appease him, the abbot plucked a petal from a lotus blossom that had been left as an offering on an altar. Giving the lotus petal a blessing, the abbot then handed it to the addict, who promptly ate it.

The next morning, the abbot expected to find the addict dead but was surprised to see that he was still very much alive and claiming that he had experienced only mild withdrawal symptoms the previous night. When the man once again asked for permission to stay the night and for the abbot to bless another lotus petal for him to consume, the abbot's interest was piqued. He didn't really think the lotus petal was doing any good; perhaps it was simply the addict's willingness to believe in a cure.

The addict's second night at the *wat* was easier than the first, and after several days, the abbot could see that the man was gaining strength and had a healthy appetite. Feeling that he was cured, the former addict profusely thanked the abbot, but before he could leave, the abbot made him promise not to tell anyone what had happened. The man promised to keep it a secret. Then, about a week later, crowds of opium addicts began arriving at the monastery. Not long after, the former addict returned to the monastery to explain himself. He told the abbot that he had tried not to break his promise, but when he arrived home alive and healthy, word got around and he was soon besieged by frantic opium addicts begging to know how he was cured.

The abbot, unable to turn away the suffering addicts, let them stay at the monastery and blessed lotus petals for everyone, while at the same time seeking the advice of a renowned herbalist—a Buddhist nun who happened to be the abbot's aunt. The nun produced a formula for a curative potion that she said came to her in a dream. Gathering hundreds of different herbs that grew in the craggy limestone mountains towering over the monastery, the nun then described a method for brewing the tonic to the abbot, who kept it a secret between himself and a handful of monks within the *wat*. The ingredients of this miraculous potion have been quietly passed down to the present day.

That was the story as it was given to me by a Buddhist monk six days after my arrival at the monastery. I knew none of this beforehand, but had I known the legend, I cannot say it would have inspired much confidence. I had been in Southeast Asia too long to believe in miracle cures. Superstition and the occult are part of the local color—interesting, yes—but not something I trusted my life with. In Thailand there are herbal remedies for AIDS and cancer. There are talismanic tattoos that can stop bullets. There are Buddhist and Hindu amulets that allow one to survive the most horrific car wreck. And there is this monastery that claims it has a secret potion to cure drug addiction—made from a recipe that was revealed to a Buddhist nun in a dream. I didn't know the story when I first arrived at the monastery, but even if I had, I would certainly have gone along with it. At that juncture I had little choice.

Via email I had told a representative of Wat Tham Krabok where I would wait for the driver and what I'd be wearing. Having thought it over carefully during my last pipe, I had decided I would dress "smart casual," which in Thailand works for all but the most formal occasions. Of course, when compared to the

average Westerner in Thailand—whether expat or tourist—
I would be overdressed, but that was the whole point of the exercise. If there were other *farang* addicts at the *wat,* I wanted to
immediately stand out from them in the eyes of the Thai monks.
I would be required to change into a uniform at the detox facility, but hopefully my first impression would be a good one. Like
most people, the Thai judge books by their covers. Never mind
that I was a junkie; if I dressed like a gentleman, I would be received as a gentleman junkie.

Despite all my planning, things started out badly. The driver
who came to pick me up was an older man, and he brought his
whole family—his wife and a grown-up son and daughter—
along for the ride. I wanted the trip to the monastery to go as
quickly and painlessly as possible. I had picked Bangkok's main
railway station as a rendezvous point because it was situated next
to an on-ramp for the expressway. I had chosen the time of departure because I knew traffic would be light at that hour. Bangkok traffic is so awful that if one makes a single bad decision
about routes or timing, it can end up causing hours and hours of
delay. I didn't want any unexpected surprises, but that's exactly
what I got.

In the parking lot of the railway station we all squeezed into
the cab of a pickup truck. The son took the driver's seat and
mentioned offhandedly that he first needed to go to a shopping
mall. I was too distracted to protest. We drove past the expressway on-ramp and were immediately mired in traffic. What
should have been an hour-and-a-half drive ended up taking
nearly four hours. I had no previous idea about the detox sched-
ule at the monastery, but upon arriving I learned that the delay
had caused me to miss that day's treatment. The news frightened
me. I contemplated going home and returning the following
day. Pain was what I feared, and without any kind of treatment I

was sure the night would be excruciating. But it was too late to turn back. I knew that if I went home and spread out the mat and arranged the layout and lit the lamp, I would never leave my apartment again.

The monastery's reception area was a mango orchard, the ground graveled to keep down the dust. Next to an outdoor shrine under a banyan tree was a doorway into the registration office, but the only things office-like inside were a couple of desks and filing cabinets. The space looked like a typical room in a Thai Buddhist monastery, its walls covered with religious posters and laminated portraits of unsmiling elderly monks. Although the windows were open to the outside air, the surrounding trees kept the office cool, quiet, and dark.

A Westerner with a German accent and attired in the toga-like robe of a Theravada Buddhist monk introduced himself and began checking me in. Phra Hans (*phra* is the Thai honorific for religious figures, both mortal and immortal) copied down information from my passport and explained the rules. I had to sign a commitment to stay a minimum of seven days. The treatment was free but donations were welcome. There were no phone calls or visitors permitted during the first five days while I was undergoing detox. Each day began at 4:30 A.M. and lights were turned out at 9:30 P.M. Before taking the herbal cure I had to take a Buddhist vow to renounce all drug use. And then the most important rule: The cure was a onetime thing. If I left the *wat* after treatment and had a relapse—breaking my Buddhist vow in the process—I was not going to be allowed back in for another try. There were no second chances at Wat Tham Krabok. Period.

I gave up my passport and valuables—my wallet and mobile phone—to be locked away in the monastery safe. Jewelry wasn't allowed inside the detox facility, but I was allowed to keep the

Ganesha amulet that I was wearing on a silver chain around my neck. Money wasn't allowed inside either. I traded about forty dollars' worth of Thai baht for Wat Tham Krabok scrip—banknotes crudely printed on colored paper—to pay for meals and snacks. I signed a release form and the agreement to stay at least seven days.

Next, I met the monk who supervised the detox facility, which turned out to be a fenced-in section within the much larger monastery grounds. Phra Art was a Thai of about thirty who as a civilian had been a roadie for a rock band. Like nearly all of the monks at the monastery, he first came to Wat Tham Krabok with an addiction—which in Art's case was alcoholism. Later I learned that a small percentage of addicts who took the cure, including a handful of Westerners, were ordained as monks or became nuns after treatment so they could prolong their sanctuary at the *wat* indefinitely.

Art looked through the toiletries that I had brought along, making sure the mouthwash was nonalcoholic (an unofficial Wat Tham Krabok website had explained in detail what was allowed), that the tube of toothpaste was new, and that other toiletries were still sealed. Then he watched as I undressed and changed into the detox facility's uniform, a baggy, pajama-like outfit based on clothing traditionally worn by farmers in Thailand's north. The shirt was collarless, and in place of buttons there were cloth ties that hung down the front like shoestrings. The knee-length pants were kept up by a drawstring, and were so baggy that I initially mistook them for a laundry bag and tried to put my civilian clothes into them. Both shirt and pants were made of a stiff synthetic that would dry quickly, and were dyed the same bright maroon color. On the back of the shirt were stenciled markings that any Thai would recognize as belonging to the monastery. In fact, the whole outfit was so bright and unusual that anybody wearing it outside the monastery would stand out like an escaped convict.

My shoes were traded for a pair of flip-flops that were wait-ing for me on a concrete slab outside the back door as I left the office and was guided to an open-air pavilion known in Thai as a *sala*. There, I stepped out of my flip-flops and climbed a low flight of stairs up into the pavilion. Inside, the polished wooden floor of the structure was bare except for an altar crowded with Buddhas. I sat before the altar, taking care to point the soles of my feet away from it, and waited for the monk who was sup-posed to come and read me my vow. Outside, the waning sun-light barely penetrated the tall mango trees. Inside, the *sala* was darkening, the ceiling fans were motionless, and mosquitoes buzzed my ears.

From my raised position I saw a van arrive and discharge a large, working-class Thai family made up of parents and small children, and accompanying a man in his early twenties whose limp and bruises told of a recent beating. I watched them all go into the registration office. About twenty minutes later, the man—not much more than a kid really—emerged from the of-fice wearing a maroon uniform, and joined me in the pavil-ion. A second Thai man, about the same age and class as the first and also wearing the detox center uniform, was then escorted into the *sala* by a young monk. The second man needed help lowering himself to the floor, and once he was sitting he began nodding off. I wondered what drug he was on.

An old Thai monk wearing a faded brown robe entered the pavilion and wordlessly seated himself between the altar of Buddhas and the three of us uniformed addicts as we held our hands before us in a prayer-like gesture of respect known in Thai as the *wai*. The monk was fat and in his fifties—or perhaps he was a decade older or a decade younger. Buddhist monks in

Thailand seem ageless, their lack of hair and eyebrows making their faces look smooth and enigmatic. It is amazing how much effect eyebrows have on the overall looks of a person: Shave them off and it's as though the eyes are looking through a feature-less mask. Theravada Buddhist monks adhere to a precept that forbids them from physically touching women, and purposely making themselves ugly is a way for them to avoid temptation.

The monk who would give the vow did not introduce him-self. Instead he briefly looked at a book and then began to recite, and we addicts repeated what he said in unison. The vows were in formal Thai combined with Pali, an Indian language that is to Theravada Buddhism what Latin is to Catholicism. I repeated the vows as best I could, only fully comprehending what was probably the most important passage: a long list of drugs and my promise never to touch them. My own personal poison—*yah fin* in Thai—was on the list, but I also renounced many others, in-cluding ecstasy, ketamine, and at least two types of amphetamine. While reciting, the monk used the street names for these drugs, and a combination of my ignorance of Thai slang and modern narcotics in general meant that I had never heard of some of the drugs that I was swearing off.

Once the vows were said, Art, the supervising monk, met me at the foot of the stairs of the pavilion and led me to the gate of the detox facility. "Did you understand it?" he asked in Thai, referring to the vow I had just taken.

"Not everything but I got the gist of it," I replied.

"Don't break your vow or something bad will happen to you," Art said with a smile to soften any confrontation in the threat. If I hadn't been in Thailand so long I might have read his smile as an indication that he didn't take what he was saying too seriously. Days later I heard Art say the same thing in English to a newly arrived Western addict. There was no smile that time.

Thais who are around Westerners for any length of time soon realize that the elaborate social ballet that Thais perform in hopes of avoiding conflict is wasted on these outlanders.

Of course, I took my vow seriously. I was here to do everything I was told to do. I would happily jump through whatever hoops they could produce, if only they could get me off opium without the soul-wrenching pain.

The gate into the detox facility was closed and locked behind me. Neither the gate nor the wall around the facility were imposing; they were more a psychological barrier than a physical one. Later I saw that the wall didn't even go all the way around the compound. Not that it mattered. Run and I wouldn't get too far while wearing that distinctive uniform. The residents of the area would immediately call the police just as they would had they seen a prison escapee. But again, running away was the last thing I wanted to do.

As Art was leading me to the foreign men's dormitory where I would be staying, he asked what I had come to cure. His reaction to my answer would be a recurring theme during my stay. The detox facility of Wat Tham Krabok may have been founded to treat opium addicts, but it had been a long, long time since anyone here had seen one. "Most of the Thais are here because of meth," Art explained. "The Westerners come for all sorts of reasons."

On the short walk to the dorm we passed a picnic table occupied by an elderly olive-skinned monk with an easy smile who was talking to three Thai women addicts. "This *farang* is addicted to opium," Art said to the old monk as we walked by.

"Really?" the monk asked. He looked rather amazed.

"He speaks Thai," Art said, nodding in my direction as we stopped to talk to the old monk.

"You're addicted to opium?" the old monk asked me. When

I answered yes, he smiled pityingly and said simply, "You are going to suffer."

This was not what I wanted to hear. The women at the table—all of them in their twenties—looked me over and then asked the old monk, "What exactly is opium?"

"We used to help opium addicts here a long time ago. We don't see them anymore. I've never seen a *farang* addicted to opium," the old monk replied. Then he asked me, "How long have you been smoking?"

"Daily, about three months."

"Oh, you'll be all right," the old monk said. "We used to get addicts who had been smoking opium daily for ten or twenty years. The local people used to complain that at night they could hear the addicts' screams all the way into town."

I must have looked shaken because the old monk repeated his assessment that I wouldn't have too bad a time of it. He pointed out a nearby table with a large aluminum beverage dispenser and racks of plastic cups. A sign in Thai posted next to the table read: DRINK THIS MEDICINE TO IMPROVE THE BLOOD.

"Drink as much of that as you can," the old monk said. "It's made from nine bitter herbs. That medicine will make you recover quickly."

I thanked the old monk and Art picked a cup from one of the racks and, twisting open the dispenser's little spigot, filled the cup halfway before handing it to me. "Herb tea," he said in English. I sipped at the tepid, burgundy colored concoction. It tasted ghastly. Art smiled and said in Thai, "Don't sip. Drink it fast. It tastes better in the morning when it's still hot."

I drank the contents of the cup and then filled it again, gulping down a second dose. I would do whatever I had to do— anything to keep the symptoms of withdrawal at bay. I would have drunk the old monk's urine if they'd told me it would lessen the pain. Fortunately for me, nobody was in the mood for pranks.

The dorm I would occupy was a room within a long, non-descript two-story building that from the outside looked like a typical administrative structure found in Thailand. It could have been part of a high school. The ground floor was divided into three rooms, one for women, another for foreign men, and a third room for monks. The women's room housed both Thais and foreigners, apparently because there were so few women addicts at the *wat*. There were also two parallel buildings of nearly identical length, the far one being for male Thai addicts, and a building between the two that I at first thought was unoccupied. Later I found that the middle building's sole occupants were two special cases lodged in separate locked rooms: an older Thai woman who was insane, and a young Thai man who was kept in chains after having punched out one of the monks.

Art led me into the foreign men's dorm, a large room with a high ceiling supported by two pillars. Seven wooden bunks were arranged around the walls. Except for a small shelf unit next to each bed there was no furniture. Out back behind the building was an area for hanging laundry and stalls housing toilets and showers. Art let me choose one of the two empty bunks, and I began placing my belongings onto the shelf next to my bed. The room was deserted when we arrived and Art told me that everyone was at a small eatery that produced noodles and stir-fry to be consumed at picnic tables under an awning. I had noticed the eatery as we were walking to the dorm. To my eyes everything was very basic and even a tad grubby. It was typical rural Thailand.

As I was rigging a mosquito net above my bunk, a tall, dark-haired man with an accent that I recognized as Israeli walked in and greeted me. All men of a certain age in Israel are ex-military and David looked it. He also seemed completely healthy and fit—certainly not the type of character I had expected to find at a drug detox center. "There are no mosquitoes here," David said after introducing himself.

"I'll use it anyway," I told him. "If there's a single mosquito in the room, it'll bite me." In truth, since I first used a mosquito net in the Philippines at the age of eighteen, I've always felt more secure sleeping under one and will, even when the threat of being bitten by mosquitoes is negligible.

David shrugged. "Why are you here?" he asked. It was always the first question asked at the detox center, but I found that I wasn't unhappy answering it. I felt a certain pride in the reactions I was getting—always surprise and, in the other addicts at least, a measure of admiration.

"Opium?" David smiled. "You mean . . . ?" He did a little mime act that resembled an Indian smoking a chillum.

"Yes, I smoked it," I replied.

"Wow! That's the bomb!"

I laughed, not sure what to say next. I had spent the previous week trying to turn myself against opium, believing that this was the only way to psychologically break free of it. To find that I still had these feelings of opium pride was slightly disturbing.

Before I could ask, David said, "I smoked a pipe, too. A crack pipe."

"That's interesting," I said, again at a loss for words. An Israeli crackhead? Surely that had to be as unusual as an American opium fiend. Maybe I wasn't so special after all.

Outside it was already dark. To change the subject I asked if it was too late to get a meal. David explained that the eatery stayed open until about seven, but there was a canteen selling snacks and drinks that closed around nine. "Are you hungry?" he asked. "Come, I'll show you."

While I had no desire for food, I felt surprisingly calm for having passed eight hours without smoking. According to my body clock—which was now ruled by opium—dusk was the start of the day, and for the past month or so I had always begun rolling by sundown. Perhaps the change of scenery alone had helped distract me, but I knew that things would get bad later that night. This might be my last chance to eat a meal.

The eatery was informal. There were no menus; I just poked my head in the kitchen and asked the woman in charge if she had the ingredients to cook what I was hungry for. I ordered minced pork fried with basil, a reliable standard that most every Thai cook can do well. I prefer chicken, but in the provinces the cooks simply use a cleaver to randomly chop whole chickens into bite-size pieces—leaving plenty of splintered bones that guarantee a long, slow meal.

David directed me to one of the picnic tables and introduced me to Clark, a Thai American from New York City. Clark's facial features made it obvious that his ancestors were of Chinese extraction. He was short and thin and wore thick glasses with unfashionable steel frames that made him look nerdish—but only if you didn't notice the blue ink tattoos covering his arms and chest. "That's a Russian mafia tattoo," Clark said when he noticed me staring at an odd rendition of a cat smoking a pipe on his inner forearm. I didn't ask why he might be sporting such a tattoo. Clark said he was twenty-seven but he could have passed for a teenager. He was friendly and talkative.

Clark's heroin addiction had prompted his father, who was retired and living in Chiang Mai, to buy him a one-way ticket to Thailand so he could do the detox program at Wat Tham Krabok. "I've been in and out of rehab in the States. The last time was a place in New York. I finished rehab and got out on my girlfriend's birthday. I was watching TV at her apartment while she went shopping for stuff for a party. Then I just got this idea to go out and score. Next thing I knew I woke up in the hospital. I overdosed and almost died."

Clark laughed at his own story and then told another about when he realized he was hooked on heroin. "I was just snorting it at first. I didn't think you could get hooked that way. One night I was out with my crew and I got picked up by the police for tagging a wall in Brooklyn. They put me in a holding cell with a bunch of other people and after a few hours I started sneezing and puking. I felt like shit. Then some Puerto Rican guy in the cell next to me says, 'Hey, *chino.* Are you a junkie?' And I'm like, 'Yeah, I'm a junkie!' He gave me a little piece of folded paper and inside was enough heroin for a couple of hits. In a minute I felt okay again."

"How long have you been here?" I asked, wondering how much the withdrawal symptoms between opium and heroin differed.

"This is day four," Clark said, picking tentatively at a plate of fried rice that had just been brought to him.

"You look pretty good for day four. I tried to stop a month ago and day three almost killed me."

"Yeah? You should have seen me when I arrived. I took my last hit on the plane over from New York and I started freaking out in the taxi on the way from the Bangkok airport. They had to carry me in here. I barely even remember it. I got dual citizenship but the monks found my Thai passport first, so they put me in the dorm with all the Thais."

"What's that like?" I asked.

"They lock us in at night!" Clark laughed. There was now a group of young Thai men sitting at the picnic table and watching Clark talk. When he noticed this, he turned to one of them and spoke in fluent Thai. "This guy's hooked on opium," he said while nodding toward me.

"Opium? What's it like?" one of the Thais asked Clark.

Before Clark could answer, another Thai replied, "It's nothing. It's just like ganja."

Clark grinned at this. "Did you understand that?" he asked me in English. "They don't know anything about it."

"Hardly anybody does," I replied. "I think only that really old monk has seen opium addicts before."

"I want to try it!" Clark said with wide eyes exaggerated by his thick glasses.

"Are you crazy? You're just getting off heroin." I was envious of Clark having already gotten through the worst of his withdrawal symptoms. To me it seemed incredibly stupid for him to be already thinking about doing drugs again.

My plate of pork fried in basil was brought out to me by the cook's husband. The rice was hot and the night air was relatively cool. At once a cloud of mosquitoes appeared and began dive-bombing the rice as though blood could be sucked from the steaming grains. I waved them away with one hand while spooning in food with the other. The conversation about doing drugs continued among the Thais, but I tuned it out while eating and thought about what the night would bring. After I finished, I bought a six-pack of bottled water on David's advice. "Maybe you won't feel like getting out of bed tomorrow," he said.

Back at the dorm room I met the others. Besides David, there was Jerry, an amiable heroin addict from England with an encyclopedic knowledge of old Hollywood movies, and Rudy, a clean-cut Croat in his twenties who had lived in Germany since he was five. He claimed that during a trip to Amsterdam he had smoked some kind of potent superweed that caused him to become a paranoid insomniac—which, in turn, drove him to get hooked on sleeping pills. Then there was Sheldon, a shy kid from Hong Kong barely out of high school. Like me, he had also just arrived, but had so far refused to reveal to anyone in the dorm what he had come to be treated for. Finally there was Kurt, a middle-aged German who, despite his swimmer's build, claimed he drank too much beer.

Nobody, in fact, looked or acted how I had expected desperate substance abusers to look and act. I assumed that flying all the way to Thailand from Europe or America for drug detox would be a last resort for most. I was lucky—for me the monastery was almost in my own backyard. I spoke Thai and had a fair idea of what to expect as far as conditions were concerned. For the others it must have been like taking a leap of desperation into the unknown. They were thousands of miles from home and as helpless as small children, unable to speak the language or understand much of what was going on around them. Yet none of these men struck me as hopeless, last-resort cases.

There were still a couple of hours before lights out, and I used the time to ask if anyone had passed any really bad nights in the dorm. I was particularly interested to know how Jerry the English junkie felt about it. "I must confess, I was already pretty much over withdrawal when I arrived here the second time," he said.

"You've been here before?" I asked.

"I came here with a mate of mine who did the treatment two years ago. He was sure he could talk his way back in if he could speak directly to the abbot."

"What happened?"

"The abbot turned him away. So my mate said he was going down to the islands to have a little holiday and I sort of joined him. We had some Subutex that we brought from England and I thought I'd come back here when they ran out. But we left the bloody pills on the train and didn't discover it until we were on Koh Phangan. I did my withdrawal in a little hut with a Thai lady I met. It was bloody painful but she took care of me."

"So if you were already over it, why did you come here?"

"I can't go back home without my treatment. My village is full of gearheads and soon as I see one I know I'll break down."

Now I was sure heroin's withdrawal symptoms weren't as severe as those of opium. If Jerry was able to sit it out in a hut with what was surely a Thai prostitute—and what she saw hadn't caused her to bolt and flee the scene—then Jerry certainly hadn't been through what I had been through.

Before the lights were turned out, I looked through a meager collection of books piled in a corner of the room. Some had been left behind by previous occupants of the dorm and others belonged to the monastery. Typically, there was a selection of English-language Dharma primers. Having gone through a dabbling-in-Buddhism stage years before, I remembered that even back when I had an interest in the subject such books were difficult to focus on. Once the withdrawals began, reading one would be like trying to decipher cuneiform. Finally I found a volume of the collected works of Franz Kafka—which seemed wonderfully appropriate. Perhaps I could will myself into becoming a giant bug and in that way keep the withdrawal pains from killing me.

When Art came by the dorm and asked us to turn out the lights, I went out and drank another two cups of "herb tea." I was very relieved to hear that the doors to the foreign men's dorm stayed open all night—in contrast to both the women's and Thai men's dorms. I took advantage of the open-door policy by getting up two or three times during the night and drinking more herb tea, and made at least that many visits to the toilet to pee. In between the trips outside I got some surprisingly restful sleep.

On November 22, 2007, at around one in the afternoon I wrote the following in my journal:

> It's been over 24 hrs since my last pipe & I'm surprised at how easy it's been. Feel weak & like I have a mild cold but so far the ugly symptoms that I've experienced in the past have not yet set in. I fear the night when everyone is asleep and I will be rolling around in pain.

Earlier that morning I had borrowed a reading light from Art and rigged up my bunk so that the light hung from the back of a chair. The bulb was just outside the mosquito net, which diffused the light somewhat; the chair back blocked the light and kept it from disturbing others in the room. I wasn't exactly getting prepared to read all night. I remembered from my previous attempts to quit that darkness made the pain worse. During the Halloween Massacre I had lights burning in every room for the entire three days. What worried me most was that I might begin thrashing around and have to be restrained. I was relieved that my dorm mates were a friendly bunch and seemed to like me.

The morning had started at five with the sweeping of mango leaves from the reception area. Everyone was required to do this daily task and it took about twenty minutes. Then we headed to the shrine next to the registration office, where the brooms were collected and the Thais gathered to light incense and pay their respects.

I approached the shrine, curious to see what deity was being venerated, and was told that it contained the body of the founder of the monastery. I watched but stopped short of any outward display of reverence. The Thais wouldn't have mocked or minded—on the contrary, they all take their religion seriously and feel pride when they see Westerners taking an interest. I knew this, yet I felt self-conscious until a young Thai woman who was handing out incense gave three of the sandalwood-coated sticks to me. I was emboldened by her gesture; it was as though she hadn't even stopped to think that I might not want to venerate the remains of an old monk enshrined under a ban-yan tree. I lit the joss sticks over a candle, and pushed them into a sand-filled receptacle already bristling with scores of others. Then I got down on my knees and bent forward three times, touching my forehead to the floor as I had seen Thais do count-less times during my eighteen years in Thailand. When I was finished, I walked through the crisp morning darkness back to the detox compound.

After regrouping inside the walls, we were led by a handful of monks in performing basic calisthenics. Besides being weak from the lack of opium, it had been months, perhaps years, since I had attempted any sort of exercise—but I wasn't about to start second-guessing the regimen. The ease of the previous night had quickly made a believer of me. My attitude at this point was: Don't question anything, just do it.

At eight was morning muster in front of the tallest structure in the detox compound—a giant whitewashed statue of the Buddha sitting on an ornate concrete dais. Everyone lined up shoulder to shoulder, with the non-Thais in a separate line at the very back, and then the Thais counted off. There were almost fifty people in treatment at that time, fewer than ten of them foreigners. Once roll call was completed, the giant Buddha smiled placidly as the Thai national anthem was sung without musical accompaniment.

At one-thirty everyone was called outside to drink a cup of bitter tea. This was to be followed by an herbal sauna—the men having traded their baggy red uniforms for knee-length Thai-style sarongs. It was pure luck that I chose the end of November to do detox. The weather was as comfortable as it ever gets in central Thailand, the daytime high temperatures never much above eighty degrees Fahrenheit. During Thailand's hot season, roughly mid-March through mid-June, the local temperatures were said to get over one hundred degrees for stretches of several weeks, and none of the dorms at Wat Tham Krabok were air-conditioned. I imagined that doing herbal sauna during the summer months would be like descending from one level of Buddhist hell into the next.

A daily soak was mandatory, but it instantly became my favorite event of the day. The sauna room was very basic: nothing more than a large concrete box with two rows of benches inside. A thick curtain over the door kept the steam in. Two of these sauna rooms were side by side, one for men and one for women.

Above and behind these concrete structures was a fire-fueled boiler and stacks of chopped wood. Reams of lemongrass and other herbs were fed into the boiler, and the resulting steam was vented into the rooms. The aromatic sauna was said to be excellent for the lungs and skin, as well as cause toxins to be sweated out through the pores. I huffed in deep breaths of the tangy steam, knowing that my lungs must be coated with the same oily vapors that turned the inside of my opium pipe tar black. Perspiring profusely, I wiped the moisture from my upper arms and could feel the slimy opium residue as it was oozing from my skin. At intervals of a few minutes, Art, who was waiting outside, gave the command for us to emerge from the steamy darkness and ladle ice-cold well water over our bodies from an adjacent cistern. My withdrawal from opium amplified the cold, and it was all I could do to keep from shrieking during these ice-water sluicings.

An attendant monk was stationed at each sauna to keep it in working order, chopping wood and feeding lemongrass into the boiler. At this particular sauna the monk in charge was one of the monastery's outstanding features. Phra Gordon was easily the most popular of the Westerners ordained as Buddhist monks at Wat Tham Krabok. Non-Asian monks are uncommon in Southeast Asia—but they're not unheard of. Gordon, however, was African American, and in all my time in the region I had only seen two black Buddhist monks. By saying Gordon was "popular" I mean that he was often a topic of conversation among the *farang* addicts at the *wat,* so it wasn't long before I heard his story. Jerry the English junkie told it to me a day or two after I arrived.

According to Jerry, Gordon was a Vietnam War veteran who had come to Thailand to do some traveling after his stint was up. While on a bus heading north from Bangkok, Gordon found himself stranded when the vehicle got punctures in all four of its tires. Waiting for the flat tires to be fixed, he decided to explore the area on foot. The bus happened to break down right in front of the gate to Wat Tham Krabok, and so Gordon walked the winding path up to the monastery. And there he stayed.

Jerry told me he'd asked Gordon if he planned to live at the monastery the rest of his life, and Gordon had said, "It's only a bus stop."

There were other Western monks besides Gordon and Hans, the monk who checked me in. Phra Neil, an Englishman with a face like one of N. C. Wyeth's pirates, was a former heroin addict and tended the second of the monastery's two saunas. Phra Marc, a placid Belgian of indiscernible age, worked in the kitchen and translated Buddhist texts from Thai into English. And there was Saundra—a fortyish Buddhist nun with a shaved head and white robe. She, too, had been addicted to heroin in her native England.

I would have thought that these Westerners ordained and living at the monastery would have little time for the questions of drug addicts. There was an endless chain of us, cycling through the process constantly, no doubt asking the same questions over and over—yet I detected not a hint of cynicism or boredom among any of the Western monks during my interaction with them. All were upbeat and reassuring, even though it was obvious they were extremely busy most of the time.

It was Saundra who gave me support on my first day of the vomiting cure—the principal procedure of the monastery's detox regimen. Unlike the nine-herb bitter tea that I had been quaffing since my arrival, this curative potion brewed from dream-inspired ingredients was to be consumed but not digested—after drinking, it had to be immediately purged. Saundra came to the dorm and explained to me what would take place, giving tips on how to make everything go as smoothly as possible—such as making sure I did not eat beforehand. "Some of these Thai guys eat a full meal before the cure, and you can imagine what it looks like coming up."

Although addicts who came for treatment had to take the vomiting cure for only five days, Saundra still did it regularly because she felt she still needed it—even after years of being off heroin.

Every afternoon a mechanical ringer like a schoolyard bell signaled everyone to assemble at the courtyard outside the Thai men's dorm. There, a wide cement patio was bisected by a long trough, about a foot wide and a foot deep. Along the trough, at intervals of every few feet, were stainless-steel pails filled to the brim with clear water. On the water's surface floated a bowl-shaped plastic scooper of the type rural Thais use for bathing.

When I arrived at the courtyard, dressed in nothing but my Thai-style sarong and flip-flops, there was already a crowd gathered. About a dozen others were also wearing sarongs. Like me, they were newly arrived at the *wat* and were undergoing the first five days of treatment, which revolved around the all-important vomiting cure. The rest wore red-pajama detox uniforms, indicating that they had already finished their initial five days. Saundra directed me to one of the pails filled with water, advising me to step out of my flip-flops and kneel on them so as to cushion my knees from the hard cement. I got into position, lining up with the sarong-clad addicts along one side of the trough and facing the crowd of baggy red uniforms who stood about chattering with excitement before what would be the main event of the day. A pair of conga drums sat incongruously on the patio, and one of the Thai men was playfully tapping on them. Absently, I thought perhaps the congas were left over from some recent performance to entertain the addicts.

An older Thai monk sporting what looked like crude prison tattoos arrived on the scene and walked directly over to me. This was the man all the *farang* addicts referred to as "the Medicine Monk." It was his task to dispense the secret potion. Something about his chiseled face looked familiar, but it took me a while to realize why: The Medicine Monk had a passing resemblance to Master Kan from the 1970s television series *Kung Fu*. Both Art and Saundra were standing behind me, and as the tattooed monk approached, Art told him that I could speak Thai. He also let slip that I was an opium addict and that I lived in Talat Noi, Bangkok's old opium-smoking quarter.

The Medicine Monk's face registered surprise. Little mounds

of muscle where his eyebrows should have been contracted, pushing layers of wrinkles into his forehead. "There's still opium in Talat Noi?" he asked.

"No sir," I answered. "I got it from a *farang.*"

Whether or not he was satisfied with this answer, he didn't dwell on it. The Medicine Monk asked me if I had any medical conditions or history of recent surgery. I said I did not. He then asked the same thing of a Thai man who was kneeling next to me, and then of another down the line. Glancing at them from the corner of my eye, I realized they were the same young men who had taken the vow with me the day before—we three were the only ones on our first day of the vomiting cure.

That finished, the Medicine Monk produced a large, clear-glass bottle of a type that I recognized as being used in Thailand for native rice liquor. The label had been removed, and in place of the metal twist-off cap was a rubber stopper. The bottle was filled with a muddy, reddish-brown liquid. The courtyard had become silent—quiet enough to hear the deep, resonant thump of the rubber plug being pulled from the bottle. Suddenly somebody began pounding the conga drums rhythmically and all the uniform-clad addicts broke into a bouncy Thai song at the tops of their lungs. I didn't recognize it, but I caught some of the lyrics and knew they were singing about giving up drugs: "If you can't stop, you'll die for sure," they sang.

The Medicine Monk produced a shot glass and carefully poured the potion into it as I knelt before him with my hands held in the *wai* of gratitude. He passed the glass to me and I took it with my right hand. Art stood behind me with his hand on my shoulder, *"Deum hai mot!"* ("Drink it all!") he shouted into my ear over the music. I did not stop to ponder the act or sniff at the potion, but instead knocked the dose back like it was a shot of tequila. There was a vile taste followed by withering va-

pors venting through my nostrils and a burning sensation dropping like a hot stone into the pit of my gut. I shuddered.

Art then handed me the plastic scooper brimming with
water from the pail and both he and Saundra urged me to
quickly drink it down. "Hold your body as erect as possible and
pour the water down your throat," she yelled. "Drink until your
belly is distended and then drink more."

I had expected the potion to cause projectile vomiting as
soon as it was swallowed, but that didn't happen. Instead, Art and
Saundra coached me to drink as much water as I could stand,
and then to hold it in for a minute or two. This was supposed to
allow the potion to draw the toxins from my body. When I could
drink no more, I looked around woozily. The music was still
bouncing away and some of the red pajamas were dancing and
cavorting, teasingly calling out encouragement to their friends
taking the cure.

I still had no urge to vomit despite feeling as though I had
just funneled a case of beer. Saundra advised me to stick a finger
down my throat, and so with scores of eyes upon me I did this.
The first upchucks were feeble, but they were soon followed by
torrents of rust-colored water. The vomiting became the violent,
rhythmic sort that causes one to cry out involuntarily with each
heave. On both sides of me others were doing the same, but I
paid no notice to anyone but Art and Saundra. When the vomiting became dry retching, I wiped the mucus from my nose and
the strands of saliva from my chin and attempted to catch my
breath. Before I could recover, however, Saundra demanded that
I drink more water. "You're not finished! You have to get all the
medicine out of your body. Drink more water! Just like before,
drink until you are going to burst!"

If only it were possible to stop moments like this—to be allowed to step out of them for a while and enjoy the spectacular

irony of it all. My helping to research a story for *Time* magazine about opium experimentation among Western backpackers in Laos had seemingly led to this moment. But actually, if I went really far back, I would have to admit that my insatiable love for the exotic—a desire that I had cultivated since childhood—was the real force that pulled me down the trail that had ultimately led to this moment. "Everyone gets everything he wants," Captain Willard said in *Apocalypse Now*. I wanted an exotic life. And for my sins, they gave me one.

I was more than eight thousand miles away from my place of birth, in a Buddhist monastery on the edge of a Southeast Asian jungle. A bald, eyebrowless woman dressed in a sheet and looking like some refugee from a 1970s cult was urgently giving me lessons in self-waterboarding. Was I still looking for exotic adventure?

Of course, as much as the vomiting cure felt like some torturous endgame, I knew this was my way out of the hole. This would save me. I scooped up more water from the pail and forced it down. With three fingers thrust down my gullet, I kept up the vomiting for twenty minutes until my stomach ached and my throat was raw. After the music had died down and the crowd began to disperse, I shakily got up and walked back to the dorm on rubbery legs. My dorm mates congratulated me with upturned thumbs and pats on the back, but I was too dazed to speak. Collapsing onto my bunk, I stared sideways at the bottle of mouthwash on the shelf. I was too exhausted to even care about using it. David helped me make it to the 6 P.M. muster, but I spent the rest of the evening too weak and queasy to get out of bed. One treatment down; four more to go.

On November 25, 2007, at around noon I wrote the following in my journal:

Day four. Haven't felt up to writing the last two days. Last night was the worst so far. . . . I could not lie down. The moment my head touched the pillow the pain was excruciating. So instead of lying I paced the darkened dorm wrapped in a blanket & walking wounded circles around a pillar in the middle of the room. This I did for what seemed like hours, or until my legs were no longer sturdy enough to continue. But whenever I walked over to read the clock on the wall, I was always disappointed to see how little time had passed.

Bim Nolan was right. Delirium *is* a disease of the night. But it turned out that the night I was describing in my journal was as bad as things got. At some point I crumpled from exhaustion and got a couple of hours of sleep. When the morning gong sounded I tried to get up and sweep leaves, but while standing at the detox compound gate, peering into the darkness of the mango orchard, my feverish state transformed the view into a howling, frozen wilderness. I dropped my broom and shuffled back to bed, burying myself under the thin blankets.

David asked me about it later that day. "You didn't sleep last night? I also didn't sleep. Every time I wake I see you walking round and round in circles like in *Midnight Express.*"

I should have been embarrassed at having kept David awake, but I simply felt too awful to care. However, I was fortunate that the trials of a new arrival were taking the spotlight from my own. Pierre was a boyish Frenchman in his mid-forties who spoke very little English. As it happened, nobody in the dorm spoke any French, and so Pierre, who made us understand with sign language that he was coming off a ten-year heroin habit, could take no solace from our words of encouragement.

His second night in the dorm—which was my fourth—

brought him to tears. I still could not sleep, and the fever from the previous night returned, but I found that by reading I could keep my mind off the pain in my head and legs. Actually, reading was just an exercise in clutching the book with both hands while trying to decipher the same paragraph over and over—but at least I didn't have the angry urge to launch weird Franz at the wall on the far side of the room.

One bunk away, Pierre was tossing and turning while now and then letting out a hopeless sob. He was in and out of his bunk as I had been the night before, muttering to himself in French before finally walking out the back door to where the toilets were located. I could see his silhouette as he paced between the window and the clothesline, holding his head in his hands. After a while I could no longer see or hear him, and guessed he must be sitting on the stairs leading to the bathrooms.

Then, a few minutes later, the sound of a fiercely barking dog caught my attention. The *wat* was typical in that it was a magnet for stray dogs, which were fed scraps of food by the monks during the day and, in turn, became loyal sentries at night. The noise was far away, off toward an area of the monastery beyond the detox center. The angry barking was joined by another dog's and then another's, until there must have been ten dogs barking and howling. I thought to myself: Pierre's doing a runner. I listened closely for the next fifteen or so minutes as the sound of the barking dogs receded into the distance and then faded away.

The next morning I again missed leaf-sweeping duty, but David pulled me out of bed for morning muster. Pierre was there with the rest of them, and I was reminded of the commotion I heard the night before. I figured I had just imagined it all.

Later, while I was lying on my bunk getting a Thai massage, Saundra visited the dorm to see if I was ready for the day's vomiting cure. We talked a bit and then she asked if I heard what

Pierre had gotten up to the previous night. It turned out that Saundra spoke some French, and Pierre had confessed his adventure to her.

"He ran all the way to the highway and tried to flag down some passing cars but he said nobody would stop."

"Was he using the thumbs-up gesture?" I asked. "To Thais that just means 'A-okay.' Nobody would interpret it to mean 'Stop, I need a ride.'"

"And even if somebody happened to stop, what was he going to say to them?" Saundra mimicked a French accent while making jabbing motions at the inside of her elbow. "Hairo-ween! Hairo-ween! Le feex! Le feex!" She laughed uproariously, but then quickly recovered her Buddhist nun demeanor.

"The funniest thing is," she continued, "there's a pond with a crocodile in it, and Pierre walked right past it last night."

"A crocodile? What?"

"Yes! It's the abbot's pet. There used to be two but one crocodile disappeared a while back."

Pierre, who, like me, always felt much better during the day, came in from outside and joined the conversation. Through Saundra he explained that he thought he saw a police truck pass him on the highway, so he ran back to the monastery and got back in bed. For my benefit, Pierre tried to sum up his predicament with one line of English, "For me, it is impossible."

Whether he was referring to his attempted breakout, his withdrawal from heroin, or life in general, I did not ask. I supposed it was all the same.

My days were becoming easier, but my nights were still fraught with pain. Each morning I awoke tangled in sweat-soaked sheets and with that feeling of a recently broken fever—as if an aura of heat was rising from my skin and dissipating into the cool morning air. Since the day after my arrival, I had not been able to eat more than a couple spoonfuls of boiled rice and a bite of banana per day. I was weak as a baby. All smells were overpowering to the point of making me nauseous. Take away my opium and life had become a foul stench.

Gradually, the nights became more restful. No longer was I simply passing out at dawn from the exhaustion of enduring hours of pain. I began to fall asleep earlier and earlier with each successive night. I had a recurring nightmare about a jackal with a pair of rusting scissors hanging from one of its fangs, but that was no doubt due to my choice of reading material.

On my sixth day, while recovering from the five days of vomiting, it occurred to me that I felt very different from before. It was as though the last of the opium had finally been expelled from my body. Suddenly I was famished. I ate ravenously and felt my mind sharpening and an immediate regaining of physical strength.

I walked around the detox compound and saw beauty that until now I had barely noticed. Mountains of jagged, jungle-clad limestone overlooked the monastery, and in the clear morning air they seemed so close that I felt I could reach out and pluck the blossoms from the flowering trees on their summits. To one side of the detox center, not far beyond the fence, was a circular arrangement of gigantic Buddha images that I later learned had been cast from molten stone. Towering above the treetops, the black, opalescent surfaces of the Buddhas' heads sparkled in the bright sun. Built as a grand centerpiece to the Buddhas were three colossal black stone columns that seemed to be several stories high. These were flanked by what looked like two giant wagon wheels—stone renditions of a Buddhist symbol called "the Wheel of Law." This fantastically imposing monument gave the impression that some classical deity's chariot had come plunging down from the heavens and crash-landed within a Stonehenge of Buddhas. Many of the stone sculptures were unfinished, adding to their surreal quality.

On a much more mundane level, there was a hammock strung between two mango trees at one end of the middle dorm building. The hammock was usually occupied by one of the Thai addicts, but that day the television in the canteen was showing a soccer match, and I found the hammock invitingly empty. Lying on my back, looking up at the sky through the shimmering green canopy, I felt a rising tide of joy surge through me. The next thing I knew, I was laughing. It was the first time I had felt like laughing in as long as I could remember; the first time I'd had any reason to laugh. I thought of my good fortune at having found this place—and the miracle of having survived opium withdrawal with so little pain. This was the true miracle of Wat Tham Krabok. I had experienced perhaps a quarter of the withdrawal symptoms that I had endured when I tried to quit opium on my own. It was then that I knew my ordeal was over and that I was free, and the very realization of this fact salted my laughter with tears.

It is difficult to live without opium after having known it because it is difficult, after knowing opium, to take earth seriously.

—Jean Cocteau, *Opium: Journal d'une désintoxication* (1930)

On the day before I checked out of the monastery, I met with the abbot at his living quarters, a modest bungalow just a couple of hundred yards beyond the detox facility. Although I had finished my treatment, I was not allowed to leave the facility unescorted until I officially checked out, and so Phra Marc, the Belgian monk, led me to the abbot's quarters. Marc had the serene personality that one expects in a Buddhist monk. Months after I left the monastery, I ran across a video interview of Marc on YouTube. In it he revealed that he had once abused a multitude of drugs including heroin, cocaine, crack, tranquilizers, and alcohol—and kept it up for nearly a decade—before coming to Wat Tham Krabok to clean himself out.

Marc and I were accompanied by David and Kurt, who were also nearing the end of their stays at the monastery. The abbot was waiting for us in a chair on the verandah of his bungalow, and we climbed some stairs and sat on the floor in front of him. Practicing Thai Buddhists spend a lot of time sitting on floors. A position sometimes referred to in English as the "mermaid pose" is considered the politest way to sit in front of Buddha images or

Buddhist clergy. It involves kneeling with the legs folded back to one side, and the feet—the lowest part of the body—pointed away from holy people or objects. To complete the pose, the hands should be held in the *wai* gesture. Thais practice sitting this way from childhood and can seemingly do it for hours. For many Westerners, however, having to stay in this position for more than a few minutes can feel like some diabolical form of torture.

Fortunately the abbot was used to Westerners and their inability to sit politely, and he smiled patiently as we crossed and uncrossed our legs in an effort to make ourselves comfortable. While Marc translated, the abbot explained in Thai that he was going to give each of us a mantra to help us get through the hardest part of the process: staying clean once we left the monastery. He produced tiny slips of paper, each with a short line of Thai letters that were a transliteration of a fragment of a Pali-language chant. This, the abbot said, was powerful magic. The mantra needed to be memorized and repeated whenever we felt the temptation to break our vows. Once the mantra was committed to memory, the slip of paper was supposed to be eaten. The abbot gave us a warning that breaking the sacred vow would bring about real calamity. He asked Marc to emphasize this in his translation, and the Belgian monk duly repeated the dire warning. The abbot asked if we understood. We all nodded that we did. The abbot then gave each of us a ring that had the monastery's name engraved into the silvered brass setting—a visual reminder of our time at Wat Tham Krabok that might also help with fighting temptation.

Marc mentioned to the abbot what I had been treated for, and after the usual expression of surprise, the abbot asked me to explain the process of smoking opium, confessing that he had only a vague idea of how it worked. I did my best to describe something that just a week before I had been forced to do, night and day, and that I now had taken a vow never to do again. Talking to the abbot about it made me feel very happy; it was like telling someone about your former life of poverty the day after winning the lottery. The old holy man's interest gave me joy for another reason. The fact that I was being asked about this by the abbot of a monastery that had once rehabilitated thousands of opium addicts was yet another testament to how incredibly rare opium smoking had become. Right then I realized that I could still be proud of my unusual—and now former—vice. I had given up opium, but my experiences and the knowledge that resulted from them would always be mine.

That evening, the call for the monks to gather for their nightly chanting caught my attention. It was a rhythmic banging on a gong that began very slowly but increased in tempo until it was almost as fast as a drumroll. Then it abruptly stopped before the slow rhythm began over again. The noise of the gong caused all the dogs in the monastery compound to howl in unison, and this haunting sound inspired me to ask permission to go listen to the monks chant. Saundra agreed to escort me to the wide, open hall where twice a day dozens of monks gathered to chant while the ordained disciples of Theravada Buddhism were doing the same in countless monasteries throughout Thailand.

Saundra and I sat near the back of the hall and watched as the monks entered the building one at a time, walking in a slightly bowed, feline way. Wordlessly they sat in half-lotus positions on a raised platform along one side of the room, facing an image of the Buddha on a red lacquer and gold-leaf dais. At a signal that I could not discern, they all began chanting. The resonant sound of a hall full of chanting Buddhist monks is an experience that can literally bring on goose bumps, but this time it was particularly powerful. For the first time in months, my mind was sharp and clear of the muddling effects of opium dependence. I closed my eyes, and the otherworldly sound washed over me like a cleansing wave. The chanting went on for about half an hour and stopped as suddenly as it had started. The monks then wordlessly stood up and filed out into the darkness. That night I slept soundly—my first real sleep in months.

The following day I checked out. I had brought clean clothes so I wouldn't have to wear the same ones departing as when I arrived. The addict's rubber flip-flops were replaced with a pair of black leather oxfords. I had purposely packed a shirt that I hadn't worn since before I became addicted—it was the one I wore to the opening night of Armand Hoorde's museum exhibition. I walked back into the detox facility to say my goodbyes dressed as though I was going for dinner at an upscale restaurant. I wanted people to notice the difference—to see a change in me.

David, Jerry, and Kurt were scheduled to leave in the next couple days, and we exchanged phone numbers and promises to get together in Bangkok for a meal. David knew a seafood restaurant that did a blazing crab curry. "It's the bomb!" he said. Jerry was trying to postpone his flight back to England so he could stay in Bangkok a few days. Kurt had plans to go to Koh Samui, an island in southern Thailand popular with tourists, where he had been staying prior to coming to the monastery.

On my way out, I ran into Clark, the Thai American from New York, in the canteen. He told me that he, too, would be leaving in the next couple of days. I suggested that we keep in touch, and he replied as though he thought it was a good idea but then excused himself and rejoined some Thais who were eating sun-dried pork and sticky rice. Among them was the kid who had checked in with me—the one who arrived bruised and limping. He looked even worse than when I first saw him—the whites of his eyes were a demon-like red from burst blood vessels caused by the physical trauma of repeated vomiting. I remembered his family and wondered if they would think he had endured more beatings when they saw him after treatment.

The driver that I hired for the ride back to Bangkok was not the same one who had brought me—I made sure of that. The new driver's car was an old Volvo with leather upholstery, and sitting alone in the backseat would feel like high luxury after the rustic living of the past week. Before I departed, I donated 10,000 baht to the monastery—about $300—putting half directly into a donation box and giving the other half to Art in an envelope. He said he would share it with the other monks who supervised at the detox facility. The money was the last of my savings, but I would happily have paid ten times that amount to get to where I was in so short a time and with so little pain.

During the ride back to Bangkok I felt waves of euphoria that were superior to anything I had experienced on opium. Now that I was free from its grip, the alarmist vocabulary from the Victorian-era books—words such as "shackled" and "enslaved"— seemed so apt. I remembered reading about Christian missionaries who used opium detox to make new converts among the Chinese, and I could now see how recently cured addicts might convert out of sheer gratitude. I thought about the number of Western monks at Wat Tham Krabok and wondered if any of them had even pondered Buddhism before their arrival at the monastery for treatment. Of course, a big difference between nineteenth-century China and twenty-first-century Thailand was that Wat Tham Krabok made no attempts to proselytize. I guessed that the former addicts who did decide to join the *wat* were probably not ready to go home and face their past, knowing that running into dealers and drug buddies had been the downfall of many.

When I arrived back at my apartment, I went straight to the

refrigerator, got out my little dropper bottle of *chandu,* and un-ceremoniously flushed its contents down the toilet. I didn't need to do anything else—I had done a thorough job of throwing away anything incriminating before leaving for the monastery. My apartment was a mess, however. For months I had not both-ered to do much more than the lightest of cleaning. Blankets were still hung over the windows, keeping the tropical sunlight at bay. I took the blankets down and, detecting the smell of opium on them, made a pile by the door to send to the laundry. With the room brightly illuminated, the true extent of my com-plete failure to keep up any semblance of order or cleanliness was shockingly apparent. There was several days' worth of clean-ing to do, so I divided the work into projects to tackle a day at a time.

When I had turned on my mobile phone during the ride back to Bangkok, there was not a single message waiting for me. After showering and changing, I got online and checked email—and again was surprised to see how few messages I'd gotten during the week I was away. Of course, it was a testament to how few people I had been in close contact with during the month before my detox. Except for one friend in San Francisco, I hadn't told anyone where I was going. Roxanna thought I was in Cambodia. I had used the "going to Cambodia" story with Jake Burton, too, but other than those two, there was nobody in Bangkok with whom I was in regular contact. I thought about calling Roxanna but wasn't yet sure how to phrase things. In-stead, I called Jake and told him what I had done.

"Ah, welcome back to the land of the living," he said in his ever-cheerful, Australian way. "I was beginning to get worried."

Jake then admitted that he was sorry he hadn't come over for one last smoke. When I told him what I had done with the *chandu,* he gasped.

Jake's reaction gave me a hint of what Roxanna's might be. I was sure everyone would be supportive to my face, but if a dabbler like Jake was shocked at how I had flushed my *chandu,* what would a confirmed smoker like Roxanna think? I decided not to risk telling her the truth. When I finally did call her, a couple days after my arrival back in Bangkok, I said that I had been through some ugly withdrawal symptoms while on the road in Cambodia, and that this had made me decide to take a break from opium. That was how I put it—I hadn't quit; I was merely letting my lungs clear out for a while. Despite my lie, I had no doubt that I could resist the pull of opium. I was finished with it. Roxanna, however, was my closest friend and I didn't want to say anything that might hurt our friendship. "Well, that sounds like a good idea to me," she said when I told her I was taking a break. "Maybe I should do the same."

Could she? I wondered to myself. Roxanna and I rarely talked frankly about her opium use. Did she really believe she could take a break from it? Or was this just something she told herself was possible? I remembered that Emily Hahn wrote how she was so sure that she could stop smoking at any time—until she tried. Surely Roxanna had attempted to quit at some point. But if her smoking never got out of hand as mine did, maybe she never saw any reason to quit. Perhaps she really was in control and could stop whenever she wished. It was all so frustratingly unclear. I had come so far on the opium trail, and yet I still knew so little about it.

About a week after arriving back in Bangkok, I got a call from David the Israeli. "I'm staying at Khao San Road. When do we eat the crab curry? Are you free?"

I was. I had spent the previous week getting my apartment

back in order and using the Internet to update as much of the *Rough Guide to Cambodia* as possible. My submission was way overdue, but I didn't have enough time or money to make the trip to Cambodia. Just a few years before it would have been impossible to get reliable information solely from the Net, but coverage of Cambodia had expanded and it was no longer absolutely necessary to visit in person. Of course, this wasn't something I'd be telling my editors—but at this point I had no choice. I passed twelve-hour days doing Internet searches and poring over websites, and then followed up with phone calls and email queries. It was eye-crossing work, and when David called I was very much ready for a break.

David didn't know the name of the restaurant, but from his description of the location I knew where we were going—one of those Chinese-oriented seafood emporiums with tanks of crustaceans waiting to be thrown into the pot. The place was crowded with families, and we were shown to a table on an upper floor. David had already decided what we would eat so I let him order. He asked me how I was faring without opium, and I told him that if things stayed as easy as they had been the past week, I would have no problem staying off the mat. Personally, I felt there was no chance of a relapse, but I didn't want to sound overly confident. I knew David had been to rehab many times in the past, and he surely knew much more about these things than I did.

"Do you remember Clark?" David asked. "I shared a ride with him to Bangkok."

"Cool," I said.

"Not cool," David replied.

Clark's father had come to pick him up at Wat Tham Krabok on the day of his release. Clark, however, had other plans. The day before, he had approached David and Jerry and asked if they wanted to share a ride back to Bangkok. The driver was to be a Thai who had been undergoing treatment and was also checking out. He had his own vehicle—a pickup truck—parked and waiting at the monastery.

David and Jerry agreed, and David told me about how, after checking out of the monastery, they had watched as Clark told his pleading father in no uncertain terms that he would not be needing a ride from him. The pickup with David, Jerry, Clark, and the Thai driver left with Clark's father following close behind in a sedan. Then, as David and Jerry looked on incredulously, Clark began urging the driver to speed up and lose his father.

"Me and Jerry are just looking at each other. We cannot believe it. Clark is speaking in Thai but we know what he's telling the one driving. And Clark was many times looking behind to see if his father's car is still there."

Once Clark's father had been ditched, the driver found a gas station and Clark asked David if he could borrow money to fill up the tank. Clark had not previously mentioned anything about gas, but David complied.

"I gave one thousand two hundred baht. If I hire a car and driver I will pay at least two thousand baht. So I don't mind."

But then, on the outskirts of Bangkok, David and Jerry found themselves being evicted from the vehicle. David described the scene while shaking his head in disgust. "Clark asked us to get out and wait for him there at some place where we stopped on the road. He says they will come back and get us after they go to their friend's house. But I know it's all bullshit so I tell Jerry that we will take a taxi the rest of the way."

Obviously, the Wat Tham Krabok cure didn't take with everybody. If you don't want to quit something, nobody can make you quit. I thought about the way Clark had laughed while relating his tale of overdosing on his girlfriend's birthday. Some of us are simply hell-bent on self-destruction and there's absolutely nothing anyone else can do about it. Upon hearing David's story I was sure that Clark would succeed in carrying out his death wish. The heroin in Southeast Asia is said to be much purer than in the West—certainly much stronger than what Clark was getting in New York. Perhaps as David and I were tucking into our steaming plates of crab curry, Clark was already dead.

Having a second chance at life kept me buoyed for weeks—I felt as though I had been cured of cancer. But the era of good feeling did not last.

I had read that the psychological symptoms of withdrawal would continue long after the physical ones had abated. Some of my symptoms seemed physical but were probably psychological—such as the loud ringing in my ears that came and went. I noticed this mainly at night when things were quiet, and I took to running the air-conditioning at its highest setting to drown out the noise in my ears. During the day the ringing didn't bother me so much. As long as I kept busy and there was some ambient noise to mask it, I found I could tune it out.

Opium smokers were once commonly described as "indifferent," and during the time that I was smoking quite heavily, I *was* often aloof to what was happening beyond the glow of the opium lamp. But once the narcotic was out of my system, it seemed as though the ability to feel indifference also left me. This might seem like a good thing, but living in a city of ten million people, a certain amount of aloofness is needed in order to get through each day emotionally unscathed.

Suddenly, it was very difficult to ignore life's brutality. Before

I began using opium heavily, I was able to deal with day-to-day sad realities just like anyone else—by ignoring them. Before opium, if I were walking down the street and saw a scrawny kitten poking around a pile of trash—and if at that moment I was not too distracted by other things—I would have felt a flash of pity. But as soon as I looked away and continued on my way, I would have begun forgetting. Perhaps five minutes later I'd have completely forgotten the kitten.

During the time when I was heavily into opium, such sights meant virtually nothing to me. Instead of being saddened, I saw life with the detachment of a hermitic sage. All things suffer; all things must die—there was no need to get emotional about it. But after about a month without opium, it was as though I had lost all control of my ability to put saddening sights and thoughts into perspective. I would see that same starving kitten and the sight would break my heart. I could walk on for another ten minutes and my heart would still be breaking; I could think of nothing else. And after a while all those little heartbreaks, day after day, started adding up. In time, my inability to cope with these thoughts brought on a paralyzing depression.

Despite my vow against it, I began to consider drinking alcohol to ease my mood. This in itself was rather extraordinary because I had all but given up drinking a decade earlier. Living in Bangkok during my twenties and thirties, there was no shortage of opportunities for partying. I had a group of friends, most of whom were journalists, and there was always a reason to go out on the town. At the time I probably got drunk on an average of two or three times a week. Budding alcoholism perhaps, but not unusual among young expats in the anything-goes Bangkok of the 1990s.

In 1998, at the age of thirty-six, I was in Laos doing research for a guidebook for Rough Guides. This one would be written from scratch—a first edition—and that meant I had to spend months in Laos exploring the travel possibilities. The Lao are famous drinkers, and I happened to be there during Lao New Year, celebrated in mid-April. The holiday is best described as a weeklong bender powered by a vodka-like liquor made from glutinous rice. And in Laos, there is no getting out of drinking. During this week of celebration the Lao will offer every visitor they encounter a shot of rice liquor. Foreigners are especially welcomed, and declining to partake is really not an option. The Lao believe that there are spirits everywhere—the paranormal kind—and that these animist spirits will be highly offended if any mortal refuses to imbibe a shot of new year's cheer. The result was that I spent a good portion of April 1998 either roaring drunk or with a crippling hangover. Once the haze had cleared, I realized that I had lost a notebook full of information that I had been collecting over the past couple months.

I decided then and there to dry out—vowing not to drink alcohol again until research for the *Rough Guide to Laos* was finished. Within a few weeks, to my surprise, I felt much better—better than I'd remembered feeling in a long time. I finished the book but put off starting to drink again—and this procrastination continued—simply because I no longer had any desire to drink. That is, until barely a month after I left Wat Tham Krabok, when suddenly I had this urge to hoist a bottle.

But it sounded too familiar. There's something about opiates: How many rock-star heroin addicts kicked the habit only to become prodigious boozers? I was determined not to follow the pattern. I wasn't even sure if my body would allow me to drink. Since I had stopped, there were a handful of times—usually social events such as weddings—when I had taken part in raising a glass to toast somebody or something. On all these occasions, the

only effect the alcohol seemed to have was to make me slightly
woozy—and I never had any desire for more.

So I pushed this newfound thirst for alcohol into the back of
my head by reminding myself of something my friend in San
Francisco had said when I told him about my planned detox:
"They say you can't turn a pickle back into a cucumber."

I was determined to prove this pessimistic little adage wrong.

Soon after I had telephoned Roxanna and told her that I was
taking a break from opium, she began calling me almost daily. I
was happy to talk, yet I was reluctant to pay her a visit. I didn't
crave opium; I wasn't pining for the pipe, but I did have a strong
feeling that if I were to visit Roxanna's house—the location of
at least a hundred of our shared opium-smoking sessions—
I might find that I suddenly *did* have cravings, and that those
cravings were overwhelming.

Roxanna seemed to understand all this without my having to
explain it. She never proposed that we get together. Even so,
after a while her phone calls began making me anxious. The
problem was, prior to my detox our phone conversations had
always been brief. We had never spent much time talking on the
phone because a call from Roxanna was always an invitation to
smoke opium (or, after a certain point in our relationship, the
phone calls were initiated by me in an effort to get myself invited to her place under some pretext or another). We had always done our real conversing while reclining with the layout
tray between us—and this is what I was starting to miss.

Feeling guilty about my behavior the previous October in
Vientiane, I also called Willi and told him that I was "fasting."
Since Willi had seen my overindulgences firsthand, I was more
forthcoming with him while explaining my reasons for taking a
break—but I said nothing about having taken the cure at Wat
Tham Krabok. "When you're ready to break your fast, come on

up and we'll do it in style," Willi said. I promised that I would, all the while feeling hollow inside with the knowledge that it could never happen.

As weeks became months, I found myself passing long, solitary days in my apartment. The homebody that I had become while smoking alone felt no need to reconnect with the world—at least not face to face. As before, I spent plenty of time communicating via email and browsing the Internet, but somehow I now felt lost. The things that had fascinated me before—the discoveries made during Internet searches, hours and hours spent reading nostalgic blogs, the déjà vu that I felt when staring at old photographs—all of it now struck me as annoyingly dull. I robotically clicked from one website to the next. Nothing held my attention for long. I was bored with everything.

"The mortal boredom of the smoker who is cured!" It was Jean Cocteau again. He had been there. Speaking of his former life as an opium addict, he said: "I am ashamed to have been expelled from that world, compared with which the world of health resembles those revolting films in which ministers unveil statues."

Cocteau was right. The modern world still seemed just as stupid and pointless to me as it had when I was using opium to escape it. Only now I could not escape it—except to hide in my room and measure time by meals that I had little appetite for. My mental voyages and imagined companionship had seemed so real that now, without the chemical magic to evoke them, I felt lobotomized.

My collecting—what had been my passion for years and years—had come to a standstill. I was too broke to acquire anything new. Instead, I had to concentrate on making enough money so I wouldn't have to sell off any more pieces to pay the rent. Even if I had been able to afford new acquisitions, I would have paid much higher prices than before. Opium antiques were becoming popular, and just as Roxanna had predicted, prices began rising as novice collectors had gotten into the game. Admittedly, the situation was partly my own doing: Much of the new interest was due to my book and the website I had constructed to promote it.

When demand outstrips supply, prices go up and merchants take notice. There were just so many authentic antique opium pipes out there. It didn't take long for merchants who dealt in opium antiques to start getting creative. The Chinese have a long history of making fake antiques—they've been doing it for so long, their early fakes are now real antiques. C. A. S. Williams had this to say about it:

> It is fairly safe to say that very few genuine pieces are to be found except in the hands of collectors and dealers, for the country has been all but combed clean . . . and imitations are all the more plentiful in consequence. Some of the spurious antiques, mostly porcelains, are extremely cleverly manufactured, and much ingenuity is exercised in their reproduction. . . . Marks on the bottom are often deceptive, the wrong period being frequently given in order to mislead the unwary purchaser.

The quote is taken from Williams's *Encyclopedia of Chinese Symbolism and Art Motives,* which was originally published in 1932. Of course, the author was not referring specifically to opium paraphernalia, and as it turns out, opium antiques are not so simple for Chinese artisans to copy. For one thing, China has a very limited supply of genuine examples to use as models. Much was destroyed during eradication campaigns, and what remained was then sold to foreign tourists—who removed the forbidden relics with even more thoroughness than the authorities and their bonfires.

I never had much problem telling the Chinese fakes from genuine pieces. With a couple of notable exceptions, the Chinese were not investing much effort in making reproduction opium paraphernalia, and their corner cutting was obvious to a trained eye. Newly crafted pipe bowls from the old kilns at Jianshui were so thick-walled that if used, they would have taken ages to heat up and cool down, slowing the process of rolling to a crawl. It was also possible that modern craftsmen simply lacked the know-how to make bowls properly—that the knowledge had been lost. At any rate, by the beginning of 2008, I began noticing that when it came to making fakes, the Chinese were nowhere near as sophisticated as the French.

The French take antiques seriously, and it was Parisian dealers who began to give real attention to opium antiques. A Paris auction house was the first to arrange a sale highlighting opium relics—way back in 1995. Seven years later a second auction was held—it presumably took that long for a respectable collection of opium-related lots to be gathered. Then, beginning in 2003, there was a frenzy of auctions in France featuring opium antiques, often combined with a sale of *objets du tabac*—tobacco pipes and tobacco-smoking accessories. These latter Paris auctions seemed legitimate in every way—they even had the names of house experts printed in their respective catalogs. The only problem was the offerings themselves. As the decade wore on, the fact that demand had outpaced supply became more and more apparent.

By examining the items in the catalogs I could tell that any careful selection of genuine and relevant items had been completely abandoned. This was not a matter of dealers not knowing what they were selling, as I had encountered during my early days of collecting. Instead, they seemed to be banking on the belief that buyers would not know what they were bidding on. I used my photographic archive—which consisted of thousands of images of genuine opium antiques—to compare the offerings of the French auction houses with what I had seen come up on the market over the years. I discovered many pipes and lamps that had been newly manufactured by copying existing examples. Some auction houses got around ethics issues by not giving an estimated age for their lots—their catalogs often had flowery descriptions of the history of opium smoking, but nowhere was it actually stated that the lots of opium paraphernalia were genuine antiques.

The whole situation was profoundly depressing. Even before antique opium-smoking paraphernalia could become a recognized collectible among aficionados of Chinese art, the collecting scene had been hijacked and was being poisoned by greed.

For me it wasn't a matter of recouping an investment—I had long before made the decision to donate my collection to the University of Idaho. A number of collectors tried to talk me out of the idea (Armand Hoorde sold his entire collection and offered to act as a go-between if I wanted to sell mine), but my mind was made up. I would rather live in poverty than sell my collection.

And if all this grief weren't enough, there was something else—something much more distressing than dealers resorting to trickery or sellout collectors; more disturbing than a lack of cash to acquire anything new.

Back when I could smoke opium, I used to liken preparing pipes to driving a classic car. I thought the comparison was apt. It had taken me years and cost a lot of money to gather all the components to complete my layout, and then I had learned to skillfully drive this breathtaking set of wheels. I once even mocked the collector Helmut P.—who had sampled opium courtesy of Armand Hoorde—because he did not know how to roll. Via an email exchange with Hoorde, I told the non-emailing Helmut P. that he was no different from someone who owns a fleet of rare automobiles yet does not know how to drive. Being a passenger didn't count, I sneered. Until he learned to drive, Helmut P. would never really know his vehicles or understand their many accessories. I taunted him with relish:"Learn to drive, old man. Learn to drive."

How greatly things had changed. I still had my car, but had lost the privilege to drive it. This was how my collection now seemed to me: a parked car with no hope of ever flying down the road again. Tools that I once used to manipulate the *chandu* felt dead in my hands. While sitting at my computer trying to work, I sometimes absently rolled my favorite needle between my thumb and forefinger. The exercise was about as gratifying as sitting in a parked car and turning the steering wheel to and fro. The engaging scenery was now just a memory.

I missed opium. I had to admit it. And my collection, the detritus of thousands of past addictions including my own, was everywhere I looked. I was surrounded by it. The dust-covered pieces of paraphernalia, looking forlorn and desperate, seemed to call out to me, begging to be put to use again. And then there was Jean Cocteau. Across the decades and with a knowing smile, he, too, was speaking to me: "The dead drug leaves a ghost behind. At certain hours it haunts the house."

Thus it was the master, Beelzebub opium, led his imp a devil dance constantly.

—William Rosser Cobbe,
Doctor Judas: A Portrayal of the Opium Habit (1895)

In April 2008, after five long months of avoiding Roxanna, I finally felt I was ready to pay a visit to her home. The occasion was a visitor from the States, a collector I met through eBay who had during my time of dependence bought some of my desperate offerings and kept me afloat. Justin was visiting Thailand for the first time, and after talking with him, I was impressed with what he knew about opium smoking—especially from a medical standpoint. Justin was able to explain to me in laymen's terms why I was suffering so:

"Think of the receptors in your brain as hungry little mouths. Normally they feed on endorphins, the body's natural painkillers and mood enhancers. But if you start regularly feeding those little mouths with the much more delicious opium, they'll get spoiled. Take away their daily feast of opium and expect them to be happy with endorphins instead, and your body and brain will revolt until you give the receptors what they want. And they won't give up easily. The receptors must be fed opium or some other opiate, or you're really going to suffer. After many months of life without opium, the little mouths will get used to eating endorphins again. But they still remember the taste of opium, and if you smoke it again just once, their angry demands for more will be impossible to ignore."

After some hours spent discussing this and many other details pertaining to opium, I got the idea to take Justin with me to Roxanna's house. I knew he would be very interested to see her in action, and his being there would take the pressure off me to smoke—since Roxanna would have another guest to prepare pipes for.

I called Roxanna—the first time in recent memory that I was doing the calling—and proposed the idea. She knew Justin's name because we used to talk about what I was going to sell and to whom. Justin was one of two collectors in the United States to whom I regularly sold, and I was happy that I had established a friendly relationship with him. I hoped that someday I might be able to buy back some of my pieces, but if that were to happen, it was going to be far in the future. Since I had neglected to keep in touch with editors, I was no longer being offered many freelance writing jobs, and I was still struggling to get back on my feet.

The afternoon of the following day, Justin and I took a taxi to Roxanna's neighborhood, trading the car for a pedicab once we reached the market where the lane narrowed. A pedicab was the most scenic way to arrive, and this lane was one of very few in Bangkok where they were still in use. During the ride in, Justin asked me questions but I was unable to concentrate and kept asking him to repeat them. In my mind I was rehearsing the scene when Roxanna would offer me a pipe—it was inevitable— and I would calmly decline.

"When was the last time you were over here?"

"I'm sorry, what was that?"

My mobile phone rang. It was Roxanna, asking if I could buy her a pack of cigarettes at the corner store. I said that we had already passed it, and she said never mind, she would borrow a cigarette from her Thai brother-in-law.

"We'll be there in three minutes," I said.

"Okay, the door is unlocked, just let yourself in. I'm upstairs already."

Familiar routes and familiar routines that in the past had always led to bliss. We disembarked from the pedicab and walked the concrete causeway, the hot afternoon sun making the frond-like leaves of the banana trees droop limply. At Roxanna's doorstep we ran into her brother-in-law and his wife, an amiable couple whom I had been on friendly terms with. They looked both surprised and happy to see me, and paid me a typically Thai compliment by remarking that I'd gained weight since I was last there for a visit.

I introduced Justin, and then the two of us made our way up the narrow wooden stairway. Roxanna was taking her cigarette break, and I immediately noticed the layout tray was littered with dross, indicating that she had been smoking opium for some time before we arrived. I had only seen her do this once before—when she was hosting both myself and her old Vietcong friend who was visiting from Vietnam. That day, she had smoked her fill first so she could concentrate on rolling for her guests. Remembering this, I took it to mean that today she was expecting me to smoke, too.

Roxanna and Justin exchanged greetings, and I invited him to recline alongside the layout tray. I then took a seat in a dusty wooden armchair situated in a corner of the room. The chair had been there almost as long as I'd been coming to smoke with Roxanna, but this was the first time I had ever sat on it. My place had always been on the floor.

Roxanna stubbed out her cigarette and began counting drops of *chandu* into the miniature wok while she and Justin chatted about his flight over. Just as in the pedicab, I was having a hard time focusing on the conversation and felt unable to join in. The musky smell of opium soon drove the sharp odor of cigarette smoke from the room, and I sat bolt upright in the chair, crossing my legs and arms in a subconscious effort to stiffen my resolve.

Justin was soon drawing on his first pipe—quite expertly I noticed—and the soft, sputtering sound of opium being vaporized took over my senses. A lotus pond full of croaking frogs; a summertime flame tree abuzz with cicadas; a maddening ringing in the ears; the forlorn sound of crying babies. I could not hear a thing they were saying above the din. I sat and stared, deafened and dumbstruck, and suddenly I remembered seeing my *Time* buddy Karl Taro Greenfeld staring at me goggle-eyed from a dark corner of that opium den in Vang Vieng seven years before. I remembered thinking, What's his problem?

Now I knew.

After Justin had smoked three pills, Roxanna held up the pipe and gestured with her needle, pointing it at the bowl. "Do you want one, too?"

"No, thank you," I heard myself say.

"Okay," she replied. Her tone said: Suit yourself.

The room was closed up as usual to keep out drafts that might make the opium lamp flicker, and the heat was becoming unbearable. Although I didn't think there was much chance of inadvertently breathing in any opium fumes—because I was sitting off by myself in a corner—I still felt as though I needed to get out of there. I looked at my mobile phone and saw that barely fifteen minutes had passed since Roxanna had called me. It would be awkward if I tried to leave now.

I closed my eyes and ran my detox mantra through my head, concentrating on each syllable in an effort to push out all other thoughts. The effect was not what I'd expected. Somehow the exercise was making me drowsy, and soon I felt that I was nodding off, entering that relaxing state just between sleep and wakefulness. My head dipped abruptly, causing me to snap back awake. Roxanna noticed this and asked if I wanted to take a nap downstairs in her bedroom. I jumped at the idea.

Lying on Roxanna's bed with the air-conditioning on, I found myself wide-awake again. I looked around the room and took in her life. Above her bed was the framed black-and-white photo of a very young and beautiful Roxanna in Vietnam-era jungle fatigues. Over the door was an oversized ornamental fan adorned with an Asian village scene painted in garish swipes. On the plywood wall near her vanity were snapshots of a decades-past trip to America: Roxanna and her Thai husband were riding bicycles on some tree-lined suburban street. Jamie, just an infant then, was strapped into a kiddie seat. There were photos of Roxanna's wedding—both bride and groom wearing traditional Thai dress and kneeling in what looked like a Buddhist temple. There was a small shelf with academic books about Asian ceramics, and I noted that my own book was among them. A clothes rack in lieu of a closet was hung with her silk and batik wardrobe. Besides the rack, the bed, and a vanity and stool, there was no other furniture.

The luster of romance that I had once seen in Roxanna's life was tarnished considerably now that the opium had left my system. Roxanna was sixty-two, her health was fragile, and she was working to support her son and Thai in-laws and their extended family. On top of that she had this expensive drug habit that was steadily draining her finances as well as her vitality. I decided then and there that I would talk Roxanna into doing detox at

Wat Tham Krabok. I was sure I could do it—I just needed an opportunity to talk to her privately.

After another hour, I heard Justin and Roxanna making their way down the stairs, and I came out of Roxanna's bedroom to meet them. I thanked Roxanna for her hospitality and told her that I would be calling her very soon. Justin wanted to walk out to the main road in order to have an unhurried look at the neighborhood, and as we talked on the walk back, I felt good for not having broken down and smoked. I had the strength to pass such a test, and I was sure a second time would not be so difficult—especially now that I had a mission.

As soon as I got home I called Roxanna and asked if I could come over that Sunday. She sounded delighted with the idea. "Are you going to join me this time?" she asked.

I didn't want to say no, or even worse, to sound undecided. I was afraid this would perhaps cause her to feel guilt, which might, in turn, make her nix the idea of my visiting. I had to sound sure of myself.

"Yes, I'm ready," I confirmed.

Over the next few days I rehearsed what I would say to Roxanna. I wouldn't rush into the proposal. If she had a few pipes in her system I knew it would help her to think clearly and be more receptive to my idea. I would keep from smoking by telling her that I had just eaten and needed to let my stomach settle before having a pipe. This would not seem strange; neither of us ever began smoking on a full stomach.

Sunday morning I arrived at Roxanna's with an elaborate plan that began with a lie about having been forced to eat a gift of mangoes and sticky rice. "One of the old lady vendors who I always buy from handed me a box of mangoes and sticky rice as I was on my way out to get a taxi. Somebody ordered it but hadn't picked it up and she was afraid it would go bad in the heat. I thought I would just eat the mangoes but somehow I couldn't help myself and before I knew it, I'd eaten the sticky rice, too."

"Oh, next time bring some over, I'll share it with you," Roxanna said.

I promised I would, thinking to myself that the next time I visited Roxanna, she would be off opium. We could share the mangoes and sticky rice as a little celebration. Roxanna and I went upstairs, and I immediately shut all the windows and began helping set up the layout. It wasn't even nine o'clock, but the morning air was heavy with heat and humidity. I looked at the dusty chair in the corner and was glad that I'd be reclining on the relatively cool wooden floorboards. I told Roxanna that I probably needed an hour or so for my stomach to settle and to go ahead without me. "I'll catch up soon as I feel a little less bloated," I lied.

I stretched out on the floor, leaving a couple feet of distance between myself and the layout tray instead of lying right up against it as a smoker does. I let my head rest on a porcelain pillow, but I chose to lie on my back instead of facing the tray. Soon the old ritual began. While I stared up at the asbestos roof tiles, I could hear but not see *chandu* sizzling in the copper wok. Once again I closed my eyes and fell back on my detox mantra. Roxanna said nothing. She often used to take catnaps between pipes, and she believed that I had a belly full of glutinous rice—the tranquilizing effects of which must be experienced to be believed. Just as before, concentrating on the mantra put me to sleep. When I awoke half an hour later, my head was absolutely clear.

"Well, you must've needed that," Roxanna said as she put down the pipe and lit a cigarette. "I'll roll one for you as soon as I finish this."

Now is the time, I thought to myself. I went straight to it. "Rox, have you ever tried to quit smoking? Opium, I mean."

She blew the cigarette smoke from her lungs, as always taking care to exhale away from me. "Why, yes, of course. Many times."

"Would you like to be finished with it for good? In just a few days and with almost no pain?"

"Go on," she said with genuine interest.

"There's this *wat* north of here. In Saraburi. They have this detox program . . ."

"You don't mean Tham Krabok, do you?"

"So you know of it."

Roxanna smiled. "That's where I met my husband."

"What?"

"Oh, it's a long story. Let me fix you a pipe and I'll tell you." Roxanna lifted the cap from her dropper bottle and started to count drops into the tiny wok.

"How did *that* happen? Were you doing a story about the *wat* and met your husband because he was doing detox there?" I was sitting up cross-legged now. I knew the business end of the pipe would soon be pointing at me, and being out of position to receive it would give me an excuse to delay smoking.

"No, this was long after I stopped doing journalism. In the late seventies I was living in Hong Kong working for *Arts of Asia* magazine. I got arrested for smoking opium and deported. That's when I came to Thailand and went to Tham Krabok to stop smoking. My husband was a monk there." Roxanna had finished rolling the pill and it was now stuck to the bowl.

"So the detox at the *wat* didn't work for you?"

She smiled again. "Well . . . here I am."

"So that means . . . I mean, I've heard you can only do the detox once. They won't let you go back and do it a second time."

"Yes, that's right. I already had my chance," Roxanna said.

It is said that even after his famous cure, Jean Cocteau went back and dabbled. Of all his quotes from *Opium: Diary of a Cure,* there is one that, for me anyway, was clear evidence of this: "The patience of a poppy. He who has smoked will smoke. Opium knows how to wait."

What's the harm? I suddenly thought to myself. I straightened out my legs and leaned back, the right side of my face coming to rest on the porcelain pillow. It was cool against my cheek and ear. Roxanna pointed the pipe toward me and I guided the mouthpiece to my lips. The heated bowl crackled almost fiercely as I hungrily sucked the vapors into my lungs. The pill vaporized in an instant and I held my breath for as long as I could before exhaling a near-invisible stream at the roof. It was as easy as that. Looking back, I don't know why I did it. I just did.

Without asking, Roxanna began to measure out another dose. I didn't feel any effect yet from that pipe, but it had only been a minute or so since the vapors left my lungs. I closed my eyes and waited.

"Really, it was probably the worst decision I ever made in my life," Roxanna continued.

"You mean doing the detox?"

"No, no. I mean breaking my vow never to smoke opium again. They warned me something terrible would happen if I broke that vow. I tried it just once with an old friend and it wasn't long after that I had my motorcycle accident and lost my leg."

I kept silent. Surely it was just superstition. Or the power of suggestion. Or a horrible coincidence. That vow was just to scare those meth-crazed kids into stopping. Those Buddha statues that I took the vow before were just pieces of cast bronze.

"Then in the hospital the doctors filled me up with morphine. Nobody expected me to live. My Thai family had to beg the doctors to treat me because they were all convinced it was a waste of time. I wasn't even in a room, they just had me on a gurney out in the hallway because they were expecting to release my body to my family in a short time." Roxanna finished preparing the second pipe and handed it to me. I took it and smoked the pill slowly this time, again keeping the vapors in and only letting go when Roxanna gave me a mild scolding. "That's really bad for your lungs," she said.

"I'm sorry, can you roll me another?" I asked.

During the next several pipes Roxanna told me in detail about her accident. It happened in Bangkok at the intersection near the famous Erawan Shrine. She told me of how the driver of a ten-wheeled truck had plowed into her motorcycle and then fled the scene. She described how being crushed under the wheels left her so disfigured that her Thai husband soon abandoned her. Roxanna's first prosthetic leg was a constant source of pain, but even after she had been fitted with a more comfortable one, there were still social obstacles to overcome. She told about a Thai male colleague at the ceramics museum who sought to undermine her position by using her disability against her— at one point even going so far as to order the staff to move the museum library to the third floor so Roxanna would have to climb the stairs every time she needed to look something up.

"You don't really believe that, do you?" I interrupted. "I mean, about breaking the vow causing your accident?"

"Yes, I do!" Roxanna said with widened eyes. "And I've heard stories about other people who broke that vow and had bad things happen to them, too."

Roxanna never struck me as somebody who bought into the paranormal. We had spent many hours together discussing everything under the sun, and I had never once gotten the idea that she let emotion stand in the way of reason. Life had made Roxanna pragmatic, but perhaps this was an exception to her pragmatism. Surely the horror of her accident would have made a deep impression on her. I might feel the same way about breaking that sacred vow had I gone through what Roxanna had. How else to explain being randomly visited upon by such violence and subsequent hardship?

I listened to Roxanna's story and tried to think things out, but there was something more worrying to me at that moment—more worrying even than a karmic curse. Roxanna had already prepared ten pipes for me, yet I felt absolutely nothing. There was no opium electricity, no opium tingle, not even an opium itch.

"It's the damnedest thing, Rox. I just don't feel anything."

I went home that afternoon angry and frustrated. Angry at myself for having broken my vow not to smoke opium; frustrated because I had gotten nothing out of it. I felt completely sober. There was only one noticeable effect but I wouldn't realize it until the following day: The ten pipes had ossified my intestines with constipation.

Over the next few days I thought a lot about what had occurred. I remembered having a similar experience on at least one occasion in the past—a night during which I seemed unable to feel opium's distinctive intoxication. It happened during my period of heavy smoking. Despite everything working properly and more than my usual number of pills, I simply could not get high. I remembered chalking it up to my own mood that night, thinking that I'd created some sort of psychological block. The following night I had smoked again—that very same batch of *chandu* with the very same pipe and bowl—and I got so cooked that I felt my head melting into the porcelain pillow.

I called Roxanna on Friday and asked if I could visit that

weekend. She replied that any day was good because her son was staying with friends in Chiang Mai. "Saturday's fine. Sunday's okay, too. Whichever day you decide not to come I'm going to spend at my office to escape the heat."

With beating the heat in mind (as well as being anxious to try smoking again as soon as possible), I chose Saturday morning, asking if it was okay if I arrived early. We agreed on seven, and that night I got little sleep due to the excitement of an imminent session. I wasn't worried about a relapse. On the contrary, I decided this was just the corrective I needed to keep life interesting. Perhaps once a month at most: I would smoke opium no more frequently than that. But first, I needed to get the full feeling again. Then I would lay off smoking for a month or so.

Roxanna was downstairs drinking a fruit smoothie when I arrived. This was her usual dinner, which her brother-in-law prepared and brought over from his nearby house every evening. Roxanna explained that she hadn't been hungry the night before and so had saved it in the fridge. "Do you want some?" she asked. "There's more than enough."

I declined because I had bought two bottles of Gatorade at the 7-Eleven before hailing a taxi. I got a glass from the dish rack and some ice from the little Igloo cooler that served as an icebox while Roxanna asked how I'd slept the night after our session. Normally we never discussed opium downstairs, but Jamie wasn't home and although Roxanna's neighbors could clearly be seen and heard through the slatted walls, there wasn't another English-speaker within miles.

"It was really weird. I just didn't feel anything," I said.

"Well, you haven't smoked in a long time. Maybe you need to build up a little in your system."

"Does that make sense?" I asked.

Roxanna chuckled. "No, it doesn't. Not in my experience, anyway. If you haven't been smoking you should need less, not more."

Roxanna started up the stairs and I waited until she got to the top. She climbed the stairs slowly but steadily without her cane, and I didn't want to crowd her from behind. Once I caught up with her, I closed the door behind us and started arranging the layout tray. It was just like old times. As Roxanna was lowering herself to the floor I said, "Let's wait to close the windows until you've trimmed the wick and you're happy with the flame. I'm afraid as soon as these windows are shut it'll heat up like an oven in here."

"Yes, it will," Roxanna replied simply. She began adding coconut oil to the lamp and it overfilled, spilling some onto the lamp tray. "Oh, darn," she said to nobody in particular.

Once everything was set and Roxanna began rolling pipes for me and herself in succession, she told me about a trip to America that she would soon be embarking on. It was one of her academic junkets, something that she did a couple times a year. These trips usually involved Roxanna speaking about Southeast Asian ceramics at some university. The way she excitedly talked about these events made it obvious that Roxanna really enjoyed the opportunity to share her passion and see colleagues from around the world. During the time that I had known her, Roxanna had traveled a number of times: to the Philippines, to Singapore, and, if I remember correctly, to Australia. This time it would be Seattle, to give a lecture at the University of Washington.

"I've been working on my talk for weeks now. Do you want to hear it?"

"Sure." I was a bit preoccupied, worrying because I had already smoked four pipes and still didn't feel anything. Perhaps if I concentrated on listening to Roxanna's lecture, the buzz might creep up and pleasantly surprise me.

"Could you go downstairs and get it? You'll see it on my bed in a blue plastic folder. Oh, and could you bring me up a cigarette?"

I popped downstairs and into her bedroom, grabbing a single cigarette from the pack on her vanity. I caught a glimpse of her old snapshots tacked to the plywood wall, curling in the tropical heat. I felt a pang of something. Was it guilt? I really could have pressed Roxanna to go back to Wat Tham Krabok. It was doubtful the monastery still had records of people who took the cure so many years before. Her current passport number would be different from the one she used back then. The *wat* would probably have taken her back no questions asked.

I walked out the bedroom door but as I mounted the stairs, my thoughts had already turned to something else: smoking. When I entered the upstairs room I saw that Roxanna was now standing. "I can't do this lying down," she said. "I need to pretend I'm behind a podium to get some real practice."

So I handed her the folder and took her place on the floor beside the layout tray. "Do you mind if I roll for myself?" I asked. "I need some practice, too."

"Go right ahead," she said.

While Roxanna was reading her lecture, I began preparing a pipe as though none of the past year had ever happened. I pushed the guilt I'd felt earlier out of my mind. Things happen for a reason, I told myself.

My own interest in ceramics was very narrow: If it was a component of an opium pipe or some other piece of opium paraphernalia and it happened to be ceramic, I was interested— otherwise, I paid little attention to it. So while I listened to Roxanna speaking, the details were lost on me. Yet, I could appreciate her passion for the subject. There was pride in Roxanna's voice as she sought to share her knowledge of a subject that, no matter how esoteric, was hers.

"The Ming Gap." My fondness for idiosyncratic juxtapositions of words made the term stick in my head, but I only had the most basic understanding of what it referred to. It didn't matter. What the Ming Gap meant to me was how much Roxanna and I had in common. We had both exiled ourselves on these exotic shores and then set about educating ourselves about some little-known Asian subject that had inspired us. Our passionate enthusiasm made us both experts in our respective fields, and we had both gone to great lengths to share our discoveries with others. And then we had both stood by and watched as others sought to profit monetarily from our beloved subjects, resorting to trickery that clouded the field with counterfeits and misinformation.

I focused on my rolling while Roxanna gave a detailed chronology of a Ming dynasty export ban, a centuries-long gap in Chinese trade that caused Southeast Asian cultures to develop their own ceramics. I forced myself to wait long minutes between pipes, hoping to seem interested and not distract her with my greed. When Roxanna had finished her lecture she slowly lowered herself to the floor and placed the folder at the head of the layout tray. "How was that?" she asked.

"Captivating," I replied. "I just hope there's not a snap quiz."

Roxanna smiled. "It needs work, but I'll be able to polish things up during my flight to Seattle."

"Would you like me to roll you one?" I asked. "I'm a little rusty but it's coming back."

"Sure. I'm ready for one."

Roxanna then began to tell me about a problem she was having at the museum. It was a recurring dilemma that centered around a colleague of hers—the one who was actively trying to undermine her authority among the museum staff. "He deals in ceramics on the side," she said.

Roxanna explained to me again about how the vast majority of pieces that made up the ceramics museum's collection belonged to the founder of Bangkok University. It was a fabulous collection, but the museum founder, like many rich collectors, had become the target of dealers and middlemen trying to pass off reproductions as genuine antiquities. And it so happened that Roxanna's colleague was one of these.

"He sold some purportedly rare pieces to the founder, some for huge amounts of money. I'm apparently the only one who can see that these ceramics aren't genuine. They're copies, but they were very well made and artificially aged. The founder has no idea."

Roxanna paused as I handed her the pipe. She closed her eyes for a moment after exhaling. I had heard this story a number of times before, but with each telling I was struck by how heavily the dilemma weighed on her.

"These reproduction pieces are now in the museum collection. Well, I thought as long as I can keep them out of sight, it's not a big problem. But now my colleague is insisting that we display these pieces in the museum right alongside all the genuine ones. This gives him credibility as a dealer. When I wasn't there he had the staff switch some of the displays around. Can you imagine? I have to deal with this every day!"

There was a sharpness in Roxanna's eyes that I saw only when she got started on this subject. She was genuinely angry about it. "Things have gotten so confused," Roxanna said, shaking her head before letting the matter drop.

I thought of the times that I myself had informed collectors of bad acquisitions, and how the news was not always well received. Perhaps I have an oddball way of looking at the problem. If it were me, I would prefer to know that I'd made a mistake so that I could learn from it—rather than having that mistake go unnoticed and perhaps be repeated. For many collectors, however, it seems that ignorance is bliss. In the past I had advised Roxanna to approach the museum founder—the person who had hired Roxanna to be the director—and at least let him know about how her colleague was using her disability against her.

This time I said nothing. I was still preoccupied with my inability to feel the opium. I had smoked another six pipes during Roxanna's lecture—for a total of ten—and I could now feel only the slightest tingle in the back of my neck. This was way off. At ten pipes after a five-month break I should have been flying. Was it possible that the monastery's cure had caused some chemical change in my brain? Stubbornly, I kept rolling.

"How many has that been?" Roxanna asked.

"Ten."

"Oh my. You're going to make yourself sick."

"How? It's having almost no effect on me. I don't even itch."

"Why don't you try some dross? I boiled up a batch a couple weeks ago. There's a jar of it in my room."

Dross. I had to snicker. Roxanna had access to the world's best *chandu* yet she saved and recycled her dross by a process of boiling and filtering. The result was a jar of smokable black gunk. Willi had always flushed his dross down the toilet, and after my experience in Europe, I'd never had any urge to try smoking it again. Roxanna said hers was "first dross," meaning it was the residual waste of opium that had only been smoked once. Apparently in the old days there were people who got a third life out of opium by smoking "second dross," or the dross of the dross. That, however, made no sense to me. The whole idea behind the opium pipe's unique design and vaporization process, besides preserving heat-sensitive alkaloids, was to remove the impurities and elements such as morphine that put a drag on opium's lively high.

When it came to smoking pure dross, it was only for the desperate: addicts too poor to afford anything else. In *Opium-Smoking in America and China,* H. H. Kane tells of a hardcore "opium fiend" in Manhattan who would scrape the dross from pipe bowls and eat it. And Cocteau had this to say about the practice: "The vice of opium-smoking is to smoke the dross."

"How about this idea?" I said to Roxanna. "What if I take some dross home with me? What would you charge me for it?"

"Oh, I'm not going to sell you dross. If you want it, just take it."

As soon as I said it, I knew it was a supremely stupid idea. I changed tack: "Maybe I'll do that during the time when you're in the States."

"Okay," Roxanna said. "I'm leaving in two weeks so we can get together again next weekend if you want."

The following week I found myself thinking about opium almost constantly. If there had been a way to set the alarm clock for Friday and sleep the week away, I would have done it. Instead I spent my time pondering the events that had brought me to this point in my life—and coming up with reasons to rationalize my return to the opium fold. I decided that it probably all came down to genetics. Not some gene that predisposed me for addiction, but one that hardwired me for collecting and a preference for things Asian. Could such traits be genetically inherited? I knew that some traits, such as being a night owl, were regarded by most people as a matter of temperament. Though seemingly a result of nurturing, my nightly tendency to work into the wee hours came to the fore when I was in my thirties—long after I had left home and was living abroad. During one of my trips to San Diego in the 1990s, I was surprised to learn that I shared this preference for working late nights with my mother. Couldn't such character traits be genetically passed down from our ancestors, sometimes even skipping a generation or two? And if this was so, I reasoned, why couldn't my great-grandfather be the source of both my acquisitive and Orientalist tendencies?

I thought of that miniature silk shoe from China that had fascinated me as a child. I had totally forgotten about it when, after having lived in Southeast Asia for over a decade, I flew to San Diego following the death of my grandmother. While paying a visit to my grandfather, I was surprised to see *two* matching silk shoes in the glass cabinet. My uncle explained that he had found the missing shoe while going through my grandmother's belongings, and this mention of the silk shoes caused my grandfather to launch into a family history that was previously unknown to me.

He related how his father had once been a "coolie driver"— that was the very term my grandfather used—in California's Central Valley, the boss of a team of Chinese laborers in charge of digging irrigation canals. Edgar Prentis Martin must also have been a collector of sorts, because the silk shoes in the cabinet were surrounded by a dozen jade miniatures that I had never before seen. The jades had been packed away in a box for decades but, thanks to my uncle, my great-grandfather's small collection of Chinese antiques was reunited and on display. My grandfather surmised that his father's curios must have been acquired from his workers, but I thought it more likely that he collected the pieces during trips to the Chinatowns that were once a part of nearly every city and town in California.

Dear old great-granddad. If nobody else could relate to my

predicament, I was certain that he would have understood me. Perhaps I was simply following in his footsteps. The difference between us was simple: Early twentieth-century California had exotic adventure at every turn, but I was born too late for that and had to go farther afield. And if the old "coolie driver" had enough interest in the culture of his underlings to acquire a collection of Chinese jades, was it a stretch to think that his curiosity might also have led him to an opium den? The time frame was right. I decided that Edgar Prentis Martin must have been an opium smoker. And if this were so—if great-granddad had indeed kicked the gong around—he, too, would have experienced how opium worms its way into the brain, planting itself deep like an indelible memory. Was it possible then that a taste for opium could be passed on in the genes? I was suddenly sure that it was—and my life was beginning to make sense to me.

Then there was Roxanna. If I were able to do and see half the things she had done and seen since coming to Asia, I might be worthy of holding her opium pipe. The mere act of having a session with Roxanna was one of those once-in-a-lifetime experiences. How did I ever lose sight of that? The pathos that I sensed while in her bedroom that day was nothing more than the melancholia of a mind longing for opium. There was nothing hopeless about Roxanna. She was a survivor. Someone to be emulated, not pitied. A genuine old Asia hand. A role model. Roxanna had come out to Southeast Asia proficient in plucking chickens and was now, due solely to her inquisitiveness and determination, a world-renowned expert on Asian art. Over the thirty-five years that she had been in the region, everything around her had changed, but Roxanna had discovered a private means to escape the boredom and beastliness of the twenty-first century—and I was very fortunate to be in on her secret.

By the time the weekend had arrived, I was convinced. I was

in my mid-forties; my youth was finished. Besides my opium experimentation, I hadn't done anything interesting or note-worthy in years. Paying the bills by writing about my adventures—boating up the Mekong from Cambodia into Laos, or following George Orwell's footsteps in Upper Burma—was something I no longer had the drive or the energy to do. With the exception of Jake Burton, all my Bangkok journalist friends had long ago left the region, going home to America, Canada, and New Zealand. Tremendous changes over the past decade—especially advances in communications, information dissemination, and air-travel affordability brought about by the Internet—had made it possible for waves of Westerners to come out to Southeast Asia and stay. Being a stranger in a strange land no longer took much effort. Bangkok was teeming with expats, but I no longer knew anybody nor had the desire to make new friends. To me, that now seemed like a young person's pursuit. Instead, I would take up an old man's hobby once traditional among the Chinese. Being a devotee of the poppy was the most romantic way I could think of to live out the rest of my life—and now it felt like destiny.

At Roxanna's I briefly entertained the idea that I might talk her into letting me take some *chandu* home before she left on her trip to Seattle, but in the end I agreed to take the dross. Due to my past experiences I knew that the high morphine content of the dross would carry a mind-numbing kick, and I was by now desperate to feel *something*.

Back at my apartment, I spread out the mat and set up my layout tray. It was a real joy to be arranging all the accoutrements as I had done so many times before—guided by the inlaid mother-of-pearl patterns on the hardwood tray. I had left Rox-anna's house after some thirteen pipes, but the buzz was hardly noticeable. I wanted to sample the dross after the slight effects of

The cover of an issue of *Real Detective* magazine from 1939. By the time this
issue hit the stands, thirty years had passed since America's nationwide opium-
smoking ban was enacted, and its strict enforcement had made the habit increasingly rare in the United States. (From the author's collection)

Roxanna's *chandu* had subsided, so I slid the prepared layout tray
under my coffee table and waited until midnight, killing time by
poking around the Internet.

At twelve, the neighborhood night watchman's banging out
the hour caught my attention, and I left my computer and
brightly lit bedroom for the darkened living room. I pulled the
layout tray from under the coffee table and positioned the gooseneck lamp so that its beam made the accoutrements sparkle in

the darkness. I placed my Billiken mascot in one corner of the tray and propped up the little framed portrait of Miss Alicia de Santos so that her beseeching eyes were upon me. I fed a Billie Holiday disc into the stereo and turned the volume down until it was barely audible. It was Sunday night—technically just a few minutes into Monday morning—and the river was silent. There were no droning tugs pulling sand barges, no booze cruises entertained by cover bands whose fixed sets played like long, forced encores. Chinatown, nine stories below my window, was absolutely still.

The dross cooked up somewhat like *chandu,* but the beautiful color and delicious fragrance were missing. There was no golden "hair" produced by pulling the needle over the wok's inner surface, the cooked opium fuzzy on the tip of the needle like a miniature stick of cotton candy. Instead, what stuck to the needle was a black blob. The dross smell was harsh and reminded me of the burning coal stink that permeates some cities in China. Rolling a dross pill was not unlike rolling opium, except that when heating the pill before sticking it to the bowl, I had to pay careful attention to keep it from bursting into flames and dropping into the lamp. The taste was dreadful, and as soon as I inhaled that first breath through my sugarcane pipe, I knew that smoking dross would ruin the stem's sweet flavor—seasoned by months of smoking the finest *chandu.* Despite all this, I never once harbored the idea that perhaps I should stop before I started.

Two hours into the session I began feeling nauseous and decided I had better hang it up for the night. My elaborate preparations to make this experience exactly mirror my pre-detox smoking sprees only added to my frustration—the scene was perfect except for its most important aspect: my being high. If only I could get back to the way it had been. I pushed the layout tray back under the coffee table and went to bed, resolving to try again in a couple of days. The next morning I called Roxanna to complain. She was preoccupied with packing for her trip to Seattle, and I could tell from her voice that she was losing patience with me and my sorry story.

On Wednesday evening—the night of May 7, 2008—I tried again, this time stubbornly rolling until I lost count of the number of pipes I had smoked. When dawn arrived, my head ached and my ears were ringing furiously. I was vexed at having spent another night rolling without reward. I went to bed but could not sleep. Sometime after eight o'clock that morning, I remembered that Roxanna would be at the airport waiting for her flight to Seattle. I sent her a text message: *This stuff isn't working!*

She texted me back immediately: *STOP!*

It was the last time I would ever hear from Roxanna Brown.

16

I didn't heed Roxanna's warning. Instead, I decided that an air
leak in my sugarcane pipe was keeping the dross from properly
vaporizing. I spent an hour meticulously resealing the pipe's
saddle and then gluing a new collar onto my favorite bowl. I had
made up my mind to smoke the entire bottle of dross before
Roxanna returned so that I would have an excuse to buy some
chandu from her. I didn't think she would refuse me this time. I
imagined that her talk at the University of Washington would
be well received and that she would return home in a jubilant
mood—and this would be perfect timing for me to ask another
favor of her.

The blankets were up on my apartment windows again, and
I smoked in a perpetual faux twilight with nary a break. I ordered a medium-sized pizza every other day, and that was enough
to satisfy my dross-stunted appetite. The intoxicating effect of
the dross seemed to be only about a third of what it should have
been—that is, what it used to be before I took the cure. I made
up for it by smoking perhaps two or three times as many pipes

as I had before. I was never really sure of my daily intake because I couldn't be bothered to keep count. Only tourists keep count, I thought to myself with a smirk.

Roxanna wouldn't be staying in the United States for long after her talk at the university. She had mentioned something about visiting relatives, but trips to the States are shockingly expensive for anyone accustomed to the cost of living in Thailand, and I expected her to be back within a week or so. Seven days after my text message exchange with Roxanna, I got a phone call from her son. Instantly I sensed that something was wrong. And then he told me: "My mom is dead."

On the few occasions that Jamie and I had conversed in the past, I had always spoken English with him, but the shock of this news caused both languages that he and I had in common to fail me. It took what felt like long minutes for me to recover, and then all I could manage was an incredulous, *"What?"*

We didn't talk long. He told me what he knew, which was very little. He said the news was online. As soon as I hung up, I immediately went to my laptop and did an Internet search for Roxanna's name. I then stared numbly at a list of headlines. News of her arrest and subsequent death in custody had already been online for days, but I had been too busy smoking dross to notice.

I struggled against a strong feeling of disbelief to stay focused, reading the backlit lines word by word while adverts incongruously blinked and jiggled in the periphery. According to the news stories, Roxanna had been charged with "wire fraud" for allegedly allowing her electronic signature to be used in a tax fraud scheme. Her arrest was to be the first of a wider investigation into the smuggling of Southeast Asian antiquities into the United States, an investigation that had included raids on major museums on the West Coast. Roxanna was placed in a federal detention facility in Seattle on a Friday—two days after our text message exchange—and she was found dead in her cell at around two the following Wednesday morning. I counted the hours between her arrest and her death and knew immediately what had killed her.

Later, over the course of weeks and then months, details of Roxanna's story would come out. She was detained by federal agents in her Seattle hotel room the day before her speaking engagement at the University of Washington. After four hours of interrogation, Roxanna was arrested and being taken away just as a colleague from the university arrived at her hotel room to take her to dinner. Knocking at her door, Roxanna's colleague was astonished when federal agents emerged, saying they were on "official business" as they hustled Roxanna into an elevator. In an effort to explain the awkward situation, Roxanna told her colleague that she had "made a mistake" and "faxed her signature" before the elevator door slid shut and put an abrupt end to the conversation.

Because Roxanna was arrested on a Friday evening, she could not appear in court until the following Monday. In the interim she was to be held at the five-hundred-bed Federal Detention Center at SeaTac near the Seattle airport. During the check-in process she was given a brief medical screening. Records of the screening were later obtained by Maria Cantwell, the Democratic senator from Washington, at the request of one of Roxanna's colleagues who, on behalf of Roxanna's family and friends, was looking for answers. The review indicated that, among other things, Roxanna was taking medication for depression and chronic constipation. The latter is a side effect of opium use that I, too, experienced whenever I was smoking daily. Opium slows one's digestive system to a crawl, which is why there is runaway diarrhea during withdrawal.

According to other inmates at the detention center who were quoted in the papers, Roxanna became ill over the weekend with "flu-like symptoms," including nausea, vomiting, and diarrhea. She was deemed too sick to attend her court hearing on Monday but managed to make the hearing in a wheelchair the following day. Because of Roxanna's dual citizenship, the judge considered the sixty-two-year-old woman with one leg a flight risk and denied bail.

Roxanna was returned to the detention facility where her symptoms worsened. Medication was given to her but to no effect. Fellow inmates allegedly reported to a guard that Roxanna was vomiting something that "smelled like excrement." Badly in need of a shower, Roxanna at one point used a plastic chair as a walker, inching along the prison corridors to get to the shower room, when she lost her balance and fell onto the floor. According to one inmate, this happened right in front of a guard who did nothing to help. "The officer watched this happen and simply gave her dirty looks," was how the inmate was quoted on the website of the *Seattle Weekly*. Some of the inmates then helped Roxanna to the shower, even turning on the water for her because she was too weak to do it herself.

That night, the detention facility was put under lockdown as usual at ten, and sometime later, inmates in neighboring cells heard Roxanna's frantic screams for help. The sound was so alarming that one of the inmates later told a reporter that she began praying for Roxanna. A guard told Roxanna through her cell door that she would have to wait until morning for medical attention, but Roxanna did not live to see another day. Paramedics were finally called and opened her cell door around 2 A.M. An inmate in a neighboring cell could see Roxanna when the cell door was opened. She saw Roxanna "on the floor, with her eyes open, but clearly dead."

Reading between the lines, I tried to piece together Roxanna's last days. While traveling, Roxanna switched to eating
opium instead of smoking it. She carried the liquid *chandu* in a
tiny brown dropper bottle, a smaller version of the one we used
during our smoking sessions. Because just a single drop under
the tongue was the equivalent of several pipes, Roxanna didn't
need to bring much opium along with her. She never overin-
dulged while eating opium, taking only enough to keep the
withdrawal symptoms at bay. Roxanna rarely discussed this most
inconvenient aspect of her addiction, but she once told me that
on one previous arrival at an American airport she had been sent
to secondary inspection. The official who searched her didn't
give her bottle of *chandu* a second look. Nobody, including the
authorities, knew what high-quality opium looked or smelled
like, and a limping, elderly woman was beyond suspicion in most
situations anyway.

I surmise that Roxanna must have had an opportunity to
flush her *chandu* down the toilet during the time she was being
interrogated in her hotel room. While checking in at the detention facility, she might have kept quiet about her addiction—and
a modern-day doctor would know nothing about the subtle
characteristics that mark an opium addict. Did Roxanna think
she could ride out the withdrawal on her own? She must have
known what would happen if she admitted the truth: a forced
regimen of methadone, the synthetic opioid that is used as a
heroin substitute. Methadone is just as addictive as opium, and its
withdrawal symptoms are said to be worse and last longer than
those of natural opiates.

Roxanna had a very high threshold for pain. During one of
our sessions—the opium as usual allowing us to converse with
unemotional candor—she confided to me that her old injuries
still caused her considerable and constant pain. Waking up from

a period of sleep was the worst, she said, when the pain throughout her body was so overwhelming that she admitted her first
thoughts upon awakening were often of suicide.

My own opium use was always recreational—even when I
rationalized it as a form of "research." For Roxanna, opium took
away pain and gave her the strength to persevere. Could she have
used other painkillers? Sure. Would an addiction to Vicodin or
Oxycontin be better for her overall health? I'm not a doctor, but
it seems to me that the way opium vapors are absorbed into the
bloodstream through the lungs and not via the stomach lining
might in itself make opium preferable to taking pills. Then again,
I know of no studies into the long-term effects of opium vapors
on the lungs. I should also point out that I am not trying to justify Roxanna's opium use, or anyone else's, on the theory that
the narcotic is superior to modern painkillers. I'm too familiar
with opium's self-serving nature to be an advocate.

Roxanna had endured many lifetimes of pain, but what I had
difficulty understanding was how she could have ridden out her
withdrawal without revealing her secret. Once the symptoms
started in earnest—by Monday or Tuesday—Roxanna would
have needed superhuman strength of will not to cry out for the
one thing that could take away the torment: opiates.

But Roxanna knew what she was up against—her interroga-
tors would have made sure of that on the day they arrested her.
If convicted of all the charges, she would face thirty-six to fifty-
six months in prison. Going to prison at age sixty-two with a
physical disability that caused her constant pain would have been
daunting even for somebody as experienced in overcoming obstacles as Roxanna. She would also have lost her job at the ceramics museum and, with it, the ability to provide for her son
and Thai family. But perhaps worse than all of this would be the
shame of having her addiction exposed and what that could do

to her name. In the West, where opium has been all but forgotten, the reaction might be curiosity or amazement at an addiction to something so quaint. In Southeast Asia, however, the word "opium" resonates extremely negatively because opium poppies are still grown in the region, and the harvest is made into heroin. With such a black mark on Roxanna's name, she would probably have been stripped of her Thai citizenship and perhaps been unable to return to Thailand even if she were found innocent of the federal charges in the United States.

The threat of all this was perhaps enough to make Roxanna think she should hide her addiction and hope she could get through withdrawal while in detention. It is said that only eight to ten days are needed for the physical symptoms of opium withdrawal to subside. The symptoms of heroin and opium withdrawal are very similar except that the former are, from what I understand, rarely life threatening. Roxanna somehow managed to stay mum throughout the torturous ordeal, and the prison authorities were clueless. One would think medical authorities in a federal detention facility should be familiar with such symptoms. Then again, Roxanna's profile was nothing like that of the typical junkie.

I remembered my own experience during the Halloween Massacre, the feeling that my internal organs were bloating up inside me to the point of popping—and this after a mere eleven weeks of daily smoking. Roxanna had been smoking regularly for years. Her symptoms would have been many times worse than mine. The cause of death was initially speculated to be a heart attack. I pictured the medical team performing the autopsy, opening her abdomen and finding a mass of ruptured guts. I could imagine the shock on their faces.

The postmortem stated that Roxanna died from an infection caused by a perforated gastric ulcer—also known as peritonitis.

During my research for this chapter, I noticed a footnote in
H. H. Kane's *Opium-Smoking in America and China* that tells of
two smokers in late-nineteenth-century New York City dying
from a similar condition:

> Since writing this chapter and within a few days two
> opium-smokers, one a white man, the other a Chinaman,
> have died. Both died from the same cause, acute suppura-
> tive peritonitis, commonly known as inflammation of the
> bowels. Although opium was not the direct cause of
> death, the gastric and intestinal irritation, irregular eating,
> and marked constipation produced by it was undoubtedly
> the real, though remote, and certainly the predisposing
> cause of it.

Kane sounds sure of himself, so perhaps my initial assumption that opium withdrawal killed Roxanna is wrong. In the end
it doesn't matter. She's gone. Despite the ridiculously petty
charges brought against her by the U.S. government, Roxanna
will still be remembered by many as an unsurpassed expert in
her field. She will be remembered as an estimable colleague and
a cherished friend. For me she will always be the epitome of an
old Asia hand. The world is a far, far less interesting place without Roxanna Brown.

I have never seen a copy of Roxanna's autopsy report, but I
know the date and approximate time of her death. Doing the
math, I discovered that during the very time Roxanna was in her
death throes, I was having my best smoking session in recent
memory. While my body was weightlessly suspended as though
floating in a warm sea, Roxanna was thrashing on the cold floor
of a prison cell in a puddle of her own bodily fluids.

Epilogue

Opium is a charismatic lover who takes you to heaven, giving you years of warmth and affection, and then, like a schizophrenic, inexplicably and without warning begins putting you through hell. You are alarmed but, desperately wanting to recapture the happiness of the early times, you give opium another chance and then another—yet your lover becomes more and more abusive. Going back to the good old days is simply not possible. You give up and try to leave, but your lover threatens to kill you, beating you half to death just to drive the point home. Finally, and with much physical and mental anguish, you make your escape . . . but before long you miss your lover with a heart-searing desperation. Do you go back? Of course you do. Given the opportunity, nearly everyone does. Opium is a force.

And so my nineteenth-century addiction has a twenty-first-century conclusion: Edgy abstinence and comfortless sobriety. It is no accident that my story lacks closure. Such tidy modern notions are unknown to the former opium addict. Feelings resembling grief and nostalgia fill my waking hours, and many times Roxanna's corpse has visited me in my dreams. She's always eager to show me blueprints of a house that will be built with money that her son was awarded—the result of a wrongful death suit against the U.S. government. The Roxanna of my recurring dream is optimistic and doesn't know that she is dead. Only I seem to notice that her skin is the very same pale blue that elderly ladies use to color their hair. Invariably I awaken from these dreams with an unvoiced sob burning in my throat and a desperate urge to fill my lungs with opium vapors. I am convinced that only upon my own death will this deviltry cease.

Yet despite all this, despite everything that has happened, I cannot despise opium. I have tried. It might be easier to stop longing for opium if only I could bring myself to loathe it—but I can't. It is easier to hate myself for having lost the rare opportunity to ride the magic carpet; for having become careless and been obliged to jump off; for having allowed the magic carpet to fly away without me.

The majority of my collection is now in storage at the University of Idaho, but I've kept a couple of pieces that were once components of my personal layout. My old Yixing pipe bowl rests on my desk next to my computer, and now and then I pick it up and give it a sniff. Sometimes I imagine that I can hear the gentle burbling of vapors passing through its hollow interior. When the cravings get particularly keen, I tell myself that when health is lost to disease or old age, I will find a way to once again light the lamp, take up the pipe, and roll myself into sweet oblivion.

Acknowledgments

I am greatly indebted to the friends who assisted me over the past couple of years while this book was being written. To thank everyone by name would take up several pages, and I'm tempted to forgo the customary list of names—doing so would greatly lessen the chances of my leaving somebody out. But there are some friends whose help, particularly during a recent period of ill health, was so great that I can honestly say without them this book would never have been written: Jack Barton, Maria Beugelmans, Jeff Cranmer, Patrick Deboyser, Sarawan Dever, Gregory Dicum, Yves Domzalski, Dylan Ford, Karl Taro Greenfeld, Yishane Lee, Gabriel Mandel, Narisara Murray, Matthew Pennington, Craig Stuart and Susan Kim-Stuart, and Andy Young. I also wish to thank everyone who contributed to the "Steve Fund." You know who you are, and this is your book as much as it is mine. I hope you all find it a worthy expression of my gratitude. Lastly, I'd like to thank my editor, Susanna Porter, and my agent, William Clark, for their patience and encouragement throughout this project.

Selected Bibliography

Anslinger, Harry J., and William F. Tompkins. *The Traffic in Narcotics.* New York: Funk & Wagnalls, 1953.

Black, Jack. *You Can't Win.* New York: Macmillan, 1926.

Blofeld, John. *City of Lingering Splendour.* London: Hutchinson, 1961.

Boyle, Jack. "A Modern Opium Eater." *The American Magazine,* June 1914.

Cobbe, William Rosser. *Doctor Judas: A Portrayal of the Opium Habit.* Chicago: S. C. Griggs, 1895.

Cocteau, Jean. *Opium: Diary of a Cure.* Translated by Margaret Crosland and Sinclair Road. London: Peter Owen, 1957. First published in French as *Opium: Journal d'une désintoxication,* 1930.

Cooke, Mordecai Cubitt. *The Seven Sisters of Sleep.* London: James Blackwood, 1860.

Dickie, James. "Opium Lamps: Variations on the Opium Smoking Theme." *Arts of Asia,* January–February 1997.

Farrère, Claude. *Black Opium.* Translated by Samuel Putnam. New York: Robert Fairberg, 1931. First published in French as *Fumée d'opium,* 1904.

Graham-Muhall, Sarah. *Opium, the Demon Flower.* New York: H. Vinal, 1926.

Hahn, Emily. "The Big Smoke." *The New Yorker,* February 15, 1969.

Halcombe, Chester, and B. Broomhal. *China's Past and Future; Britain's Sin and Folly.* London: Morgan and Scott, 1904.

Hawkins, John A. *Opium Addicts and Addiction.* Boston: Humphries, 1937.

Hervey, Harry. *King Cobra: An Autobiography of Travel in French Indo-China.* New York: Cosmopolitan, 1927.

Hodgson, Barbara. *Opium: A Portrait of the Heavenly Demon.* Vancouver, B.C.: Greystone Books, 1999.

Kane, H. H. *Opium-Smoking in America and China.* New York: Putnam, 1882.

La Motte, Ellen. *The Ethics of Opium.* New York: Century, 1924.

Lee, James. *Underworld of the East.* London: Sampson, Low, Marston, 1935.

Lee, Peter. *The Big Smoke.* Thailand: Lamplight Books, 1999.

McLeod, Alexander. *Pigtails and Gold Dust: A Panorama of Chinese Life in Early California.* Caldwell, Idaho: Caxton Printers, 1947.

Merwin, Samuel. *Drugging a Nation.* New York: Fleming H. Revell, 1908.

Millant, Richard. *La drogue: fumeurs et mangeurs d'opium.* Paris: René Roger, 1910.

Morrison, Arthur. "Hidden London." *Strand Magazine,* December 1899.

Murphy, Emily F. *The Black Candle.* Toronto: Thomas Allen, 1922.

Nguyen, Te Duc. *Le livre de l'opium.* Paris: Trédaniel, 1979. First published as *De l'opium, sa pratique,* 1902.

O'Leary, Frank, and Morris Lipsius. *Dictionary of American Underworld Lingo.* New York: Twayne, 1950.

Olivier-Lacamp, Max. *Le kief.* Paris: B. Grasset, 1974.

Partridge, Eric. *A Dictionary of the Underworld.* London: Macmillan, 1949.

Quirmbach, A. P. *From Opium Fiend to Preacher.* Toronto: Musson, 1907.

Rapaport, Benjamin. "The Chinese Opium Pipe: The Art and Beauty of an Evil Custom." *Arts of Asia,* March–April 1995.

Ross, Edward Alsworth. *The Changing Chinese.* New York: Century, 1911.

Tosches, Nick. "Confessions of an Opium-Seeker." *Vanity Fair,* September 2000.

Wegars, Priscilla, ed. *Hidden Heritage: Historical Archaeology of the Overseas Chinese.* Amityville, N.Y.: Baywood Publishing, 1993.

Williams, Samuel Wells. *The Middle Kingdom: A Survey of the Geography, Government, Education, Social Life, Arts, Religion, etc., of the Chinese Empire and Its Inhabitants.* New York: Wiley and Putnam, 1848.

Yangwen, Zheng. *The Social History of Opium in China.* Cambridge: Cambridge University Press, 2005.

ABOUT THE AUTHOR

STEVEN MARTIN was born and raised in San Diego. After four years in the U.S. Navy, he moved to Thailand. A freelance writer, he has written articles for the Associated Press, Agence France-Presse, and the Asian edition of *Time*. He has also contributed to guidebooks for Lonely Planet and Rough Guides. Martin has gathered one of the world's largest, most diverse collections of antique opium-smoking paraphernalia, and has written an illustrated book on the subject, *The Art of Opium Antiques*. His expertise has led to consulting work for museums and films, most recently for HBO's period drama *Boardwalk Empire*.

ABOUT THE TYPE

This book was set in Bembo, a typeface based on an old-style Roman face that was used for Cardinal Bembo's tract *De Aetna* in 1495. Bembo was cut by Francisco Griffo in the early sixteenth century. The Lanston Monotype Company of Philadelphia brought the well-proportioned letterforms of Bembo to the United States in the 1930s.